THE REVIEW *of* CONTEMPORARY FICTION

NOVEL-WRITING PLAYWRIGHTS AND PLAYWRITING NOVELISTS

SPRING 2014 / VOL. XXXIV, NO.1

REVIEW OF CONTEMPORARY FICTION
Spring 2014
Vol. XXXIV, No. 1

The *Review of Contemporary Fiction* is published three times each year (March, August, November). Subscription prices are as follows:

Single volume (three issues):
Individuals: $17.00 U.S.; $22.60 Canada; $32.60 all other countries
Institutions: $26.00 U.S.; $31.60 Canada; $41.60 all other countries

ISSN: 0276-0045
ISBN: 978-1-56478-704-0

Indexed in *Humanities International Complete, International Bibliography of Periodical Literature, International Bibliography of Book Reviews, MLA Bibliography,* and *Book Review Index.* Abstracted in *Abstracts of English Studies.*

The *Review of Contemporary Fiction* is also available on 16mm microfilm, 35mm microfilm, and 105mm microfiche from University Microfilms International, 300 North Zeeb Road, Ann Arbor, MI 48106-1346.

Address all correspondence to:
Review of Contemporary Fiction
3404 North Ben Wilson Street,
Victoria, TX 77901

www.dalkeyarchive.com

CONTENTS

THE REVIEW *of* CONTEMPORARY FICTION

FOREWORD

While many of our more experimental contemporary novelists have written occasional plays, these plays have typically received relatively little critical attention from academics who study their novels. Conversely, many contemporary playwrights have written novels which have received scant attention as well. Samuel Beckett is, of course, an obvious exception in this respect, as his work across both mediums has received significant critical attention. Indeed, the fact that much of the best of this criticism deals with both forms simultaneously by looking at aesthetic and philosophical issues which transcend his work across these two mediums, only makes this oversight in the academic literature more compelling. And so it is with Beckett in mind that this edition of *The Review of Contemporary Fiction* looks to consider other novelists and playwrights who have worked in both mediums, albeit in a more limited fashion than Beckett. The expectation is that looking at such cross currents in the works of the various subjects will open up new avenues for discussion, ultimately leading to fresh observations about each author's better-known work as well as a deeper understanding of each of these two genres.

A project such as this will inevitably force us to consider the various aesthetic differences between fiction and drama. In looking for similarities, differences, and resonances across these mediums, it is hard to ignore the fact that from a strictly narratological standpoint, drama has received much less critical scrutiny of late than fiction. As Ryan Claycomb explains, "despite consistent exhortations by Brian Richardson, Manfred Jahn, Ansgar Nünning and Roy Sommer, and Monika Fludernik, we are still at the very beginning of a process that theorizes dramatic narratives." And while a special edition such as this one—which is meant to be as much about fiction as it is about drama (in a journal devoted to contemporary fiction, no less)—isn't going to alter this imbalance, it is a study which in its own way refuses the tendency to allow drama to be "cordoned off from the study of narrative" (Claycomb 159).

As noted in several of the essays, it turns out that one of the reasons authors decide to work outside of their more familiar genre is related to dissatisfaction with their usual medium. In Joseph H. O'Mealy's essay on Alan Bennett, for instance, we learn that working in fiction for Bennett is part and parcel of a "late style" which, quoting Edward Said, O'Mealey argues provides Bennett with "a permit . . . to kick [his] heels up." Focusing on Don DeLillo's late work in his discussion of *Love-Lies-Bleeding*, Graley Herren notes how "DeLillo uses the medium-specific conditions of printed prose and performed drama to explore his signature obsessions in strikingly different ways." Herren goes on to note that while many of DeLillo's novels end right back where they have started, DeLillo takes full advantage of his new dramatic medium, and with it "the infinite loop of dramatic time."

While not attributing Philip Roth's playwriting to a late period in the novelist's life, Mike Witcombe suggests that a notable turn towards experimentation is associated with the moments in which Roth turned to drama, arguing that "Roth would appear to have a renewed interest in playwriting during the phase of his career in which his writing is most commonly considered to be experimental." Perhaps more importantly, Witcombe carefully explores and explains the way in which the overlooked plays fill in recognizable aesthetic gaps between the novels, an observation which should prove valuable to Roth scholars seeking to understand the arc of his career as a novelist.

That the aesthetic potential of one genre can be re-imagined in another is further established by Neil Murphy's explanation of how John Banville first reworked Kleist's *Amphitryon* as the play *God's Gift*, before revising it once again into the novel *Infinities*. Murphy provides a compelling exploration of the various and different ways in which drama and fiction are diegetically disorienting, arguing that the techniques of drama—including "characters' speech (dialogue, soliloquies, asides etc.), direct address to the audience, and stage directions"—are matched in *Infinities* by "an array of defamiliarising techniques."

In some cases, however, genre specific challenges prove so prohibitive that writers are perhaps best off choosing and sticking to a medium that suits their needs. In my own essay on Tom Stoppard I argue that the metanarrative elements Stoppard attempts to employ in *Lord Malquist and Mr. Moon* ultimately find their more natural form only in Stoppard's early plays. Jane Wong Yeang Chui's essay on Pinter's novel *The Dwarfs* (later rewritten as a play of the same name) elucidates the various power dynamics Pinter makes use of vis-à-vis the very space of the stage, while also arguing that the novel is a very different environment in which to explore the relationships between space and power. While Wong clarifies that much is lost in the transition from novel to play, it is also clear that Pinter, like Stoppard, finds the best environment for pursuing his particular aesthetic ideals in theater.

Conversely, Michelle Wang shows that even while Alasdair Gray—who in the 90's would rewrite some of his earlier radio plays as fiction—also has various medium-specific talents, he ultimately proves himself well able to channel his talents both ways: "I suggest that Gray's plays are more successful when they are attentive to medium particularities and that in addition to the similarity of subject matter in his fictional and dramatic work . . . such attention to medium differences is a critical point of similarity between Gray the novelist and Gray the playwright."

While essays such as these are essential to understanding fiction and drama's "unique narratological elements" it is also important to consider various non-narrative characteristics of these two mediums as well, especially given that drama is every bit a performative medium as it is a narrative one. While unconvinced by the quality of Jack Kerouac's *Beat Generation*, Kevin Riordan uses the play as a lens through which to examine the way performance subsumes Kerouac's entire socio-aesthetic oeuvre, from the performative manner in which his novels were composed to the way narrative voice features so prominently: "Kerouac finds characteristic verve, adding, clarifying, and exclaiming, choreographing ideas in something like improvising-live." Riordan pushes this observation further still, ultimately making the case that the novels serve as something of a script for future performances.

Expanding the scope to the way in which socio-economic factors also influence theatre performances, William Boles's analysis of the financial machinations which brought Irvine Welsh's *You'll Have Had Your Hole* to the stage after the runaway success of his *Trainspotting* explains how the decision process which went into choosing and developing the play very likely "kept a good play by a no-name author off the board and produced a bad play by a celebrated author, all in the hopes of enticing a new audience to [the] theatre." Moreover, Boles comes to an intriguing understanding of why some plays written in much the same mode as *Trainspotting* succeeded (plays by Mark Ravenhill and Sarah Kane, for instance), while Welsh's aesthetic sensibilities vis-à-vis (motiveless) revenge fantasy and fulfillment were entirely unsuited for the leap to the stage.

However, no collection such as this one would be complete without a discussion of Beckett—and in this case, it seems only fitting that two essays be included, one examining what his novels owe to his work in theatre, and one examining what his plays owe to his novels. To this end, Bartosz Lutostański argues that the theatrical elements of concurrency, monologue, and scene are fundamental to the aesthetic technique Beckett employs in the novel *Molloy*, while Michelle Chiang focuses on how the duality (and consequent subjectivity) of time in *Malone Dies* and *The Unnamable* become a theatrical and structural motif in Beckett's "mimes" (*Act Without Words I* and *II*).

Finally, while Suzan-Lori Parks is well-known for her plays, in Jeffrey Severs's discussion of her only novel, *Getting Mother's Body*, he explains that "the novel, not the play, is in several senses Parks's 'first' genre." While going on to note numerous ways in which one genre feeds the other in Parks's work, Severs discusses a Parks quote which serves as a fitting epigraph for this entire special issue: "Parks encourages writers to 'cross fertilize' or 'cross-train': 'novelists and those in the novel corner read the poets and the playwrights, playwrights and theater professionals read the novelists, and so on.'" As critics, I believe we would be well-served not only by recognizing and discussing such cross-training when it happens, but by engaging in more of it ourselves, especially when it comes to writing about the work of authors who have engaged in this sort of cross-training themselves. [DANIEL JERNIGAN, 2015]

GRALEY HERREN

DELILLO VARIATIONS: A CONTRAPUNTAL READING OF "COUNTERPOINT," *THE BODY ARTIST*, AND *LOVE-LIES-BLEEDING*

The eccentric genius Glenn Gould is one of the guiding muses in Don DeLillo's contemplative 2004 essay, "Counterpoint: Three Films, a Book, and an Old Photograph." Gould first earned international acclaim in the mid-1950s for his recording of Bach's *Goldberg Variations*. This notoriously complex piece is structured as a variation set: Bach establishes an aria, follows it with thirty variations on the initial theme, and returns to the beginning with an aria da capo. The filmmakers of *Thirty Two Short Films about Glenn Gould* likewise adopt a contrapuntal approach for their character study of the mercurial artist. DeLillo constructs his "Counterpoint" essay in similar fashion, using juxtaposition and variation to develop thematic relationships between solitude, madness, art, and death in the lives and works of Gould, Thelonious Monk, and Thomas Bernhard.

DeLillo's own oeuvre invites contrapuntal consideration as well. Early in his career, he seemed determined to reinvent himself with every novel, experimenting with one subgenre after another: the artistic apprenticeship novel (*Americana*), sports (*End Zone*), music (*Great Jones Street*), science fiction (*Ratner's Star*), and cloak-and-dagger thrillers (*Players* and *Running Dog*). The highly accomplished mature works of DeLillo's mid-career—*The Names*, *White Noise*, *Libra*, *Mao II*, and his magnum opus *Underworld*—cemented his reputation as the most penetrating literary chronicler of late-twentieth century American life. Throughout his diverse works, DeLillo returned again and again to certain predominant themes, and in his post-*Underworld*, twenty-first century work for page and stage, these recurring preoccupations have crystallized into urgent obsessions. The late DeLillo aesthetic focuses unblinkingly on the role of the artist to interrogate and mediate time, identity, and mortality. But to say that DeLillo returns obsessively to these core themes is not to say that his work has become redundant or predictable. In fact, what is most remarkable is the striking variety and medium-specific nuance he brings to bear on each new variation upon his themes. In "Counterpoint" DeLillo observes, "Gould's second recording of the *Goldberg Variations* was made twenty-six years after his first rendition and is somber and slower, far more contemplative. He is not only reimagining Bach but engaging in a form of *corrective self-dialogue*" (44, emphasis added). The same dynamics of corrective self-dialogue animate DeLillo's late work. Taking my cues from DeLillo, Gould, and Bach, the present essay takes a contrapuntal approach to three late works, the essay "Counterpoint" (2004), the novella *The Body Artist* (2000), and the play *Love-Lies-Bleeding* (2005). DeLillo uses the medium-specific conditions of printed prose and performed drama to explore his signature obsessions in strikingly different ways. Each of these reflexive self-dialogues is provocative in its own right but considered in counterpoint, the "DeLillo Variations" constitute an important triptych within his late oeuvre. Performance art is central to all three works; indeed, DeLillo's increasing attention to performance constitutes one of the central features of his late aesthetic.

"Counterpoint: Three Films, a Book, and an Old Photograph" appeared in the journal *Grand Street* four years after the publication of *The Body Artist* and several months before the stage premiere of *Love-Lies-Bleeding*. This work of creative non-fiction serves effectively as a thematic bridge between the other two fictional works. The three movies referenced in the title are *The Fast Runner* (based on an Inuit legend about Atanarjuat), *Thirty Two Short Films about Glenn Gould* (a film which includes dramatic enactments as well as interviews with people who knew the enigmatic virtuoso), and *Straight, No Chaser* (a documentary about jazz innovator Thelonious Monk). The titular book is *The Loser*, a novel about Glenn Gould by the relentlessly intense Austrian writer Thomas Bernhard. The old photograph refers to an image hanging on the wall of DeLillo's writing room. It captures the Mount Rushmore of the 1950s New York jazz scene: Monk on piano, bassist Charles Mingus, drummer Roy Haynes, and saxophonist Charlie Parker playing in the Village in 1953. The essay riffs back and forth between these eclectic artists, developing motifs close to the heart of DeLillo's own work.

Among the essay's several photos, the first is most emblematic: a naked runner sprints across a frozen white landscape, fleeing for his life from a distant pack of pursuers. "In *The Fast Runner*, Atanarjuat, racing, naked, is a man reacting to a primal danger; there are other men who want to kill him. But he may also resemble an individual trying to reestablish his sense of isolation, his natural place in the landscape" ("Counterpoint" 46). From the beginning, most of DeLillo's works have featured at least one major figure who feels hounded into retreat by a hostile world. In his first published interview, he was asked by Tom LeClair about the tendency of his characters to withdraw from the world. DeLillo explained, "They feel instinctively that there's a certain struggle, a solitude they have to confront. The landscape is silent, whether it's a desert, a small room, a hole in the ground. *The voice you have to answer is your own*" (8, emphasis added). Ascetic withdrawal into meditative isolation is, according to DeLillo, a fundamental precondition to producing art. He identifies this same impulse in Glenn Gould, a Canadian by nationality and a lone wanderer of the metaphysical North. According to DeLillo, "The artist is an adept of solitude living at the edge of that psychic immensity, the otherworld of ice and time and wintry introspection" ("Counterpoint" 38). Following a compass that always points away, an inner compulsion toward solitude so crucial to artistic achievement, involves great personal risk. The ascetic places himself at odds with society, a stance DeLillo defines in terms of *counterpoint*: "In older cultures, the solitary man is a malignant figure. He threatens the well-being of the group. But we know him because we encounter him, in ourselves and others. He lives in counterpoint, a figure in the faint distance. This is who he is, lastingly alone" (47–49). The group may feel threatened by the individual's secession, and the loner is also threatened by the corrosive effects of prolonged isolation. Solitude can foster genius, but it can also breed madness and crippling loneliness. As DeLillo notes, "The prisoner is thrown into solitary. He is alone, confined, sequestered. This is the harshest punishment the state allows, short of outright execution" (46). DeLillo's vacillation between a romanticized image of the remote artist and a cautionary image of the indigent prisoner serves to remind that quests which begin on the mountaintop in search of enlightenment can end in the madhouse of psychic disintegration and self-annihilation.

The voice you have to answer is your own. DeLillo's opinion has not altered since he made that declaration to LeClair, though his estimation of the cost for this self-dialogue has increased with age. At the heart of "Counterpoint," DeLillo launches into a verbal jazz solo riffing on various dead-end attempts to explain away or pathologize the solitary lives led by Gould, Monk, and Bernhard:

> First there is the gradation of language, a sense of deepening threat played out in the terms themselves. Introspection, solitude, isolation, anxiety, phobia, depression, hallucination, schizophrenia. Then there are the human referents. He is free from convention; or there is something scanted in his humanity; or he is trapped in a modern context, bearing some taint of estrangement that makes him uneasy in the world; or it's a result of upbringing maybe; or he's a goddamn genius—leave him alone; or the matter is strictly clinical, a question of brain chemistry; or it's a natural state in fact, some dread that lingers in the early brain, the snake brain, outside the slanted limits of all the things he has shored against it. (49)

But for all these pigeon-holing rationalizations, DeLillo distills the artist's solitary quest down to a single driving question: "How close to the self can we get without losing everything?" (49)

Who or what or where is "the self"? How does one get close enough to it to risk losing everything? The postmodern era with which DeLillo is most commonly associated has little truck with antiquated absolutes like the essential, unified self. However, this does not prevent several characters in his recent work from reopening the closed subject of the Subject, the True Self. For instance, war theoretician Richard Elster is introduced into the novel *Point Omega* through his observations on the "true life": "The true life is not reducible to words spoken or written, not by anyone, ever. The true life takes place when we're alone, thinking, feeling, lost in memory, dreamingly self-aware, the submicroscopic moments" (17). Later Elster describes the true life like a Proustian epiphany of the self's confrontation with its own mortality: "A moment, a thought, here and gone, each of us, on a street somewhere, and this is everything. [. . .] It's what we call self, the true life, he said, the essential being. It's self in the soft wallow of what it knows, and what it knows is that it will not live forever" (63). Delfina Treadwell, the confession-seeking, death-dealing talk show host in the play *Valparaiso*, invokes the concept more crudely and succinctly: "Then call it the self. I want your naked shitmost self" (91). Of course, Elster and Delfina are dubious sources of knowledge, so we shouldn't necessarily take their words for it. DeLillo's depiction of identity is more complex, contingent, elusive, diffuse, and, most interestingly in the present context, more *performative*.

His most revealing commentary with respect to the dangerous pursuit of self comes in his reflections on fellow novelist Thomas Bernhard. DeLillo makes no claims to membership among the madmen-geniuses he studies in "Counterpoint." But he does know a thing or two about writing, so he speaks with hard-won authority when he turns from Gould's classical music and Monk's jazz to Bernhard's novel *The Loser*. He pushes a provocative line of inquiry: "To what extent is Bernhard himself speaking to the reader?" ("Counterpoint" 41) As with all rhetorical questions, the answer is asserted in the asking: Bernhard expresses himself to the reader through the guise of his narrator. Here DeLillo the reader commits the very offense that DeLillo the novelist has consistently discouraged in numerous interviews; namely, he equates the novel's narrator and characters to mouthpieces for the novelist himself. In so doing, DeLillo indirectly sheds significant light on his own creative process and that of the artist-characters who preside over several of his works. "There are shadings of identity among author, narrator, and character. There is the doubling of Bernhard/Gould and also the split between Bernhard the pianist and Bernhard the novelist" ("Counterpoint" 41). These shadings of identity between the artist and his/her creations, the propensity of art to reflect and replicate the artist—one's self-image, fantasies, fears, and obsessions—is fundamental to understanding multiple DeLillo works for page and stage. It is particularly telling that DeLillo identifies this aesthetic of projection, reflection, and deflection not by pointing to it in his own work (where it is manifestly evident), but by locating it in the work of an artist he admires (Bernhard), who was himself identifying with another artist they both admired (Gould). Most revealing of all, DeLillo conceptualizes this relationship between creator and creatures in terms of *acting*: "Where is the novelist? He is sitting in a room in Vienna or Salzburg writing lines for a narrator who is not him, but is him, but isn't. In the end the narrator is an uncredited actor playing Thomas Bernhard in much the same way that a flesh-and-blood actor plays Glenn Gould in *Thirty Two Short Films*" ("Counterpoint" 42). The sequestered novelist draws closer to the self by creating and acting out the roles of other selves, a performance of self-dialogue. As Samuel Beckett, in *Endgame*, described the primal creative impulse, "Then babble, babble, words, like the solitary child who turns himself into children, two, three, so as to be together, and whisper together, in the dark" (126). *The voice you have to answer is your own*. Through his penetrating meditations on the art of others in "Counterpoint," DeLillo provides his clearest articulation of the performative aesthetic that animates his late work, an approach he had already begun developing in the earlier novella *The Body Artist*, and a method he subsequently returned to in variant form in the play *Love-Lies-Bleeding*.

Readers enter the novella *in medias res* amidst breakfast banter between a husband and wife. We cannot appreciate the significance of this encounter until the obituary appended at the chapter's end. The breakfast scene chronicles the final morning Lauren Hartke spent with Rey Robles, her filmmaker husband who committed suicide later that same day. Lauren is identified as "the body artist" at the conclusion of Rey's obituary (*Body Artist* 31). In retrospect there are several prior indications establishing her habits of mind as a performance artist. She does not simply browse the newspaper; she absorbs the stories and is gathered into the lives of people she reads about. "She tended lately to place herself, to insert herself into certain stories in the newspaper. Some kind of daydream variation" (16). "Variation" here connotes contrapuntal experiments in rearrangement like those expressed musically in the *Goldberg Variations*. At times it is difficult to determine who is rearranging whom. Is Lauren projecting herself into the lives of others? Or is she hyper-receptive to being acted upon by the experiences and voices around and within her? "She had a hyper-preparedness, or haywire, or hair-trigger, and Rey was always saying, or said once, and she carried a voice in her head that was hers and it was dialogue or monologue [. . .] a voice that flowed from a story in the paper" (18). The boundary separating Lauren from others is porous, dappled with shadings of identity, where "an incident described in the paper seemed to rise out of the inky lines of print and gather her into it" (20), and where "there are people being tortured halfway around the world, who speak another language, and you have conversations with them more or less uncontrollably until you become aware you are doing it and then you stop" (21). Ink is to Lauren what drink is to an alcoholic: one story and she's besotted with voices. Critic Mark Osteen has described *The Body Artist* as "DeLillo's most penetrating analysis of the process of artistic generation" (65). One wonders how closely Lauren's process of creative inspiration mirrors that of her author. Certainly the two share common talents, including a finely tuned ear for speech, a willingness to allow new work to develop slowly at its own pace, and an openness to following different paths and shapes dictated by the characters. However, a fundamental difference is announced in the title. DeLillo is primarily an artist of language, but Lauren is a *body* artist. Her body is her medium of expression.

Lauren maintains a rigorous training ritual to prepare her body for art. She stretches and strains her muscles, sands her skin, waxes off her body hair, and applies bleaching cream to her skin. "This was her work, to disappear from all her former venues of aspect and bearing and to become a blankness, a body slate erased of every past resemblance" (86). In the wake of Rey's suicide, one might interpret her austere measures as symptomatic of unresolved grief; she is slowly dwindling to nothing, annihilating her past and erasing her identity. However, her training regimen was apparently well-established long before Rey's death. Her discipline and commitment cannot merely be dismissed as melancholia. She certainly suffers for her art, but she also makes an art of suffering, much like Kafka's hunger artist, whose influence is palpable throughout *The Body Artist*. Furthermore, Lauren's willful erasure serves a practical artistic function. She aspires to become a blank cipher or tabula rasa in preparation for reinscribing her "body slate" with new characters. Her process sounds comparable to a painter priming a new canvas, or DeLillo rolling a clean sheet into his trusty Olympia typewriter.

In the final analysis, however, Lauren's body cannot be reduced to the same object status as a canvas or a piece of paper—it is a body; she is a living, feeling person. Corporeality and mediation emerge as major sources of tension in *The Body Artist* after Rey's death. For all the seeming banality of the opening breakfast scene, the first chapter establishes that Lauren was *not* a solitary artist so long as she had Rey. She has her voices too, yes, her inner murmur and the vicarious voices she weaves together in "daydream variation." But as DeLillo subtly emphasizes in the breakfast scene, Lauren experiences most people and events at a distant remove. She encounters others via the newspaper in narratives that are already mediated. The singular, sustaining exception is Rey. She is grounded by direct contact with the material body of her husband. *The Body Artist* is DeLillo's shortest novel, but it is also his most sensual, crackling with supercharged physical sensations. For instance, when Rey lights up a cigarette at the kitchen table, it sends Lauren into a sensual reverie about his body: "It was agreeable to her, the smell of tobacco. It was part of her knowledge of his body. It was the aura of the man, a residue of smoke and unbroken habit, a dimension in the night, and she lapped it off the curled gray hairs on his chest and tasted it in his mouth. It was who he was in the dark, cigarettes and mumbled sleep and a hundred other things nameable and not" (21-22). Rey helps to anchor Lauren bodily in the material world, and she suddenly becomes unmoored after his suicide.

Enter Mr. Tuttle. After Rey's suicide Lauren returns to their rental home and discovers a small male of indeterminate age and aspect. She nicknames him "Mr. Tuttle" after an awkward science teacher from high school. The silliness of the name bears no resemblance to the seriousness of his impact on Lauren. Perhaps DeLillo intended "Mr. Tuttle" as a rough homophone for

"Mortal" or "Mortality," for Lauren soon associates him with her dead husband. Not that he looks or acts like Rey at first. She initially mistakes him for a sandy-haired child. Even after she concludes that he is older, he retains the air of a sleepy foundling, a perversely inscrutable variation on Goldilocks. It is his voice that eventually binds him to Rey. When Mr. Tuttle first attempts to speak in his own voice, his stilted gibberish is barely decipherable. His first words, "It is not able" (45), sound less like a Zen koan and more like a poor imitation of "E.T. phone home." At one point Lauren wonders half-jokingly, "Am I the first human to abduct an alien?" (85). But she snaps to attention when she discovers that Mr. Tuttle can recite entire monologues and dialogues involving Rey. At first she suspects he was eavesdropping on conversations and memorizing them with pitch-perfect mimicry: "This was not some communication with the dead. It was Rey alive in the course of a talk he'd had with her, in this room, not long after they'd come here. She was sure of this" (63). Later she suspects Mr. Tuttle is capable of channeling her dead husband in the present, conjuring him from the dead. "It was Rey's voice all right, it was her husband's tonal soul, but she didn't think the man was remembering. It is happening now. This is what she thought. She watched him struggle in his utterance and thought it was happening, somehow now, in his frame, in his fracted time, and he is only reporting, helplessly, what they say" (89).

Is Mr. Tuttle the hallucination of an unhinged mind? Is he a warped external projection of Lauren's inner fantasy to reunite with Rey? David Cowart observes, "So far as the reader of [*The Body Artist*] knows, only Lauren ever lays eyes on or converses with her visitor" (204). He further speculates that "in Mr. Tuttle Lauren encounters, as a projection of her own unconscious, the artist in herself, temporarily obtunded or disoriented by late catastrophe" (206). To be sure, no rational explanations adequately account for this strange visitor, or even confirm his existence. Yet Lauren is drawn inexorably to Mr. Tuttle, not as a ghost or a delusion, but as a substantial corporeal being. She regards him as a bodily portal through which she might reestablish a carnal connection with Rey. In one of the most revealing scenes in *The Body Artist*, Lauren expresses her desire to physically enter Mr. Tuttle as a means to reenter Rey:

> Rey is alive now in this man's mind, in his mouth and body and cock. Her skin was electric. She saw herself, she sees herself crawling toward him. The image is there in front of her. She is crawling across the floor and it is nearly real to her. She feels something has separated, softly come unfixed, and she tries to pull him down to the floor with her, stop him, keep him here, or crawls up onto him or into him, dissolving, or only lies prone and sobs unstoppably, being watched by herself from above.
>
> She could smell his liniment on her body, his muscle rub, and then he was all through talking. (89-90)

This passage captures Lauren's abject desperation, her physical need, her loosening grip on the distinctions between fantasy and reality, and her identity dissociation. But notice an important rhetorical move here: "She saw herself, she sees herself crawling toward him." The narrative voice abruptly shifts from past- to present-tense verbs and continues on in that new temporal mode for the rest of the paragraph—only to plummet back into past tense in the final sentence, after the spell is broken. This passage signals one of DeLillo's primary preoccupations in *The Body Artist* and in much of his twenty-first century work: *Time.*

The novella opens with the line: "Time seems to pass" (9). The present verb tense is again notable, but more striking still is the verb itself. Time only *seems* to pass? DeLillo began testing the boundaries of time and space in his fiction as far back as the mid-seventies in *Ratner's Star*. In recent years the relationship of time and space has become a recurring preoccupation. Samuel Chase Coale has studied the Harry Ransom Center's archival material and found abundant evidence of DeLillo's interest in quantum theory and physics. "There were his interpretations of and quotations from articles on Einstein, Bohr, Heisenberg, Schrödinger, and others" (Coale 5). He connects the opening of *The Body Artist* with a manuscript note quoting Hermann Weyl: "The objective world simply is; it does not happen" (ctd. in Coale 7). The idea here is that time does not unfold gradually in a chronological sequence of moments but instead already exists all at once on what we might conceive of spatially as an infinite plane, encompassing all past, present, and future. To draw a comparison near at hand, think of time as a book. All the things that happen in that book have already been committed to print. At any given moment in the reading experience, future events that one has not yet read are already fixed (just flip ahead and see), while events that have previously happened continue to exist (flip back and they're still there). These bedrock truths apply to all books, of course, but few novelists exploit this built-in space-time dimension as deftly as DeLillo.

His clearest articulation of the quantum theories undergirding his recent work came in a 2003 radio interview with Michael Krasny. The interviewer asked about the subject of déjà vu in *White Noise*, and DeLillo began to open up about his broader theories on time. "Time is a great mystery to most people, including philosophers, cosmologists, and others. [. . .] It occurs to me, and I think it has occurred to physicists who work in this particular area, that it may well be that time exists—past, present, and future—simultaneously. And that it is simply a question, for the sake of our self-protection, of completely reformulating the nature of time in order to survive."

DeLillo then posed the questions, "Is it possible that the experience of déjà vu is somehow connected with the idea that time exists in one continuum, and that it is just a question of our gaining access to it? Is it possible for us to gain access to the future? Does déjà vu suggest that we are able to do this, that there is some kind of leakage from the future into our current sense of perception?" Krasny asked what DeLillo's instincts as a novelist told him with respect to time as a single pre-existing continuum, and his reply was fascinating:

> I think there is much on this subject that we simply haven't been able to understand. It's the way in which we construct our own universe. The way that the universe itself is totally different, we are told, from our perceptions of it. We create the universe in a way; we create the world around us. And I don't know that anyone can attempt to discuss this in any great, accurate detail. But it seems

> to be a fact, if we can use the word "fact," not that it doesn't exist, but that it exists in a way that may be totally alien to the ability of humans to survive it.

As an artist, DeLillo has long been a creator of worlds, and he often writes about artist-characters who are themselves creators of worlds inside worlds. But here DeLillo radically extends his understanding of creation to include all of us. Each human effectively creates a variation of the world through individual perceptions. Furthermore, we distort time and space because we could not survive staring into the Medusa's head of a space-time continuum which retains our ineluctable past, augurs our inevitable future, and contains our unavoidable death.

Mr. Tuttle is a creature fully steeped in this alternate understanding of time. He finds himself stranded in our alien world and struggling to adapt, like a Tralfamadorian stuck in the amber of human time. The first hint of Mr. Tuttle's different temporal bearings comes through his inability to grasp verb tense. He observes, "It rained very much," but Lauren corrects him: "It will rain. It is going to rain" (46). He apprehends past, present, and future equally and at once, rendering meaningless distinctions between what has happened, what is happening, and what will happen. She gradually speculates, "Maybe this man experiences another kind of reality where he is here and there, before and after, and he moves from one to the other shatteringly, in a state of collapse, minus an identity, a language [. . .]. She thought maybe he lived in a kind of time that had no narrative quality" (66, 67). Time that has no narrative quality is time that does not happen but merely is. Connecting Mr. Tuttle's worldview with the opening passage of the *The Body Artist*, Lauren reflects, "Time is supposed to pass, she thought. But maybe he is living in another state. It is a kind of time that is simply and overwhelmingly there, laid out, unoccurring, and he lacks the inborn ability to reconceive this condition" (79). Lauren resists Mr. Tuttle's relationship with time. Yet she is so mired in grief and thwarted desire that she is gradually forced to reconsider the existence of time that does not pass.

Ultimately, Lauren learns to work through her suffering and assimilate Rey's death. Art is crucial to that process. Mr. Tuttle becomes the principal muse and culminating character for a new work of performance art. During her interrogations of Mr. Tuttle, Lauren began recording their conversations, which eventually served as a kind of artist's journal guiding her toward the development of *Body Time*. As this suggestive title indicates, Lauren brings her distinct connection with the body into contrapuntal dialogue with Mr. Tuttle's distinct connection with time. DeLillo includes a review of the piece by Lauren's friend and theater critic Mariella Chapman titled "Body Art in Extremis: Slow, Spare and Painful." The reviewer observes, "Hartke clearly wanted her audience to feel time go by, viscerally, even painfully" (106). Lauren explains, "Maybe the idea is to think of time differently [. . .]. Stop time, or stretch it out, or open it up. Make a still life that's living, not painted" (109). The idea of a "still life that's living" perfectly captures the demands Lauren makes of her body, manipulating herself like an organic canvas for portraying various characters. As Chapman describes it, "Hartke is a body artist who tries to shake off the body—hers anyway. [. . .] Hartke's work is not self-strutting or self-lacerating. She is acting, always in the process, of becoming another or exploring some root identity" (107). Paradoxically, the more Lauren removes her ego from her art by surrendering herself to other bodies and voices and allowing them to speak and move through her, the closer she comes to reintegrating her shattered identity.

Commenting on the novella's experiments with identity, Mark Osteen observes, "*The Body Artist* also traffics in metempsychosis: both the literary kind, whereby patterns and motifs from previous texts are revived, and the human kind, whereby human beings return to life in altered forms" (65). Focusing on *The Body Artist*'s experiments with time, David Cowart argues, "Mr. Tuttle is not unique in either his shuttling backward and forward in time or his ability to act as a recording device to replicate or reproduce the world's discourse. The literary artist can do these things as well—and in narrative that need not proceed in a linear fashion" (205). Both critics are right in terms of DeLillo's literary achievement, but Lauren's achievement within the novella hinges upon the specifically *performative* nature of her art as distinct from the literary. DeLillo once admitted in an interview with Adam Begley, "When my head is in the typewriter the last thing on my mind is some imaginary reader. I don't have an audience; I have a set of standards" (91). But for Lauren, who seeks to restore her severed physical connection to the world which she lost when Rey died, the presence of a live audience is an essential component to her performance art. The relation of live performance to time is crucial as it is a temporal relation that is significantly different from printed fiction. One does not have to be a ghost, a space-time alien, or a supernatural foundling to inhabit a reality that simultaneously encompasses past, present, and future: one can be a performing artist. Each performance takes place on a fixed stage and "seems to pass" in the singular, unprecedented, unrepeatable *now*. And yet, no matter how fully the performer immerses herself in the now, there is no escaping the fact that a version of tonight's show happened last night, and another version will happen again tomorrow night. Though a hundred incremental changes could differentiate Saturday's performance from Friday's and Sunday's, the physical stage and the written script generally remain fixed. Thus, the conditions of stage performance constitute a relatively stable space-time continuum encompassing past, present, and future.

DeLillo has worked in the performing arts as a playwright, though he has not achieved nearly the same level of critical and popular acclaim in this medium. His full-length plays *The Day Room* (1986), *Valparaiso* (1999), and *Love-Lies-Bleeding* (2005) have all received multiple productions and largely positive, if muted, receptions. Of these plays, the latter work about the dying artist Alex Macklin is the most accomplished, though also the least understood. Reviewer Tony Adler snarkily voices the gripes of many detractors in his review of the Steppenwolf production of *Love-Lies-Bleeding*:

> As a playwright, Don DeLillo makes an excellent novelist. This isn't as damning as it sounds. There's some merciless, meticulous writing in DeLillo's new *Love-Lies-Bleeding*. The language is interesting for the way it traps anguish in frozen, formal diction. The characters

> each have their own weight and mass. The premise provides an elegantly simple mechanism for exploring primal issues. It's all very strong. It just doesn't belong on a stage.

Adler rehashes familiar complaints about static, verbose fiction writers who try and fail to translate their talents from page to stage, and then he sends DeLillo's would-be audiences across town to see a better show:

> Coincidentally, you can find out how a real playwright handles the same formal challenge by seeing Edward Albee's *Three Tall Women*, currently at the Apple Tree Theatre. Albee takes a comatose old lady and divides her up into her young, middle-aged, and dying selves, giving them rein not only to argue with one another but to scare the old lady's son as he observes his deathbed vigil. The result is funny, profound, and visually dynamic. Theatrical.

Adler is right to compare DeLillo and Albee's formal challenges—staging a death by splitting the dying person into three selves—but he ignores the metadramatic dimensions of *Love-Lies-Bleeding* which prevail in DeLillo just as surely as in Albee. Critics and audiences have generally been so distracted by the topical euthanasia plot that they have failed to appreciate *Love-Lies-Bleeding* as a bold theatrical experiment in time and self-dialogue.

DeLillo uses the same term to describe Alex Macklin that he applied to Lauren Hartke's body art: *in extremis*. That is, at the furthest extreme, in the final agony, at the brink of death. Having suffered two massive strokes, the seventy-year-old Alex can no longer speak or walk. But his younger selves—the sixty-nine-year-old Alex (featured in Act 1, Scene 1 and Act 3, Scene 9) and the sixty four year-old Alex (featured in Act 2)—still exist at other points in the space-time continuum and remain capable of speech and movement. DeLillo never explicitly spells this division out in the dialogue of the play. Instead he uses the medium-specific tools of theater to communicate this concept. The stage directions note, "Two actors appear as Alex. One plays the character in three episodes that precede the main action. The other plays Alex *in extremis*, a helpless figure attached to a feeding tube" (1). Alex *in extremis* sits separately on the side of the stage in distinct lighting. He occupies the same stage at the same time while an episode from his past is reenacted in the opening scene. Unlike Albee's *Three Tall Women*, the three Alexes never directly interact with each other in *Love-Lies-Bleeding*. In the first scene neither the seventy-year-old catatonic Alex nor the sixty-nine-year-old partially incapacitated Alex overtly acknowledges the other's presence. Nevertheless, the audience is made visually aware of their simultaneous presence. We are effectively positioned to see through the temporal perspective of Mr. Tuttle. This dramaturgical precedent establishes the conceptual paradigm for understanding the entire play.

Within the closed, inner world of *Love-Lies-Bleeding*, the action is filtered entirely through the perspective of the artist Alex Macklin. His gaze is fixed squarely upon his death. The first scene turns back the calendar a year, just after Alex suffered his first stroke. The sixty-nine-year-old Alex fixates on the first dead body he ever saw as a child, a man on a New York subway train. He recalls to his wife Lia: "Gray like an animal. He belonged to a different order of nature. The first dead man I'd ever seen and there's never been anyone since who has looked more finally dead" (8). What was becoming clear to Alex after his first stroke, and what is manifestly evident for Alex *in extremis* after the second stroke, is that he, too, will eventually become a gray, lifeless, dying animal. As an eleven-year-old kid, he received his first premonition of death, and the play dramatizes his fulfillment of the prophecy.

Viewed from a perspective that comprehends time as always already existing, Alex is both always alive and already dead; it's just a question of what position he occupies in the space-time continuum at a given point. Here Murray Jay Siskind's theories on déjà vu in *White Noise* are apropos for *Love-Lies-Bleeding*. "Why do we think these things happened before?" Murray asks. "Simple. They did happen before, in our minds, as visions of the future. Because these are precognitions, we can't fit the material into our system of consciousness as it is now structured." Murray theorizes that in déjà vu, "We're seeing into the future but haven't learned how to process the experience. So it stays hidden until the precognition comes true, until we come face to face with the event. Now we are free to remember it, to experience it as familiar material." This phenomenon is felt most sharply with respect to our inevitable mortality: "Most of us have probably seen our own death but haven't known how to make the material surface. Maybe when we die, the first thing we'll say is, 'I know this feeling. I was here before'" (145-46). Seventy-year-old Alex is in a position to look back at the dead man on the subway and appreciate this as a premonition of his own death. He's been here before. *Love-Lies-Bleeding* consists largely of a dramatic staging of what Alex *in extremis* sees when he goes back to the future of his death.

Does Alex see a preordained future, or does he creatively construct it? That is, does Alex flip ahead to read a script already etched in the stone of time? Or does he use his imagination to invent that script—a subjective fantasy of what his loved ones might say and do to hasten his death, and a self-dialogue with his former and future selves? The most honest answer is that DeLillo invites both interpretive possibilities, mutually exclusive though they are, and allows both to remain open. As an artist, as a creator of worlds, DeLillo equips his artist-figures with the same creative license to generate their own worlds. Like Beckett before him, who transformed the theater space into a mindscape in plays like *Endgame* and *Not I*, DeLillo's *Love-Lies-Bleeding* may be understood as a self-contained solipsistic fantasy world of Alex's own device. The episode that lends greatest credence to this interpretation is Act 2.

Set six years prior to the main action, Act 2 features sixty-four-year-old Alex in full health and top form, flirting with his ex-wife Toinette and discoursing on his latest artwork. He reluctantly explains to her why he has a crew blasting into a desert mountain: "A room, a cube. I don't have a name for it. First we cut a passage in. A tough narrow entranceway, cramped, with jutting rock. [. . .] A chamber, a cubical room. Fashioned out of solid rock. Precise dimensions. A large empty room. Six congruent square surfaces. Painted. Ocher and amber. Old colors. Burnt brick. Lampblack. All six surfaces, every square inch" (59). On one level, this artwork represents the apotheosis of DeLillo's classic "men in small rooms" conceit. On another level, the project fits within a much older tradition of cave art. In an earlier scene (chronologically later), Alex's wife Lia recalls his deep admiration for the cave temples of Ajanta in India (37). On the meta-level of self-dialogue, Alex's cave room also harkens back to the underworld caves of *Ratner's Star*. There, Jean Sweet Venable connects ancient cave art to a primal artistic confrontation with mortality:

> wondering what it would take to "remember through" the ochre and soot of cave art to the very reason why these earliest of artists descended to the most remote parts of caves and applied their pigments to nearly inaccessible walls, the intricate journey and the isolated site being representative perhaps of the secret nature of the story told in the painting itself, all fiction, she thought, all fiction takes place at the end of this process of crawl, scratch and gasp, this secret memory of death. (394)

Alex seems to have been remembering his death for much of his life, and there is no mistaking the morbid implication of his underground room as a self-constructed grave. Toinette reminds him that he has been germinating this idea for years. She recalls him talking in bed about "Art that's hidden in a mountain. An incredible, you said, sort of stone enclosure that you would drench with paintings of your dreams" (60). Alex harbors doubts about his plans, fretting "Should the room be painted at all? I have my doubts. I always have my doubts. The paint's a mistake. The paint is excess. A bare room inside a mountain. [. . .] I want to throw off doubt, stop thinking, stop caring, just be, just work. Throw off who I am, goddamn it. A bare room without a signature" (61). If Alex is digging his own grave, he seems determined to make it an unmarked one. Like Lauren Hartke, he struggles to remove ego as an obstacle to creating his art. He longs to erase the epitaph from his headstone, detach the dreamer from the dream. In Act 3, Lia laments, "What powerful work he had it in mind to make. Untitled, unfinished. But not nothing" (83). This eulogy implies that Alex's greatest work was never completed.

Or was it? A variation of Alex's artistic vision to construct an inner sanctum for his dreams may ultimately be realized, not inside a desert mountain, but in the theater itself. The hermetically sealed auditorium lends itself to appropriation as a solipsistic dreamscape. Bert O. States famously characterized the phenomenology of theater as "great reckonings in little rooms." The little room that hosts a production of *Love-Lies-Bleeding* is capable of housing no less than the psychic immensity of Alex Macklin's mind reckoning with death. *M'illumino d'immenso*. Alex and Toinette mull over possible English translations of this verse from Giuseppe Ungaretti. "I glow, I shine, I bathe myself in light," begins Alex. "I turn luminous in this vast space." Toinette counters, "Do we want space in the physical sense? Or spiritual immensity? Something unnamable." But Alex cautions, "Let's not get too ambitious. We'll keep it local. This space and this light" (64). In the literal and the metatheatrical senses, *this* space and *this* light is a phenomenological self-reference to the performance conditions on stage as those lines are being delivered, a stage coterminous with Alex Macklin's mind.

Like so many DeLillo works, *Love-Lies-Bleeding* bends back on itself to end more or less where it started. The final exchange picks up the conversation between Alex and Lia that began the play, with the sitting figure hovering again on the periphery. Alex emphasizes his growing detachment from life. Lia tries to keep him grounded in the real through physical touch—playing Rey to his Lauren—but he is irreversibly losing his grip on the present: "You're the one blessing I know. All I can see and hear. The last of the body. There's more of you than there ever was of me. Everything's running backwards now. This is what consciousness is beginning to mean" (94). The body artist Lauren Hartke moved through death by way of art to return to life and reintegrated identity. In this later corrective variation, Alex Macklin withdraws further from others as he approaches death, culminating in radical detachment. The play's closing image starkly depicts "The sitting figure in isolation" before fading to black (97). One could read this final tableau as an image of death, Alex's final isolation fading into the void of darkness. But it is crucial to note how this concluding image brings the play full circle back to its beginning, a cyclical movement in time which does not suggest termination so much as repetition. From his very first excursion into drama, DeLillo has been attracted to theater as a medium for experimenting with cyclical time. In an interview about his first play, *The Day Room*, he told Mervyn Rothstein, "it seemed natural to me beginning a play that theater itself would be one of the subjects I was interested in" (21). Elaborating upon the metadramatic elements that appealed to him, he added, "I'm interested in the way the play forms a kind of unending circular structure—it bends back on itself" (23). By the time he conceived *Love-Lies-Bleeding* almost twenty years later, DeLillo had matured into a playwright fully capable of self-reflexively exploiting the infinite loop of dramatic time. Tom Stoppard wisely noted in *Rosencrantz and Guildenstern Are Dead* that every exit is an entrance somewhere else (28). The final exit of tonight's performance is an entry into the beginning of tomorrow night's performance in theoretically endless recirculation. Alex Macklin's end is also his beginning. He is not so much dead at the end of *Love-Lies-Bleeding* as he is poised to reenact his dying yet again.

In the liner notes to his *Goldberg Variations*, Glenn Gould addressed what he considered to be the timelessness of the piece, not in terms of its enduring legacy, but in terms of the internal structure of Bach's variation form. Gould proclaims, "the theme is not terminal but radial, the variations circumferential not rectilinear," resulting in "music which observes neither end nor beginning, music with neither real climax nor real resolution." These observations apply equally well to DeLillo's variations. His works for page and stage revolve around a persistent set of core themes in a radial, circumferential manner. His agenda is not to resolve the irresolvable themes of time, identity, death, and the function of art. Rather, through a relentless process of self-dialogue, he returns again and again to themes from his previous work and rearranges them into inventive new variant compositions.

WORKS CITED

Adler, Tony. "DeLillo off the Page." *Chicago Reader.* Chicagoreader.com, 11 May 2006. Web. 13 Apr. 2014.

Beckett, Samuel. *Endgame. The Complete Dramatic Works.* London: Faber and Faber, 1986. 89-134. Print.

Begley, Adam. "The Art of Fiction CXXXV: Don DeLillo." 1993. *Conversations with Don DeLillo.* Ed. Thomas DePietro. Jackson: U of Mississippi P, 2005. 86-108. Print.

Coale, Samuel Chase. *Quirks of the Quantum: Postmodern and Contemporary American Fiction.* Charlottesville: U of Virginia P, 2012. Print.

Cowart, David. *Don DeLillo: The Physics of Language.* Athens: U of Georgia P, 2002. Print.

DeLillo, Don. *The Body Artist.* New York: Simon & Schuster, 2001. Print.

—. "Counterpoint: Three Movies, a Book, and an Old Photograph." Grand Street 73 (2004): 37-53. Web. 13 Apr. 2014.

—. *Love-Lies-Bleeding.* New York: Scribner, 2005. Print.

—. *Point Omega.* New York: Simon & Schuster, 2010. Print.

—. *Ratner's Star.* New York: Vintage, 1976. Print.

—. *Valparaiso.* New York: Scribner, 1999. Print.

—. *White Noise.* New York: Penguin, 1985. Print.

Gould, Glenn. Liner Notes. *Bach: The Goldberg Variations.* Columbia Masterworks ML 5060, 1956. Rjgeib.com. Web. 13 Apr. 2014.

Krasny, Michael. "Interview with Don DeLillo." *Forum with Michael Krasny.* KQED, San Francisco. 4 Jul. 2003. Youtube. Web. 13 Apr. 2014.

LeClair, Thomas. "An Interview with Don DeLillo." 1982. *Conversations with Don DeLillo.* Ed. Thomas DePietro. Jackson: U of Mississippi P, 2005. 3-15. Print.

Osteen, Mark. "Echo Chamber: Undertaking The Body Artist." *Studies in the Novel* 37.1 (2005): 64-81. Web. 13 Apr. 2014.

Rothstein, Mervyn. "A Novelist Faces His Themes on New Ground." 1987. *Conversations with Don DeLillo.* Ed. Thomas DePietro. Jackson: U of Mississippi P, 2005. 20-24. Print.

States, Bert O. *Great Reckonings in Little Rooms: On the Phenomenology of Theater.* Berkeley: U of California P, 1987. Print.

Stoppard, Tom. *Rosencrantz and Guildenstern Are Dead.* New York: Grove Press, 1967. Print.

WILLIAM C. BOLES

IRVINE WELSH AND IN-YER-FACE THEATRE: FROM THE RISE OF *TRAINSPOTTING* TO THE FALL OF *YOU'LL HAVE HAD YOUR HOLE*

"Welsh says that writing a play is a lot easier than writing a novel. After enduring this one, I felt like borrowing one of his characters' trademark aphorisms. **** off, you @@@@."
(Benedict Nightingale, on *You'll Have Had Your Hole*)

"We have to listen to the kids," oft spoken by Stephen Daldry, the artistic director for the Royal Court Theatre during much of the 1990s, became one of the dominant philosophies for a sweeping theatrical movement in Britain known as In-Yer-Face theatre (Sierz, "Outrage"). Daldry's theatre produced new work by young playwrights such as Joe Penhall, Mark Ravenhill, Sarah Kane, Judy Upton, Nick Grosso, Jez Butterworth and Martin McDonagh. This same dedication to hip, new writers also existed at the Bush, the Soho, the Tricycle and the National Theatre. These "kids" altered the direction of the British stage through a redefinition of what could and should be theatrical. Like John Osborne and the Angry Young Men, these authors redirected the theatre's gaze onto previously unseen characters and situations. Mark Ravenhill, author of *Shopping and Fucking*, a notorious piece in the new canon of plays, captured the tenor of these works when he said: "You only have to wait for a bus in Camden for ten minutes to come across the people I'm writing about . . . What surprises me is Londoners who claim to have no knowledge of this kind of life" ("Curtains Up"). While Osborne's Jimmy Porter focused on the previously unexplored world of the lower middle class, these young writers explored, in part, a disenfranchised youth culture. In depicting this culture the playwrights used explicit violence and sexuality, which earned the theatrical movement the moniker of In-Yer-Face. Aleks Sierz, who coined the term, described it as

> a theatre of sensation: it jolts both actors and spectators out of conventional responses, touching nerves and provoking alarm. Often such drama employs shock tactics, or is shocking because it is new in tone or structure, or because it is bolder or more experimental than what audiences are used to. Questioning moral norms, it affronts the ruling ideas of what can or should be shown onstage; it also taps into more primitive feelings, smashing taboos, mentioning the forbidden, creating discomfort. (*In-Yer-Face* 4)

Sarah Kane, author of *Blasted*, perhaps the best known and most infamous work of all the In-Yer-Face plays, stated that no rules should exist for theatre: "If you are saying you can't represent something, you are saying you can't talk about it, you are denying its existence, and that's an extraordinarily ignorant thing to do" (Bayley 25). Their extreme material, in turn, changed the composition of the theatre audience as youths now saw their own stories and concerns being theatrically explored. Daldry's comment about "listening to the kids" not only pertained to the young writers but also these new twentysomething theatregoers. Artistic directors desperately wanted to court this group, as they did not in the 1990s and still do not in the 2010s, typically attend the theatre, and their presence in the stalls only reinforced the economic, social, critical and aesthetic value of the In-Yer-Face writers. As audience taste has always played a factor in the direction of the theatre, in the mid-1990s the "kids" were steering the subject matter of plays that were being produced.

Trainspotting: The Play

It is no surprise then that Irvine Welsh's *Trainspotting*, one of the most successful and groundbreaking novels of the 1990s, became an In-Yer-Face hit when it was adapted for the stage. After all, the novel, published in 1993, just as the theatrical movement was in its genesis, featured the same focus, energy and counter culture cachet that was beginning to emerge on British stages. A *Times* book reviewer echoed the theatrical world of Ravenhill's plays in describing the tone of *Trainspotting*: "It gives voice to the silent, swaying figure at the back of the late-night bus, the one nobody wants to sit next to. It describes the lower depths from the viewpoint of the people who live down there" (Hughes-Hallett). Welsh's sketchy characters were a deliberate response to the stagnation he saw in the contemporary novel. He argued that "The middle class character is an omnipotent, all-powerful character for whom nothing bad happens to, nothing goes wrong for" (Berman 57). Welsh's characters also challenged the conventions closer to home in the Scottish novel, signaling, as Matt McGuire argued, "a shift away from the depiction of lonely artists, bus conductors and disaffected school teachers as exemplars of working-class Scotland" (21). Made up of disenfranchised, lower class, twentysomething heroin users and their friends in Edinburgh, Welsh's novel was driven by an engaging, dialect infused narrative. Because of the novel's focus on drug culture, he quickly became dubbed "the poet laureate of the chemical generation." Welsh's novel touched a nerve among youth culture, as it was featured prominently next to the hottest albums in Virgin and Tower record stores and soon became *the* book for people who did not read (and, according to at least one newspaper, it was the most shoplifted book in Britain ("Northern Stage"). Because youth culture embraced the work (at least those who bought it), *Trainspotting*, which initially had a press run of three thousand copies, rocketed to the top of the best seller list, on which it would continue to reside for the next three years. Its impact on the British publishing industry was almost instantaneous. Publishers usurped Welsh's brand by designing similar covers and touting their author as the female Irvine Welsh, the English Irvine Welsh or the Welsh Irvine Welsh. *The Independent* noted the Welshian influence, writing "Every publishing house worth its salt now has its stable of cool young cutting-edgers, turning out an endless stream of variations on the theme" (Lacey). As they were in the theatre with In-Yer-Face writers, the youth were speaking with their wallets, sending book sales of *Trainspotting* over a million copies in Britain alone and making Welsh a cultural icon and celebrity.

When Harry Gibson read *Trainspotting*, he immediately recognized the inherent theatricality of the novel's characters and situations (Boles). Alan

Riach noted this dramatic aspect in Welsh's language: "It is as if the character is both acting in a play and addressing the audience directly, at the same time. Vulnerability, fellow-feeling, selfishness, sympathy: all are evoked here and readers are responsive to a shared sense of culpable desire" (6). Prior to the play's arrival in London at the Bush Theatre in 1995, Gibson's adaptation played in Scotland, premiering in 1994 in Glasgow at the Citizens Theatre before moving to the Traverse Theatre in Edinburgh. The London premiere would prove to be fortuitous. In the fall of 1994 the Royal Court Theatre began producing in earnest the plays by this batch of new, young playwrights. Within months of one another Joe Penhall's *Some Voices*, Judy Upton's *Ashes and Sand*, Sarah Kane's *Blasted* and Jez Butterworth's *Mojo* all opened in Sloane Square. The London theatrical audience as well as the fans of Welsh's fiction were primed and prepared for the premiere of *Trainspotting*. Dominic Dromgoole, who was the artistic director at the Bush when *Trainspotting* arrived, was enthusiastic, just like Daldry, about the younger clientele—"drawn from the clubbing and popular music scenes" (Scullion 80)—coming to the transfer production in Shepherd's Bush. However, after the first couple of nights he was not as keen, calling these young punters "a fucking nightmare" (Dromgoole 279). Why? During the production "they smoked cigarettes, joints, even heroin (something of a theatrical first), they talked amongst themselves, picked fights, spilt drinks and created whatever mayhem they could" (279). At one point a number of the audience members walked out, crossing over the stage on their way out the door. A few minutes later, they returned, having only left to go to the bathroom. When the run ended at the Bush, Dromgoole and his staff asked, "How can we get them back to the clubs, raves, etc. Where are all those nice people in sweaters?" (279). Despite or because of the audience, *Trainspotting* was a hit and transferred to the West End, where it played twice, had a national tour, and found international success. Gibson's adaptation showed the marketability of not only Welsh's *Trainspotting* but also the In-Yer-Face writers, who would now find their own plays moving from the smaller London venues into the larger houses in the heart of the West End.

You'll Have Had Your Hole: The World Premiere and Aftermath

In-Yer-Face and *Trainspotting* were aesthetically and philosophically copacetic. After all, as Robert A. Morace wrote, Welsh was a writer "in whose rhythm can be heard the sneer of punk and the rhythms of rave and hip-hop, in whose design can be seen the influence of visual culture and whose intense physicality provided an alternative to the increasing abstraction of modern literature and life" (26), all of which spoke to a younger audience and mirrored the influences of the new breed of playwrights. When Welsh announced he was writing his first play, *You'll Have Had Your Hole*, for the West Yorkshire Playhouse to be premiered in February of 1998, it seemed destined that the author who had ensnared youthful readers into the world of his fiction would seamlessly make the transition to plays, bringing with him not only his compelling characterizations, dark humor and timely observations but also a large crowd of paying youths. The hope was that Welsh's play, in turn, would match or perhaps, even better, surpass the buzz of works being produced by the In-Yer-Face movement, including *Popcorn* by Ben Elton, *Shopping and Fucking* by Ravenhill and *The Beauty Queen of Leenane* by Martin McDonagh, all of which had become critical and economic successes on the West End. However, it was not to be. *You'll Have Had Your Hole* turned out to be, perhaps, the biggest failure of not only Welsh's career, but also for the In-Yer-Face era.

The title stems from a scene in Muriel Spark's *The Prime of Miss Jean Brodie*. Welsh explained that the titular character says at one point "'You'll have had your tea.' It's an Edinburgh expression. People from Edinburgh are so mean, they automatically assume you've had your tea and won't be wanting anything from them" (Deevoy). Welsh's title is far removed from Spark's novel; instead, the focus for the two main characters in Welsh's play is sexual conquest. Two small time gangsters, Docksey, recently released from prison, and Jinks, his partner, have captured Dex, another gangster, and strung him up in a soundproof recording studio. Previously, Docksey and Dex had killed a family man who had not paid off his gambling debts to serve as an example to other gamblers who owed money to their boss. The crime has weighed on

Docksey, but not on Dex, and Docksey wants to learn why Dex has not been affected by the brutal murder. While Dex is literally hung up in the air, Docksey plans to seduce Laney, Dex's girlfriend, while Jinks aims to have his way with the suspended criminal. The scenes shift between Jinks's torture of Dex and Docksey's seduction of Laney. Eventually, both men "have their hole," after which Jinks gleefully declares to Dex his HIV positive status. Docksey then reveals to Dex that his real reason for abducting him was that Dex grassed on him, sending him to prison. However, in a moment of surprising compassion Docksey kills Dex, so that his tortured existence at the hands of the sadistic Jinks can come to an end. The play concludes with Jinks turning the tables on Docksey and stringing him up to get revenge for the quick killing of his playmate.

Audience members familiar with Welsh's fiction at the time, including a second novel, *Marabou Stork Nightmares*, considered by some to be his best work, and two collections of short stories and novellas, could easily anticipate the brutal content of the play, and the advertisements placed outside the West Yorkshire Playhouse made clear to those uninitiated with Welsh that the work belonged to the In-Yer-Face movement. The Playhouse banners dared its audience to "Experience It Live, Uncensored, and Too Close for Comfort" (Chadwick). Underneath the heading were boxed images of pliers, a female form, a syringe and a sound system, visually linking the work to violence, sex, drugs, and rock 'n' roll.

Irvine Welsh's first solo theatrical foray, unsurprisingly, was national news, enticing the London press to travel to Leeds to see the world premiere. It might have been better if the reviewers had stayed home, as the play was brutally panned by all who saw it. Charles Spencer's scathing review featured the most quoted reaction to the piece, stating that *You'll Have Had Your Hole* was "the most obnoxious and contemptible play I have ever sat through. It is also one of the most incompetent." Spencer contrasted Welsh's work with other In-Yer-Face writers, noting that unlike plays by Ravenhill and Kane, who presented worlds with a distinct sense of morality, Welsh's play "offers only pornography and unspeakable cruelty." This aspect of the play was picked up by other reviewers. *The Scotsman* remarked that the work was "the most abusive and violent play Welsh could have dreamed up" ("The Voice"), while Nick Meo said "unless you enjoy rape and torture, there is nothing much here for you." *The Sunday Times* called the play "both nasty and empty" as well as "pointless" (Peter).

Throughout the 1990s the critics had become more and more accustomed to the shocking and sensational theatrical material to be found in the In-Yer-Face productions, but what really stunned them in regard to Welsh's play was its poor execution and writing, especially considering how mesmerizing and compelling Welsh's writing had been in *Trainspotting* and how easily his provocative language and characters transferred to the stage in Gibson's version. It was precisely that linguistic talent that was missing, as noted by Benedict Nightingale, who said the play was "lacking in wit, inventiveness and verbal flair." Charles Spencer continued his barrage against the work, noting that Welsh demonstrated no understanding of how to write a play as the work displayed the "poverty of both his imagination and his dramatic skills." Neil Cooper was so befuddled by the writing that "what caused [him] to reel was how anyone allowed such a slackly-written piece of fluff on to a stage at all." Paul Taylor of *The Independent* thought that on a macro level there was potential in Welsh's premise, but it was "the intermittent artistic incompetence of the piece, not its morality, that offends," plus the play featured "some dreadful schlock-sentimental writing."

Perhaps more significantly, the European arts community weighed in on the quality of Welsh's writing. Due to the growing international recognition of the strength of British drama, *You'll Have Had Your Hole* and *Shopping and Fucking* were both selected to have their productions travel to Belgium for an international arts festival. Lieven Struye, the director of the festival, traveled to Leeds to see the world premiere of the play that was set to be a prime highlight of his event. As he sat in the audience, he quickly found the play problematic "because the staging just wasn't convincing" (Adamson). He explained that for the festival: "We want convincing staging and convincing acting and the feeling of the play did not come through to the audience" (Adamson). That night he decided to remove the play from the festival schedule. When he read the reviews of the production, he felt vindicated in his decision. Welsh dismissed all the criticisms, telling Alan Jackson:

> It was probably a mistake to open in such a mainstream theatre, because it meant that drama critics from the nationals, most of whom are of a certain age, class and outlook, reviewed it for people who weren't going to be interested in it. I think those critics heard Scottish accents and swearing, saw people doing nasty things to each other, and were too repelled to engage with the material in any serious way.

When the play transferred to London in 1999, Welsh incorporated the bludgeoning reviews into a savvy, marketing move: "We were happy to use the negative review to publicise the play, working on the premise that condemnation from the out-of-touch is as valid an endorsement as praise from the hip" ("Why I Hate Theatre"). His advertising ploy succeeded. In London the play brought in younger audiences, despite problems in the structure, character, and writing, but at what cost?

Jude Kelley, the artistic director of the West Yorkshire Playhouse at the time, later acknowledged that "Irvine wrote a bad play" (Rosenthal). While she disavowed selecting the play "just for the box office," she also admitted that "it brought in hundreds of young, first-time theatregoers" (Rosenthal). Pursuit of the elusive youth compromised Kelley, forcing her to produce material that would not have been produced otherwise. As Cooper aptly surmised about the economic nature of Kelley's decision: "It is the Irvine Welsh brand name that has pulled the self-same punters through the door for *You'll Have Had Your Hole*, not the work itself." In other words, Kelley kept a good play by a no-name author off the board and produced a bad play by a celebrated author, all in the hopes of enticing a new audience to her theatre. And yet, the choice to produce the work was a keen publicity move, as the West Yorkshire Playhouse became the cultural center of the English theatre scene for the month of February as interviews with Welsh, the actors, and Kelley ran in the nationals prior to the subsequent reviews. The result: a world premiere, a boffo box office and free national advertising for the Playhouse. With such attention on the bottom line, rather than aesthetics and theatrical viability, Kelley and others involved with the production certainly deserve part of the blame for the play's failure. However, Welsh deserves the majority of the blame precisely because the piece he presented to the West Yorkshire Playhouse was so highly problematic.

The Failure of *You'll Have Had Your Hole*: Shock, Revenge and Motivation

Why did this play by Welsh, a writer embodying the cultural zeitgeist of the 1990s, fail so spectacularly? Unsurprisingly, Welsh and his supporters blame the reviewers, especially since the intended audience was not older, middle class journalists. Others blame Kelley and greedy producers aiming to make money off the Welsh brand. However, tangible problematic writing elements can be identified and isolated, including Welsh's mistaken thought that a shocking act of on-stage anal rape as the crux of his plot would emulate the violent success of In-Yer-Face playwrights; his half-formulated use of revenge, a compelling and successful staple in his fiction; and his questionable motivation for writing the play. Ultimately, all of these factors contributed to Welsh's failure to transfer the narrative and literary power of his fiction to the dramatic genre.

Even though the In-Yer-Face movement achieved notoriety thanks to explicit depictions of violence and sexuality, the plays incorporated such material as a complimentary component to their narratives, characterizations and thematic developments. After all, being shocking for the sake of being shocking has its limitations. Like Welsh's work, two of the most representative plays from the era, *Blasted* and *Shopping and Fucking*, feature onstage sodomy and in comparing these works one sees that, unlike Kane and Ravenhill, Welsh fails to integrate the shocking action within the larger framework of his play.

In the middle of *Blasted* a soldier bursts into a Leeds hotel room and takes Ian, a reporter, prisoner. Kate, who is in the bathroom, escapes unseen out the window. The two men have a terse conversation about the nature of war, as the soldier challenges Ian's ability to comprehend its horrors, which the soldier has seen from both sides—as a perpetrator of brutally violent sex acts against innocent victims and as a witness to the aftermath of the sexual butchering of his girlfriend. In a display of his military and masculine power and need for sexual release he holds Ian at gunpoint and proceeds to rape the reporter, all the while crying over his lost love. The soldier's act has numerous repercussions throughout the play as it is a mirror to the various shades of violence between Ian and Kate that occurred earlier in the hotel room (Ian sexually assaulted Kate a number of times, including one scene where he held a gun to her head just as the soldier does to Ian) and foreshadows the continuing sexual violence to be inflicted on Kate when she acquires food and drink from a soldier. In addition, the act is endemic of the conflict of war, specifically "Kane wanted to draw comparisons between acts of rape in the play against the part mass rape played" in the war in Serbia (Saunders 48). Performed without dialogue, the rape of Ian links together the play's violence, which occurs on as well as offstage, reifying Kane's exploration not only of the brutality of war but also of relationships, this latter being a unifying component across all of Kane's plays. While shocking, the act is not present simply for the sake of being shocking but is an integral element of her theatrical aesthetic.

Mark Ravenhill's *Shopping and Fucking* offers a scathing critique of capitalism and the transactional nature of sex in the 1990s. These two thematic elements synthesize in the play's penultimate scene, featuring the fatal sodomization of the underage rent boy Gary, who pays for his body to be violated. Throughout the play Mark defines relationships as mere transactions, a concept reified multiple times through other characters, including Robbie and Lulu, Mark's previous lovers, who start a phone sex business to pay off an ecstasy drug dealer. During the numerous phone calls they receive the two create detailed fictional stories to fulfill the sexual needs of their callers. Gary, too, needs to have his own sex story fulfilled, but unlike the callers, his is a terminal one, as he wants someone to penetrate him anally with a sharp instrument. He tells Mark: "I've got this unhappiness. This big sadness swelling like it's gonna burst. I'm sick and I'm never going to be well" (85). His unhappiness with his short, brutalized life, having been sexually abused as a child, leads him to pay for his own death. By paying Robbie and Mark to sexually brutalize him, he fulfills his own fantasy, while also equating sex with a specific sum of money. The detached transaction that brings about Gary's demise provides Mark not only with an epiphany about the error of his own pessimistic, transactional view of relationships, but also financially releases Robbie and Lulu from the clutches of the drug dealer, as they can now pay back everything they owe. The shocking and disturbing act of Gary's rape, first by Robbie and then Mark, although the use of the fatal instrument by Mark occurs offstage, serves as an effective narrative device, concentrating the play's financial, relational, economic, and thematic elements into one climactic moment. Narratively, Ravenhill's use of rape is as essential as Kane's.

In contrast, Welsh's use of sodomy is problematic as it exists solely for shock value. Throughout the first half of the play Jinks teases the audience with his sexual suggestions of penetrating Dex, all for the purpose of making them question whether Welsh will have his character perform the act on stage or not. In essence, the act becomes more of a "will he or won't he?" proposition, turning the focus on the playwright's intentions rather than whether the sexual act is embedded in the actions and psychology of the characters themselves. In fact, Welsh constructs a flawed premise around Dex's abduction, as the audience wonders why he would be kidnapped and tortured for his lack of distress over a murder. After all, the characters are minor members of a larger criminal organization. Murder is a key component of its financial success and longevity. In addition, if Docksey is the one who has a history with Dex, why is it Jinks that tortures him? Jinks has no emotional or historical connection to his victim, his torture and rape of Dex exist narratively merely for the sake of shock, which, in turn, elicits little emotional or intellectual investment from the audience. The scenario is fraught with problems and it is not until the play's final few minutes that Welsh reveals Docksey's real reason for abducting

Dex: revenge for having turned him into the police. Still, this reveal does not explain Jinks's involvement, except that Welsh ups the shock value by having Jinks declare his HIV positive status after sodomizing Dex. And even this twist is anti-climactic; since Jinks plans to kill Dex, the revelation lacks permanency; Dex will not even live long enough to contract the disease. In effect, Welsh, seeing the violent tenor of other In-Yer-Face pieces, provided a similar narrative thrust, but he stopped short of integration into the larger context of the play's thematic elements. The use of homosexual rape appears to be a misguided and confusing attempt at shock for the sake of shock, rather than an essential element of the play's storyline.

The crux of the play hangs on Docksey's desire for revenge, a prominent and driving narrative device in Welsh's early fiction. David Higdon argues that "much of the power of Welsh's works comes not from his realistic documentation of the contemporary 'acid house,' 'eurotrash' milieu, of the novelty of the language, but from his corrosive exploitation of the very ancient and almost universal desire for revenge to repay perceived wrongs" (422). The chapter "Eating Out" in *Trainspotting* features a waitress exacting revenge on rude male diners by mixing her menstrual blood into their tomato soup, feces into their chocolate dessert and urine into their drinks. His second novel *Marabou Stork Nightmares* is framed entirely around the revenge of Roy Strang, the novel's narrator. While in a coma, Strang tells his life story, defined through the various vengeances he has enacted upon the persons and creatures who have done him wrong, including the brutal killing of his family's dog, which attacked him as a child and left him with a limp; the revenge on a pack of students who terrorized him one night as he was picking up takeout for his family; and the extended rape of a woman who ignored him at parties. The novel's *coup de grace* is that the woman raped by Roy, who is found not guilty of the act by the courts, enacts her own revenge at the novel's end by cutting off his genitalia and sticking it in his mouth. *Ecstasy*, a collection of three novellas, features "Fortune's Always Hiding," which details the revenge of Samantha, a disabled woman born with no arms due to a drug similar to thalidomide, against the leaders of the drug company. As Higdon argues, Welsh "is interested in the individual's perception that he has the right to practice vengeance, that he can define himself and control his reputation through revenge, and that there is a large gap, a silence in the laws, within which the individual must act alone" (433). In essence, these wronged persons must create equity themselves since society has failed them. In so doing, "The individuals move fearlessly into a lawless realm to establish their own justice" (Higdon 422). Welsh's fictional pieces, then, document the battle of the underdog to exact vengeance through their individual actions.

In Welsh's fictional pieces the motivation for the revenge is identified early, driving the narrative forward and allowing the reader to engage with the psychological and emotional motivations of the characters' actions. Surprisingly, he abandons this effective narrative method in his play. Instead, revenge becomes Docksey's surprise reveal to Dex at the play's end. With the lack of a driving narrative impulse, the piece and characters stagnate, failing to move forward, which is obvious in the heavily repetitive scenes of Docksey and Jinks threating Dex. In addition, unlike his fiction's reliance on an underdog who overcomes an established power, Welsh creates three characters who all exist in the same strata of a larger criminal syndicate. None of them are disenfranchised in relation to one another. There is no underdog for whom the audience can root. Perhaps most problematic is that Welsh's play, in part, echoes one of the stronger stories in *Trainspotting* called "Bad Blood," where Davie, a minor character in the world of Renton, Sick Boy and Spud, contracts HIV from his girlfriend, who was raped by Alan Venters, who knew of his condition. Davie enacts his revenge by seducing Venters's ex-wife and becoming chummy with his son, the only person Venters loves. As Venters nears the end in the hospital, Davie arrives, bearing photos that depict the murder of Venters's son (Davie reveals later that the photos were staged). As Venters wallows in despair over his son's death, Davie suffocates him, exacting his vengeance. Between the two stories, "Bad Blood" is far more successful in depicting a man's quest for revenge. Davie's own HIV diagnosis after Venters's rape of his girlfriend justifies his desire for vengeance. It is a personal motivator and a driving narrative hook rather than a weak plot twist such as the one featured in *You'll Have Had Your Hole*. Docksey's need for revenge is not clearly articulated, never fully conveyed to the audience until the play's last moments. While Docksey does seduce Laney for revenge, much as Davie does with Venters's ex-wife, the action has no real consequences. In fact, what starts out as revenge turns to love as Docksey falls for Laney, but their story line is left open-ended, as the play closes, she sits in her flat awaiting his return. Ultimately, Welsh uses revenge, like he does the anal rape of Dex, as a purely theatrical device lacking any narrative context. Instead of channeling the highly theatrical and fantastic bouts of revenge to be found in the seventeenth century plays he studied, Welsh merely created a poor, unmotivated imitation of his more successful fictional material.

One final significant factor to consider in the play's failure was Welsh's motivation for writing *You'll Have Had Your Hole*. Welsh has been open about the reasons behind his fiction writing. *Trainspotting*, which first started as sketches written during a boring cross country bus ride in the United States, eventually became a novel because of what Welsh witnessed upon returning to Leith and seeing the dramatic changes to his friends:

> I saw a lot of people I used to know, from the scheme I'd grown up on, who were all HIV plus from sharing needles, and everyone was bangin' up on smack. You'd get guys who used to go for a pint, now they'd go and bang up . . . The place was flooded with cheap Pakistani heroin. It was so easy to get; a couple of grains for a fiver. People got so used to bangin' up that, when the supply ran down, you'd get ground-up pills . . . People were shooting up on anything in that period. (ctd. in Walsh)

For Welsh, *Trainspotting* became a personal, anguished response to the devastation he viewed. His reaction to the changing landscape of his youth can be seen in the authenticity of his writing, which is emotional, powerful, offensive, personal, caustic, ribald, and touching. However, when personal motivation and drive is absent, his work suffers greatly. Case in point: *Ecstasy*, which got the worst reception of any fictional work by Welsh in the 1990s. He acknowledged that the writing was weak and "*Ecstasy* probably deserved to get slagged off" (Ross). What went wrong? Seeing an opportunity at a cash grab and to expand the Welsh brand, his publisher wanted to release a new book to coincide with the premiere of the film version of *Trainspotting*. There was no concern over the quality of Welsh's writing. Instead, it was about hitting a deadline and serving more Welsh to his hungry audience, paralleling Jude Kelley and her theatre's production of *You'll Have Had Your Hole*. Welsh wrote to appease his publisher, not himself.

Similar to *Ecstasy*, Welsh's decision to write *You'll Have Had Your Hole* was not driven by personal passion. Instead, he admitted that "I decided upon medium before content, electing to write a play, simply because I'd never written one before. It seemed a logical step: I'd done novels, novellas, stories, songs and poems; I'd adapted and produced original screenplays and developed *Headstate*, a performance piece with Boilerhouse Theatre Company. The conventional stage-play seemed the next thing to tackle" ("Inside the Black Box"). For Welsh, writing a play was merely another item for him to check off on a list of different options to explore. As noted by reviewers, he struggled with the theatrical form, but adding to the play's failure was his casual dismissal of the power invested by the theatre in the role of the playwright. In interviews Welsh was highly commendatory of and receptive to the communal nature of the theatre, perhaps he may have been too receptive. In one interview he remarked: "You can't really write a play, you know. Not in the way that you write a novel, with that sense of total control. You're just making a series of suggestions for the company to work on, to play around with or throw out" (McMillian). Rather than accepting the playwright's responsibility for story, motivation and characterization, Welsh placed the power in the hands of the director, designers and actors, suggesting that they make the necessary narrative decisions to create a successful theatrical piece. This philosophy on the role of the playwright was perhaps best displayed when he returned to the theatre four years later, collaborating with Harry Gibson for a musical called *Blackpool*. Welsh provided a first draft of the book and then handed it over to Gibson, who workshopped and improvised material with the university students who were cast to perform the piece. Gibson then rewrote the play, incorporating material devised through the students' improvisations. Welsh, in effect, handed over his authorial control to theatre students, something literally unheard of by established theatre practitioners.

And yet, the role of the playwright is far more precise and powerful than Welsh acknowledged. After all, playwrights have more authorial control than writers in any other genre when it comes to their material. Playwrights and their estates can shut down productions, as has been done by Samuel Beckett's estate on numerous occasions and, most recently, by David Mamet in July 2014 to a production of *Oleanna* in Milwaukee, Wisconsin which altered the gender of one of his characters. Welsh underestimated the importance of his role in the creation and implementation of the play, as seen when it comes to characterization and plot, which are notably absent. Adrienne Scullion made a similar argument, stating that Welsh's plays lacked "theatrical innovation, formal experimentation [and] dramaturgical daring" (81). In essence, Welsh simply provided sketched-out material and one-dimensional characterizations with feathery motivations, relying on others to enact a coherent narrative and theatrical vision on his work.

Welsh would return to the theatre one more time in 2006 with *Babylon Heights*, which he co-wrote with Dean Cavanagh. The play, which premiered in San Francisco, is about the happenings inside a hotel room shared by actors playing the Munchkins in *The Wizard of Oz*. It did not fare well with critics. In a 2010 interview Welsh announced he was done with theatre, calling the people behind the British theatre scene "pansies and nutjobs" and "ponces that have no f****** clue about drama" (Reynolds). Other established, non-theatrical writers like Ben Elton with *Popcorn* and Patrick Marber with *Closer* were able to seamlessly transition to theatre but despite the fact that Welsh's moment to make the same move was perfectly timed with an era that reflected his fiction's vision and voice, he was unable to translate this distinct voice from the written page to the stage. Ironically, Welsh's greatest success with the theatre came not as a novelist turned playwright, but simply as a novelist relying on someone else to transform his memorable fictional characters into effective, engaging theatrical figures for audiences around the world.

WORKS CITED

Adamson, Lucy. "Euro Snub for Welsh Play." *Sunday Times* 8 Mar. 1998. ProQuest. Web. 11 May 2014.

Bayley, Clare. "A Very Angry Young Woman." *The Independent* 23 Jan. 1995: 20. Print.

Berman, Jenifer. "Irvine Welsh." *BOMB* 56 (Summer 1996): 56-61. Jstor. Web. 12 May 2014.

Boles, William C. "Ravers at the Bush: Generation Ecstasy Goes to the Theatre." *Reconstruction* 3 (Fall 2003). Web. 3 Jun. 2014.

Chadwick, Alan. "The Torture of Playspotting." *Sunday Times* 22 Feb. 1998. ProQuest. Web. 11 May 2014.

Cooper, Neil. "Theatre is Not Dead (Sorry Irvine Welsh)." *The Herald* 7 Mar. 1999. ProQuest. Web. 11 May 2014.

"Curtains Up." *Midweek* 24-27 Feb. 1997: n.p. Print.

Deevoy, Adrian. "I Had Tea with . . . Irvine Welsh." *Mail on Sunday* 21 Feb. 1999. *ProQuest*. Web. 11 May 2014.

Dromgoole, Dominic. *The Full Room: An A-Z of Contemporary Playwriting*. London: *Methuen*, 2000. Print.

Higdon, David Leon. "'Wild Justice' in the Works of Irvine Welsh." *Studies in Scottish Literature* 33.1 (2004): 421-34. Print.

Hughes-Hallett, Lucy. "Cruising for a Bruising." *The Times* 15 Aug. 1993. *LexisNexis*. Web. 18 Jun. 2014.

Jackson, Alan. "Alan Jackson Calls Irvine Welsh." *The Times* 30 Jan. 1999. ProQuest. Web. 11 May 2014.

Lacey, Hester. "It's Not Big and It's Not Clever." *The Independent* 8 Mar. 1998. Academic Universe. Web. 20 Jun. 2014.

McGuire, Matt. "Welsh's Novels." *The Edinburgh Companion to Irvine Welsh*. Ed. Berthold Schoene. Edinburgh: Edinburgh UP, 2010. 19-30. Print.

McMillian, Joyce. "Theatre's Best Shot in the Arm." *The Scotsman* 6 Feb. 2002. ProQuest. Web. 11 May 2014.

Meo, Nick. "Torture, Bondage and Rape . . . but Not Much Fun." *Evening News* 20 Feb. 1998. ProQuest. Web. 11 May 2014.

Morace, Robert A. *Irvine Welsh*. New York: Palgrave Macmillan, 2007. Print.

Nightingale, Benedict. "What a Load of Hybrid Interplay." *The Times* 26 Feb. 1998. LexisNexis. Web. 22 Jun. 2014.

"Northern Stage Pushes Things a Hole Lot Further." *The Journal* (Newcastle) 24 Sep. 1999. LexisNexis. Web. 20 Jun. 2014.

Peter, John. "The Theatre of Excess." *Sunday Times* 1 Mar. 1998. ProQuest. Web. 11 May 2014.

Ravenhill, Mark. *Shopping and Fucking*. Plays: 1. London: Methuen, 2001. 1-91. Print.

Reynolds, Rory. "Irvine Welsh Says UK Stage Full of 'Pansies and Nutjobs.'" *Deadline* 21 Mar. 2010. Web. 31 Jul. 2014.

Riach, Alan. "The Unnatural Scene: The Fiction of Irvine Welsh." *The Contemporary British Novel*. Eds. James Acheson and Sarah Ross. Edinburgh: Edinburgh UP, 2005. 35-47. Print.

Rosenthal, Daniel. "Bad Girl of the North." The Times 28 Oct. 1998. *ProQuest*. Web. 11 May 2014.

Ross, Peter. "Of Human Bondage." Sunday Herald 22 Apr. 2001. *ProQuest*. Web. 11 May 2014.

Saunders, Graham. *"Love Me or Kill Me": Sarah Kane and the Theatre of Extremes*. Manchester: Manchester UP, 2002. Print.

Scullion, Adrienne. "Welsh and Theatre." *The Edinburgh Companion to Irvine Welsh*. Ed. Berthold Schoene. Edinburgh: Edinburgh UP, 2010. 77-88. Print.

Sierz, Aleks. *In-Yer-Face Theatre: British Drama Today*. London: Faber, 2001. Print.

—. "Outrage." The Daily Telegraph 17 Feb. 2001. *ProQuest*. Web. 11 May 2014.

Spencer, Charles. "Cruel, Disgusting and Contemptible." *The Daily Telegraph* 28 Feb. 1998. Web. 11 May 2014.

Taylor, Paul. "On the Receiving End." The Independent 26 Feb. 1998. *ProQuest*. Web. 11 May 2014.

"The Voice of a New Generation or All Talked Out." *The Scotsman* 27 Feb. 1998. *ProQuest*. Web. 11 May 2014.

Walsh, John. "The Not-So-Shady Past of Irvine Welsh." *The Independent* 15 Apr. 1995. *ProQuest*. Web. 20 Jun. 2014.

Welsh, Irvine. "Inside the Black Box." The Sunday Telegraph 1 Feb. 1998. *ProQuest*. Web. 16 Jun. 2014.

—. "Why I Hate Theatre." *The Stage* 5 Feb. 1999. *LexisNexis*. Web. 18 Jun. 2014.

NEIL MURPHY

JOHN BANVILLE AND HEINRICH VON KLEIST: THE ART OF CONFUSION

John Banville's decision to adapt Heinrich von Kleist's plays, *Der zerbrochne Krug* (1811), *Amphitryon* (1807), and *Penthesilea* (1808), as *The Broken Jug* (1994), *God's Gift* (2000), and *Love in the Wars* (2005), respectively, was perhaps partly inevitable, given the recurring presence of the German playwright's work in his fiction and, more generally, the centrality of overt intertextual gestures in his work. Throughout Banville's fiction, one encounters deeply resonant allusive structures, like the framing device of the old English ballad, "Long Lankin," in his early collection of stories of the same title, the parodic big house structure in *Birchwood* (1973), the presence of Wallace Stevens's and Rilke's poetry throughout the science tetralogy, Nietzsche's philosophical significance to *The Book of Evidence* (1989), and the aesthetic mirroring of the French painter, Pierre Bonnard's artistic principles in *The Sea*, to name but a brief sampling of Banville's usage of key intertextual narrative frames. More directly relevant to Banville's dramatic adaptations, Part One of *Mefisto* (1986), "Marionettes," alludes to Heinrich von Kleist's "On the Puppet Theatre,"[1] which offers an aesthetic argument for the gracefulness of the marionette, in contrast with the materiality of human dancers.

The marionettes, or puppets, "have the advantage of being resistant to gravity. Of the heaviness of matter, the factor that most works against the dancer, they are entirely ignorant: because the force lifting them into the air is greater than the one attaching them to the earth" (Kleist, "Puppet Theatre" 414). Erich Heller further clarifies the significance of Kleist's essay as follows:

> . . . a dancer, a ballet master, is seeking out the perfect model of graceful movement, goes back beyond the child, even beyond the sphere of organic nature, to the mechanical contraption of

1 Kleist's "Über das Marionettentheater" has been variously translated as "The Puppet Theatre" and "The Marionette Theatre."

> the marionette; for in its absolute and unconscious obedience to natural laws, the laws of weight and counterweight, the marionette displays in its motions a grace that is wholly unaffected — unaffected, that is, by even the slightest trace of self-consciousness, a grace that is not obtainable by any man or woman. (Heller 47–8)

Kleist's unselfconscious puppet movement is purely artificial and quite distinct from the materiality of man; in keeping with Banville's familiar pattern of infusing his own texts with the philosophical and aesthetic fascinations of other writers, thinkers, intellectual discoverers, *Mefisto*'s Gabriel Swan acquires a puppet-like aura in the non-realist fabric of the novel. John Kenny also observes that the first part of *Mefisto* ("Marionettes") "includes scenes with broken puppets and theatrical costumes, and in his narrative Swan repeatedly refers to himself as a 'Pinocchio' who is trying to be real" (Kenny 170).

Similarly, in *Eclipse* (2000), Banville's Alex Cleave expresses *his* aesthetic fascination by spying on a naked girl from his window: "The unadorned grave beauty of her movements was, it pained the performer in me to acknowledge, inimitable: even if I spent a lifetime in rehearsal I could not hope to aspire to the thoughtless elegance of this girl's most trivial gesture" (101). Banville's long-term fascination with Kleist's "The Puppet Theatre" is again clearly evident: the narrator is besotted by the girl's absence of self-consciousness, by the objective grace that is unaffected by a consciousness of the external gaze. The fictive universe, it is implied, has its own world-rules and, in certain moments of abandon, the residue of human self-awareness evaporates and one witnesses a purity of action denied to human beings—in this the marionette or puppet, for Kleist and Banville, was a perfect example of unconscious aesthetic expression. A further demonstration of the aesthetic assimilation of Kleist into Banville's work is registered in the fact that Cleave was, or had been, an actor who froze on stage while playing the part of Amphitryon, in a moment of almost total loss of self, precisely at the point in Kleist's *Amphitryon* (or Banville's ironically titled *God's Gift*) in which the main character, completely bewildered by the machinations of the Gods, has lost all sense of himself. Cleave dramatically offers his own insight into his collapse as follows:

"'Who if not I, then, is Amphitryon?' I cried—it is now for me the most poignant line in all drama—and suddenly everything shifted on to another plane and I was at once there and not there" (89). Cleave's focus on the essentially ontological question in *Eclipse* becomes, as we shall see, a central facet of Banville's later adaptations of Kleist.

More playful allusions to Kleist's work proliferate in many of Banville's novels. For example, the use of the letter 'A' to designate Athena (or, possibly, Art), in *Athena* (1995), echoes the comic and deceptive identity-play with the letters 'A' (for Amphitryon) and 'J' (for Jupiter) in Kleist's *Amphitryon* (97-98). Another example would be the use of variants of the line from *Amphitryon*—"And who, except me is Amphitryon?" (116)—in *Eclipse* (89), *The Sea* (217), and *The Infinities* (60). There are numerous other references to marionettes and puppets throughout Banville's work. In addition, Banville positively reviewed Martin Greenberg's translations of Kleist ("The Helpless Laughter of a Tragedian" W9) and his fascination with the Kleistian marionette also extends to the Benjamin Black novels; Inspector Hackett, of the Quirke novels, is repeatedly referred to in terms reminiscent of a marionette, while Phoebe, in *Christine Falls*, stands with her "head bowed and her arms hanging at her side, herself a slack-stringed marionette" (189), and Leslie, from *The Silver Swan*, is described as "long and gangly, with a stooping, sinuous, flat-footed gait, his long pale hands swinging at the ends of his arms as if they were connected to his wrists not by bone but skin alone" (91).

Banville's full acknowledgement of the influence of Kleist is, of course, most emphatically offered in the adaptations of the three plays and in his rewriting of *Amphitryon* in prose fictional form as *The Infinities* (2009). Both *The Broken Jug* and *Penthesilea* offer intriguing insights into how certain aspects of Banville's aesthetic, via Kleist, find expression on stage but this essay will primarily focus on both *God's Gift* and *The Infinities* because both play and novel are versions of Kleist's play, which is itself an adaptation of Molière's comic version of the Greek myth. Thus, several interpretative shifts, from Kleist to Banville, and from drama to fiction present themselves as questions of critical significance. Banville's double appropriation of the tale establishes a deeply resonant texture that exceeds any simple notions of adaptation and also offers an opportunity to evaluate the relative merits of Banville's prose and dramatic rendering of Kleist. Kleist's own reconstruction, or "reworking" of Molière is also significant; according to David Constantine, Kleist's version differs most clearly from that of his predecessor in its infusion of serious subject matter into what was essentially a ribald comedy, a seriousness that is primarily located in the "developed character of Alcmene, and, as in *Jug*, it is incongruous in a context of coarse comedy" (Constantine 431). In this essay, I will trace the narrative-aesthetic implications of the multi-adaptive process involved in the move from Kleist's *Amphitryon* to Banville's *God's Gift*, and thereafter to his *The Infinities*.

Banville's adaptation of Kleist, or his "version," as the subtitle of *God's Gift* declares, offers insights into his tacit approval of Kleist's specific focus and also reveals some key ways in which he overwrites Kleist. Thereafter a comparative evaluation of *God's Gift* and *The Infinities* will focus on Banville's employment of drama as a vehicle for an aesthetic that has long been expressed in prose fiction, and also offers us the opportunity to consider the relative merits of how two distinct narrative forms engage and re-invent Kleist's original.

Banville's insistence on the status of his own work as art, and on the pursuit of beauty as the proper aim of the artist, has long characterized his observations in interviews and commentaries about the intention and value of his fictions. Central to his understanding of art is the distinction between meaning—or what he names "translatable content"—and significance, to which he has frequently alluded (Schwall 15). Echoing Nietzsche's rejection of the pursuit of "the identical" as a feasible artistic aim, Banville disputes the first principle of representative narrative fiction as a replica of life: "Nothing is translatable really. I don't think anything has meaning, in the sense that I define it" (ctd. in Schwall 15). In this context *meaning* suggests a mode of knowable signification or representation, or a sense of art as a vehicle of comment, opinion and rhetorical purpose. Alternatively, Art's *significance* lies in its capacity to "make vivid for the reader the mysterious predicament of being alive" (Elborough), and aims to "go beyond mere human doing to the question of what it is to be, the question of being in the world. And that's what all artists do, however they work" (Haughton and Radley 858). At the heart of such observations lies the perennial aesthetic question of the value of content, or subject-matter, in works of art, the tension between competing oppositions of utility and beauty, logos and mythos. The aesthetic philosopher, Gordon Graham, for example, points to the obvious limitations of paraphrasing when compared with the actual works of literature from which the activity is derived, to demonstrate that the literary text cannot simply be reduced to content (142). In addition, he argues that "a novel is not to be thought of as providing us with a faithful reflection of experience or a skillful summary of it, but as obliging us to view some aspect of experience through an image which allows us to attain an illuminating perspective on it" (144). The key point here is that art has to illuminate experience, rather than to reflect it, as with Banville's assertion that art may have *significance* rather than *meaning*.

This is, in a sense, akin to what E. L. Doctorow alludes to when he argues for the cultural and historical translatability of Kleist's drama: "A Kleist play may be set in ancient Greece, in Holland, or in seventeenth-century Prussia, but the fortress of consciousness is where the action occurs; inevitably, the walls are breached and the ramparts overrun" (vii). The inherent significance of the dramatic enactment lies not in its representational value but in the deeper capacity to illuminate the more fundamental question of being—embodied in Amphitryon's/Ashburningham's ontological confusion and uncertainty about the essence of personal identity. The primary significance of Kleist's *Amphitryon* and Banville's *God's Gift* lies precisely in the inherently unnerving tension of Doctorow's "fortress of consciousness," and despite several commentators noting the historical and cultural significance of Banville's *God's Gift* being set in Ireland in 1798 (Friberg-Harnesk 73), and his *The Broken Jug* being set in the Irish Famine (Fattori 80), Kleist's work is primarily of interest to Banville not because it offers him a plot to imbue with ideological implications but because of a shared sense of the essential strangeness of human existence, or as Kleist claimed in a late letter, "The world is a strange set-up. And we are not at home in it. God, if he exists, is incomprehensible

. . . There seems to be some mismatch between the way we are and the way the universe is constituted" (ctd. in Constantine xviii-xiv). He also claimed that "everything in me is confusion," while Constantine argues that this is also embodied in Kleist's characters: "Their confusion is legendary. Their patterns fail them; playing familiar roles they discover that the lines no longer make much sense. The usual categories collapse" (Constantine xxi). Constantine could have been writing of Banville's characters' similar confusion, or as Freddie Montgomery of *The Book of Evidence* puts it: "I have never really got used to being on this earth. Sometimes I think our presence here is due to a cosmic blunder, that we were meant for another planet altogether, with other arrangements, and other laws, and other, grimmer skies" (26-7). Similarly, with respect to *Amphitryon*, Goethe argued that "Kleist, in his delineation of the main character, aims for a confusion of emotions" (ctd. in Hinderer xi). Banville has frequently claimed that the world's strangeness, and his characters' puzzlement in the face of it, best defines his work (Friberg 206), and the philosophical and comic energy of both Kleist's and Banville's "Amphitryon" plays lies in a relentless ontological confusion and loss of a coherent sense of self. Granted, this is predicated on the primary narrative level of a comic gesture derived from a marauding Greek God but the metaphorical power of the myth, for both Banville and Kleist, lies in the world of the fraught mind, or Doctorow's "fortress of consciousness," rather than in the literal immediacy of the represented context on stage.

On its most obvious level, Banville's adaptation simply registers another way to permit Kleist's resonance to be felt in his intertextual universes. Furthermore, as previously mentioned, the fundamental embracing of ontological confusion as a central motif links the two authors on several key levels. In some respects, however, *God's Gift* both extends and reframes Kleist's *Amphitryon*. Firstly, as Friberg-Harnesk points out in some detail, the transference of the Theban wars to an Irish setting is a fundamental adjustment, as is the re-naming of some of the central characters: "Amphitryon and his wife Alcmene, of Kleist's play, become the English General Ashburningham and Lady Minna; the servant Sosias and his wife Charis become Souse and Kitty" (73).

However, reconstitution of Thebes to Wexford and the Theban wars to the 1798 rebellion is perhaps not as significant as first appears to be the case. The retention of Mercury and Jupiter universalizes the context and Banville's version, while historically-specific, is far less detailed than Kleist's and rarely extends beyond a backdrop. In fact, some of the Ireland-specific references are indicative of typically Banvillean anachronistic play, as is the case with the reference to the song "The Auld Triangle," from Brendan Behan's play *The Quare Fellow* (1954), which is mentioned by Mercury: "Let's go and see the rebels being flogged / And hear the old triangle jingle-jangle" (23). The historically-specific 1798 setting could not have featured a Behan song, of course, but the cross-temporality of Mercury reaches across all limits, as is often the case in Banville's intertextual universes.

Banville also makes more use of stage directions as a narrative device than does Kleist in a few key areas. Rarely extending beyond very basic scene-setting in Kleist, the stage directions in Banville, perhaps typically for a novelist (Beckett's elaborate use of stage directions looms large), occasionally offer more detail, some of which alludes to Banville's prose fictions. For example, the directions at the beginning of Scene 2 make reference to "golden light," (18) as a quite dramatic depiction of events is provided. A few lines later, Jupiter himself tells Minna that "this day that's starting now will be / A day out of your days, a golden day, / The light of which will burn throughout your days" (21), and Minna herself refers to having been upon "some golden mountaintop" (35). The golden world, or *Le monde d'or*, is also, of course, the painting that lies at the heart of Banville's *Ghosts*, ascribed in that novel to the fake painter, Vaublin (a near anagram of Banville). The descriptions of *Le monde d'or* in *Ghosts* speak of an otherworldly existence, of an artistically framed world, pastoral in imagery, godly in appearance, that Freddie aspires to and, as Joseph McMinn claims, "*Le monde d'or* serves as a kind of visual parable of Freddie's world, a landscape, even an escape, he yearns for, but one which he will never enjoy" (McMinn 124). So in *God's Gift*, Banville finds a way to infuse his narrative with allusions to his extended house of prose fiction, and simultaneously manages to generate the same sense of non-realist fictive otherness that one finds so often in the novels; to extend the thought one step further, we realize that if the golden world in the play is intertextually invented by the fake painter Vaublin (Banville), then the depiction of the landscape here is effectively a self-reflexive acknowledgement of the novelist's own artistry. Kleist's *Amphitryon* is not party to such intertextual echoes, of course.

There are other differences between the two plays: Banville's *God's Gift* is a significantly truncated version of Kleist's play, offering two acts rather than three; in particular there is a significant diminishing in emphasis on the heavy comic play between Sosias and Mercury in the opening scenes and a stripping away of detail pertaining to the war and the role of the citizens and officers in the final scene. Furthermore, while Banville's Minna remains relatively prominent, she is certainly less so than Kleist's Alcmene, particularly in the closing scenes. Crucial too are the respective differences between the endings: In Banville, there is far greater emphasis on the difference between the worlds of Gods and men, with Mercury sneeringly referring to the human world as the "(With a contemptuous wave) bright world of beauty, hope and joy," only for Jupiter to reply that the human world is "warmer, though, than our cold lifeless Heaven" (72). The distinction between worlds extends beyond the literal heaven/earth opposition in Banville's version, with numerous references to a distinction between the real and the artistically-constructed, with Souse, from the outset, remarking that "The sun appeared, and then went down again, / As if some hand had pulled it by a string" (11). Similarly, there are several instances of direct address to, or gazing at, the audience (16; 65) as Banville self-reflexively breaks the fourth wall (in keeping with his novelistic narrative habits) while characters are frequently described as artistically-conceived entities like statues (46) and paintings:

> "He seemed a living portrait of himself,
> A Painting by a master, showing him
> Exactly as he is and yet transformed!
> Standing there, he was—I don't know what:
> A dream; a fantasy; and yet a man. (51)

In this, *God's Gift* enlarges the Kleist version with the familiar Banvillean usage of a variety of metaphorical structures (science in tetralogy, art in the frames trilogy, acting in the three Cleave novels, and painting in *The Sea*) and the play thus becomes as much a commentary on the difference between imaginative zones, between the theatrical and the real. Of course, a play in which many of the main characters are either acting, or being acted to, or are unsure of their own selves, is perfect subject matter for a novelist whose work has always been populated by fakes who live self-reflexive theatrical existences in worlds that are self-evidently staged. The fact that Banville eventually chose to re-write his own adaptation of Kleist's *Amphitryon*, as *The Infinities* (2009), testifies to his residing interest in the imaginative possibilities of the mythic frame and also suggests that there were other, unfulfilled, possibilities that might be explored in prose fiction.

Drama, of course, has fundamentally different narrative properties to fiction, ensuring that the embodiment of the Amphitryon story in *The Infinities* and *God's Gift* must necessarily take quite different shape in each. Most obviously, perhaps, as H. Porter Abbott points out, the move from fiction to stage and film, involves, in one sense, a reduction in narrative content: "Adaptation to the shorter, continuous forms of stage and screen is, then, a surgical act" (115), although this may enhance the clarity of the key issues because the "finished form" may depict what "readers of the novel often find themselves struggling to understand: the story's constituent events. We see much more clearly than in the novel how one event leads to the next . . ." (115). The "constituent events" in Kleist's and Banville's dramas, and in *The Infinities*, are all directly intertwined with the ontological confusion at the heart of the lead characters and, while the narrative method is different the essential focus doesn't change. However, given the marked difference in narrative focus between drama and fiction, there are significant adjustments made, particularly in the artistic framing of the subject matter. Drama, as discussed by critics like Richardson and Claycomb, among others, has its own repertoire of narrative devices and is not simply a narrative-less form (2001; 2013). Claycomb, for example, declares that "most performed plays relate narratives, in that on a specific occasion (the performance) someone (the actors and production staff) represents something that happens (the plot of the play) to someone (the audience) for a specific purpose" (159). Other diegetic elements of drama include characters' speech (dialogue, soliloquies, asides etc.), direct address to the audience, and stage directions. The visual spectacle of the stage and its arrangement of spatial imagery also formulates meaning. Furthermore, Brian Richardson, arguing for a distinct narrative poetics of drama, insightfully suggests that the performative nature of the play radically impacts on the notion of representation in the work:

> [H]earing words being uttered in an auditorium defamiliarises the more usual (and usually mimetic) conventions of representation. Likewise, deep traditions of stylization (verse drama, and so on), nonillusionistic theater (for example, asides), and the material conditions of the playing space (lighting effects, coughing) all work against the illusion of representation. (Richardson 685)

The otherness that is created via Richardson's defamiliarised dramatic representation is a special attribute of theatre that distances one from realism no matter how authentic the representative zeal aspires to be. Fiction, as we shall see, also offers an array of defamiliarising techniques.

Banville's *The Infinities* is effectively a rewriting of both Kleist's and Banville's dramatic versions of the Amphitryon myth. But the novel doesn't simply re-interpret and transplant the same story; it enlarges the metaphorical possibilities offered by Kleist's dramatic model. Banville does so by adjusting the emphasis of the role of Mercury (here named Hermes). He also adds several alternative narrative layers by permitting both young Adam, via free indirect discourse, and old Adam, via first person narration, to offer their interiorized perspectives. There is also a significant increase in the cast of central characters and—perhaps most importantly—a more comprehensive positioning of the events of the basic plot in Banville's complex, allusive fictive universe. For example, the motif of the house has long been a centrally important feature of Banville's worlds. In Banville's early novel *Birchwood* (1973), alluding to Henry James's "house of fiction," Gabriel Godkin promised to remain in his "house" alone and to "live a life different from any the house has ever known" (170), a statement that Banville later claimed was the "only direct statement I've *ever* made in any book that I have written" (ctd. in Schwall 19). All of Banville's work occurs in one elaboration or another of this house of fiction of endlessly re-imagined dimensions and features, replete with revisited obsessions, character types and imagistic patterns. In *The Infinities*, we find ourselves in yet another variant of the house:

> They round a bend and the house comes into view. Really it is, Adam sees, not for the first time, an impossible sort of folly, square and mad-looking, with its yellow-painted walls and pale-blue shutters and that winged tin figure—ahem!—atop the single turret. Viewed from this perspective the entire structure seems to lean slightly to one side, drunkenly (105).

Populating the house are cast members who are familiar from other Banville novels; the vaguely demonic Benny Grace, with "goatish hoofs" (177) is a revised version of Carlo Grace (a "grinning goat god" (125)) from *The Sea* who was, in turn, a revised version of Felix (*Mefisto, Ghosts*), Andreas (*Doctor Copernicus*), and several others. There are also numerous references to clowns, a familiar presence in Banville; here, for example, even young Adam and Petra, are dressed in "clownishly ill-fitting pairs of pyjamas" from their childhood (11), and many other references to the essential fakeness of the landscape abound. And, similar to *God's Gift*'s allusion to Banville's *Ghosts*, via *Le monde d'or*, *The Infinities* frequently makes direct references to Banville's fictional universe. Again, cheekily alluding to *Birchwood*, we are told that the peculiarly childlike Petra is "nineteen and so much younger than her years, and yet possessed too of an awful ancientness—'That one,' Granny Godley used to say of her darkly, 'that one has been here before'" (9). Granny Godley is clearly a reincarnation of Granny Godkin from the early novel—and she is correct, Petra has been here before, in Banville's world, as Flora, as Cass Cleave, and many other female figures in Banville whose recurring expressions of otherness is as constant as any other feature in his work.

All of this intertextual play serves primarily to remind us of the essentially invented landscape that we inhabit and, again as a familiar mechanism in Banville, the world frequently appears to coalesce into that invented visual universe of paintings. For example, Hermes guides us to see the world in such a fashion at one point:

> What a striking tableau we must have made, a genre scene by one of the minor Dutch masters, me in the bright doorway and she in the smouldering dimness of the room and the still-life chicken on the table; look at the cat, the crockery on the dresser, delph, they call it—from Delft!—the red and black floor-tiles, and that glimpse of the sunlit day behind me in the door, mute and calm as money. Poor Ivy braced a hand on the table to support herself and looked at me with a look so needy and defenceless even I experienced a qualm. Something to say? I had nothing to say. I was just amusing myself, toying with one of my creatures, as so often is the way.
>
> Turning to go, I nodded in the direction of the jug. "That milk," I said, "is gone sour." (87-8)

Apart from the familiar (for Banville) allusion to Dutch still-life portraits, the final remark, of course, is a playful reference to Vermeer's *The Milkmaid* (1657/8)—the milk is sour because it has been still for so long in that other universe of art that we frequent so often in Banville's work.

A brief description of these literary devices and games is offered, in part, as a demonstration of the manner in which Banville weaves so many diverse interrelated elements into the texture of his fictional worlds, worlds that are multi-layered in temporal and spatial terms, and which frequently bring storyworlds into collision with other fictional realms, both painterly and literary. His godlike figures, Hermes, Benny Grace, Zeus himself, all contribute an obvious extra-real dimension but it is in the multi-textured world of art that Banville's universes acquire their true complex identities. Hermes may be a god but figures like old Adam, himself a revenant from numerous Banvillean parables about the creative imagination, exhibit the ghostly behavior of the re-born (from other texts)—they are themselves and others simultaneously. Here, for example, is a depiction of him at work:

> A plain steel desk and a bentwood chair, a block of graph paper in loose sheets and a plentiful supply of pencils, of course, his famous Ticonderoga No. 4, extra hard, yellow with a green band and pink eraser, specially imported by the boxful; these are, were, the tools of his trade, the implements of the Arcanum. When he was famous first, caricaturists pictured him as a monk in a windowless bare cell, wild-eyed and hydrocephalic, hunched with his pencil over a gridded page of parchment; also as a spaceman in a globular helmet popping out of a hole in the sky. (43)

He could be any number of Banville heroes, or Banville himself perhaps, at work—but the key issue here is how feasible such forms of representation and multi-layered approaches are possible in drama.

The theatricality of Banville's fictional prose world is immediately obvious, from clownish dressing to puppet-like movements, and to numerous references to performances and imitations. At one point, for example, Hermes suggests that,

> Adam feels light-headed, weightless, seeming to float an inch above the floor. He supposes it is to do with the supply of oxygen to the brain, or lack of it. His sister is right, he is not used to being up at this hour—*everything is different*—when the world looks like an imitation of itself, cunningly crafted yet discrepant in small but essential details. (13)

Direct connections to Kleist are also evident in the shape of Helen playing the part of Alcmene (or Alceme, as declared by Helen) in a version of *Amphitryon*—the version in which she is acting is, of course, set in Vinegar Hill during the 1798 rebellion, Banville's own version. And yet, the nature of the adaptation, or version, of the "Amphitryon" play (of either Kleist or Banville) remains a complex problem. The more obvious changes from Roman to Greek names, to location, historical dates, and other surface details are less significant than the key structural differences between drama and fiction, particularly Banville's layered form of the novel genre.

As mentioned earlier, H. Porter Abbott argues that film (and drama) in adaptation acts as an interpretive gesture of a novel by emphasizing "the story's constituent events" (115), and argues that "the story line move[s] with greater clarity and simplicity in a film. One way to describe the difference [between novels and films] is the quality and degree of retardation, or the slowing down of the narrative discourse, that the media can tolerate." He concludes that "its tolerance is much more restricted than that of novels" and the audience cannot tolerate the expansiveness of the novel form on stage, although he does concede that much "figurative flexibility" is also lost in drama (116). Porter Abbott's observation holds good for prose fictions that are heavily dependent on the allegorical or metaphorical implications of complex plots. However, Banville's fiction, including *The Infinities*, is comprised of a multiplicity of narrative threads that defy any simple notion of extracting key constituent elements. It is clear why Banville has always found in Kleist a kindred artistic and philosophical voice, a fellow champion of the idea that existence is defined, in its truest form, by the way we negotiate our ways through labyrinths of confusion, and not by seeking merely to resolve the confusion into order. The way that ontological confusion is contextualized in fiction here seems more potent in its execution, primarily because the form of Banville's novel is more complex. One of the achievements of Banville's multi-textured fictional world is the sense that existence itself is inherently mysterious in ways that extend far beyond the overt actions of characters. For example, near the close of *The Infinities*, Hermes, Banville's expression of the creative imagination in the novel, offers a final statement about the world that we have just encountered:

> This is the mortal world. It is a world where nothing is lost, where all is accounted for while yet the mystery of things is preserved; a world where they may live, however briefly, however tenuously, in the failing evening of the self, solitary and at the same time together somehow here in this place, dying as they may be and yet fixed forever in a luminous, unending instant. (300)

The surface reality of the world, the aesthetically reconceived surface reality, can be more comprehensively rendered in the prose fictional world, particularly in the dense verbal tapestries of Banville's non-realist, richly complex, world. Both Banville's and Kleist's plays depict the confusion of self, and the overt strangeness of the human capacity to grasp the complexity of being; drama well illustrates the comedy and tragedy of our tentative grasp of the existences that we laud so highly. But *The Infinities* takes us beyond the confusion of self, it guides us through the maddening labyrinths of existence that offer context to our confusion—in the very air itself the insubstantial nature of being begins to lose focus in Banville's poetical fictions and for all the world-depiction that is possible, for all the immediacy and the here-and-now qualities of drama, it may well be that, in certain instances, the novel form, as conceived by Banville at least, may offer a more comprehensively imagined rendering of a world that has no boundaries, that has confusion and mystery at the very core of its ontology.

WORKS CITED

Banville, John. *Athena*. London: Secker & Warburg, 1995. Print.

—. *The Book of Evidence*. London: Secker & Warburg, 1989. Print.

—. *The Broken Jug: after Heinrich von Kleist*. Oldcastle: Gallery Books, 1994. Print.

—. *Ghosts*. London: Secker & Warburg, 1993. Print.

—. *God's Gift: a version of Amphitryon by Heinrich von Kleist*. Oldcastle: Gallery Books, 2000. Print.

—. "The Helpless Laughter of a Tragedian," *The Irish Times*, 3 Dec. 1988: W9. Print.

—. *The Infinities*. London: Picador, 2009. Print.

—. *Love in the Wars: a version of Penthesilea by Heinrich von Kleist*. Oldcastle: Gallery Books, 2005. Print.

—. *Mefisto*. London: Paladin, 1987. Print.

—. *The Sea*. New York: Alfred A. Knopf, 2005. Print.

Black, Benjamin. *Christine Falls*. London: Picador, 2006. Print.

—. *The Silver Swan*. London: Picador, 2007. Print.

Claycomb, Ryan. "Here's How You Produce This Play: Towards a Narratology of Dramatic Texts," *Narrative*, Vol. 21, No. 2 (May 2013): 159-79. Print.

Constantine, David. "Introduction" in *Heinrich von Kleist: Selected Writings*. Ed. and Trans. David Constantine. Cambridge: Hackett Publishing Company, 2004. Print.

Doctorow, E. L. "Foreword," to *Heinrich von Kleist: Plays*. Ed. Walter Hinderer. New York: Continuum, 1995. Print.

Elborough, Travis. *Fully Booked: Q&A with John Banville*. 29 Jun. 2012. Web. 8 Apr. 2015.

Fattori, Anna. "'A Genuinely Funny German Farce' Turns into a Very Irish Play: *The Broken Jug* (1994): John Banville's Adaptation of Heinrich von Kleist's *Der zerbrochne Krug* (1807)" in *Angermion: Yearbook for Anglo-German Literary Criticism, Intellectual History and Cultural Transfers/Jahrbuch für Britisch-Deutsche Kulturbeziehungen*, (Vol. 4:), Nov. 2011, 5-94. Print.

Friberg-Harnesk, Hedda. "In the Sign of the Counterfeit: John Banville's God's Gift" *Nordic Irish Studies*, Vol. 9 (2010): 71-88. Print.

Friberg, Hedda. "John Banville and Derek Hand in Conversation," in *Irish University Review*, Vol. 36, Number 1 (Spring/Summer 2006): 200-15. Print.

Graham, Gordon. *Philosophy of the Arts: An Introduction to Aesthetics*. New York: Routledge, 2007. Print.

Hugh Haughton, Bryan Radley. "An Interview with John Banville. *Modernism/Modernity* 18, Number 4 (Nov. 2011): 855-69. Print.

Heller, Erich. *The Poet's Self and the Poem: Essays on Goethe, Nietzsche, Rilke and Thomas Mann.* London: Athlone Press, University of London, 1976. Print.

Hinderer, Walter. "Introduction," to *Heinrich von Kleist: Plays.* Ed. Walter Hinderer. New York: Continuum, 1995. Print.

Kenny, John. *John Banville.* Dublin: Irish Academic Press, 2009. Print.

Kleist, Heinrich von. "On the Puppet Theatre," in *Heinrich von Kleist: Selected Writings.* Ed. and Trans. David Constantine. Cambridge: Hackett Publishing Company, 2004. Print.

—. *Selected Writings.* Ed. and Trans. David Constantine. Cambridge: Hackett Publishing Company, 2004. Print.

—. *Amphitryon in Selected Writings.* Ed. and Trans. David Constantine. Indianapolis: Hackett Publishing Ltd.: 2004. Print.

McMinn, Joseph. *The Supreme Fictions of John Banville.* Manchester: Manchester University Press, 1999. Print.

Porter Abbott, H. *The Cambridge Introduction to Narrative.* 2nd ed. Cambridge: CUP, 2012. Print.

Radley, Bryan. "John Banville's Comedy of Cruelty," *Nordic Irish Studies*, Vol. 9 (2010): 13-31. Print.

Richardson, Brian. "Voice and Narration in Postmodern Drama," *New Literary History*, Vol. 32, No. 3, Voice and Human Experience (Summer 2001): 681-94. Print.

Schwall, Hedwig, "An Iridescent Surplus of Style: Features of The Fantastic in Banville's The Infinities," *Nordic Irish Studies*, Vol. 9 (2010), pp. 89-107. Print.

—. "An Interview with John Banville," by Hedwig Schwall. *European English Messenger* 6, 1 (1997): 13-19. Print.

KEVIN RIORDAN

BEAT GENERATION AND THE DRAMATURGY OF THE AMERICAN ROAD*

Across the span of his novels—which he considered a single project, the "Legend of Duluoz"—Jack Kerouac daringly dramatizes America's physical and spiritual landscape. His characters perform across the continent, seeking like doomed tragic heroes a lost father or a lost love or just the thrill of new-highway speed. And with his persistent engagements with music, photography, and religious ritual, Kerouac enriches the novelistic discourse with appeals to other modes in order to richly memorialize this fleeting post-war mise-en-scène, with its hobo circuits, smoky jazz bars, and all-night diners.

With the 2005 rediscovery and publication of Kerouac's only play, *Beat Generation*, it seemed that Kerouac's thick description of America would find explicitly dramatic form for the first time; and, following on its author's fame, the play could be auditioned for a place in the canon of American drama. In a 1957 letter to his agent, Kerouac himself makes an attempt to position his foray into dramatic writing: "it is now a real play, an original play, a comedy but with overtones of sadness and with some pretty fine spontaneous speeches that are as good as Odets" (*Beat Generation*).[1] Yet despite what Kerouac hails as its reality and its originality, *Beat Generation* does not quite work as a script for performance. While his novels feature well-wrought action and character, crisp scene changes, and figurative sound and light cues—that is, all of the elements of theatrical writing—his play is comparatively *not very dramatic*. Unusual for Kerouac, the dialogue and the action in *Beat Generation* are hindered by formal restraint; the three acts seem static and arbitrary, and there are few stage directions to inspire the dramatic imagination beyond the play's spoken lines. The work's comparative limitation, then, is that unlike Kerouac's novels it seems to behave too safely within a too-narrow set of genre expecta-

* I'd like to thank Nick Hengen Fox, Josh Garrett-Davis, and the anonymous reader for their astute and detailed comments, and a further nod to critical co-pilots along the way, in particular: Chris Ingraham, Kyle Fruh, Janice Huang, Dan Farbman, and Garon Taylor-Tyree.

1 This quotation from Kerouac's letter is reproduced on the back cover of the Thunder's Mouth Press print edition.

tions. In other words, it is a "real play" that neither embraces nor challenges what that designation entails.

Cast in a different light, however, *Beat Generation*'s theatrical shortcomings strangely reveal the impressive if understated theatricality of Kerouac's novels. Kerouac's significant engagements with other art forms—abstract painting, cinema, bebop—find pronounced form in the novels, so much so that the Legend of Dulouz resists being read as *just* a series of novels. With their ekphrastic appeals and their formal ambitions, these books aspire towards something beyond the novel form. They implicate the reader as a kind of spectator *and* participant and, in their incorporation of features from the spatiotemporal arts, they propose a kind of dramaturgy for the beat generation that is strangely absent in—but is now illuminated by—*Beat Generation*.

Kerouac's experiment with playwriting offers a dramatic critical framework that invites a rereading of the author's life and work from a more theatrical point of view; and this perspective provides one way to reconcile Kerouac's sometimes at-odds popular and literary legacies. Whether in terms of his legendary typing sessions (a kind of durational performance) or the subsequent road trips his novels have inspired, Kerouac's work offers an exemplary sense of modern print *dramatically* serving "both as a record and as an instigation" (Worthen 10). A Kerouac novel, like other performance texts, documents one event while it produces others. And as people continue to follow his stories—often quite literally taking to the road to play his characters—all of his writing, from a certain spectatorial distance, begins to read like a dramatic script. In this way, *Beat Generation* exposes how Kerouac's work is something not only to read but something to go out and do, as his writings artfully act as both records of performed moments and instigations for other performances still to come.

Beat Generation on Page and Screen

Beat Generation resurfaced in 2005 when Kerouac's agent Sterling Lord was preparing his own memoirs. According to the biographers of Kerouac and Lord, Kerouac wrote the play in a single night in 1957, after the completion but before the publication of *On the Road* (Glaister). He sent the manuscript out widely—as a struggling writer does—to theaters and agents as well as to the likes of Allen Ginsberg and Marlon Brando, but it received little interest. Shortly thereafter, with the sudden success of *On the Road*, Kerouac's career took off and seven of his already finished—but previously neglected—novels were published swiftly between 1958 and 1960, as publishers tried to capitalize on the cultural sensation that Kerouac's prose seemed to both document and produce. Consequently, *Beat Generation* and Kerouac's brief ambition as a dramatist were soon forgotten.

Despite the play's apparent disappearance, its third act was adapted for film in 1959. In collaboration with the photographer Robert Frank and the visual artist Alfred Leslie, Kerouac adapted the play's last act for the film *Pull My Daisy*.[2] Critically praised and hailed as the beginning of beat cinema, *Pull My Daisy* features Ginsberg and Gregory Corso, with Kerouac credited as the writer and voice-over narrator. Initially, the film was to take the play's—and the milieu's—title, but MGM Studios had copyrighted "Beat Generation" for a B-movie already in production (Sargeant 14). While *Pull My Daisy* depicts a gathering of poets casually discussing God and jazz, Hollywood's *Beat Generation* would follow a serial rapist and so further tarnish the subculture's already suspect public image.

As in his fiction, Kerouac's dramatic writing relies on the mythologizing of his and his friends' lives. The third act of Kerouac's *Beat Generation* and *Pull My Daisy* riff on the same real-life episode from Neal and Carolyn Cassady's attempt at suburban respectability in Los Gatos, California (Sargeant 13). The Cassadys invite a respectable bishop to a dinner only to have their deadbeat friends arrive and linger, making for an awkward, and potentially comical, scenario. Kerouac indeed classified the play as a comedy in his letter to Sterling Lord.[3] It would be hard to imagine his making a similar generic claim about his fiction, and this provides an initial indication of his different approach to playwriting.

2 Kerouac's engagement with photography is perhaps most directly expressed in his introduction to Frank's *The Americans* (1959), written during this same period.

3 In the "world premiere" staged reading of *Beat Generation*, the Merrimack Repertory Theater followed this extra-textual stage direction, pursuing the script's humor. Artistic Director Charles Towers suggested that the comedy was the key to the work, "once I realized it's a comedy, all of a sudden the thing made sense to me. It's not that kind of heavy, slow, jazz, Beat heaviness. It's just really a bunch of guys having fun together" (ctd. in Brown).

In his famous advice for writers, "Belief & Technique for Modern Prose," Kerouac lays out a "List of Essentials" for crafting prose and, perhaps by extension, drama (57). Kerouac here aphoristically and ungrammatically provides tips on craft such as: "In praise of Character in the Bleak inhuman Loneliness." In many of his statements about writing Kerouac protests the playing by any formal rules, comedic or otherwise. In this same oft-cited list from 1959, Kerouac also riffs: "Something that you feel will find its own form"; "Remove literary, grammatical, and stylistic inhibition"; and "Composing wild, undisciplined pure, coming in from under, crazier the better." Across these different takes, feeling finds form and inhibition is to be avoided. And movies here—if not yet plays—will be an important part of the project: "Bookmovie is the movie in words, the visual American form."

To open his book on beat cinema, Jack Sargeant stresses Kerouac's interest in film and his anxiety with novels, as it was traditionally understood. Sargeant cites a Kerouac letter declaring that "the 'novel form' is dead" (13). Kerouac here proposes that his books—or his bookmovies—instead are "poetry sheeted in narrative steel, a new kind of narrative . . . [that] aims at the flow of feeling unimpeded." For a moment, Kerouac waxes futurist with steel sheeting, the time-based "flow" and the immediacy of the spatiotemporal arts. In the late 1950s, theater and film offer Kerouac a way to develop a live "flow of feeling unimpeded." In this light, Kerouac's framing *Beat Generation* as a comedy that compares favorably to Clifford Odets's work—the most significant of which had come two decades earlier—signals an uncharacteristically conservative approach that perhaps impedes his play's flow.

Just Listening to *Beat Generation*

The complete three-act *Beat Generation* takes place in three locations: in the first act, off-duty brakemen drink wine and play chess at the Bowery; in the second, they head off to the horse races; and in the third, they find themselves out of place at the Cassady home. There are fourteen characters who correspond—like in the novels—more or less directly to Kerouac's friends on the beat scene. Amongst the dramatis personae are avatars for the real-life

Kerouac, Cassady, Corso, and Ginsberg, but with the exception of Ginsberg ("Irwin," which is Ginsberg's actual given name) they here go by unfamiliar pseudonyms. Across his novels, Kerouac often shifts character names, including that of his own persona: Jack Duluoz, Sal Paradise, and Leo Percepied to name a few. In the novels, real people seem to be playing a number of different parts, switching roles for different productions—these castings make the beat generation seem a bit like a repertory company. But in *Beat Generation*, the correspondent identities of and distinctions among these characters become hard to discern because most characters adopt new names (nowhere else found in the Duluoz Legend) and because there is little dramatic differentiation between their voices or actions within the play.

Despite featuring some of the rhetorical flashes familiar to readers of the novels, *Beat Generation* lacks the same spontaneity of action, movement among scenes, and sustained character development. Kerouac's discomfort in the dramatic form is most pronounced at the scenes' outsets. Rather than relying on stage directions or subtler spoken cues, the characters bluntly announce themselves. Act 1 opens with Buck: "Here I am sitting in Jullius Chauncey's kitchen in a clear morning in October 1955" (2). Act 2 starts, "here we are at the racetrack now"; and two pages later, a reminder, "old buddy, see here we are at the racetrack, and there's your flags flyin on the flagpoles" (46, 48). While verbal scenic placements are of course an old convention—Rosalind reports that "Well, this is the forest of Arden" (Shakespeare II.iv.15)—Kerouac's placements abruptly interrupt the ongoing conversation. In their artificiality these statements might offer a kind of alienating effect, but they lack clear, epic purposiveness.

At the Bowery, the racetrack, and the ranch house, the characters jive energetically and, like in the novels, the talk flows freely: from women to cars to bad-paying jobs, from Bela Lugosi to Buddhist dogma to Dostoevsky. As is sometimes said critically of beat writing, the play's references are flip and they lack substance; they seem little more than accessories to a speaker's style. And unlike in the novels, the characters merely sustain a conversation, the stakes are rarely defined or raised. The distinctions among the characters—who reads Dostoevsky; who picks horses based on his dreams?—become difficult to track.

After the play's slow start over morning wine, the audience shares in the characters' anticipation for what will come next—the midday racetrack seems more dramatically promising. Milo, Buck, and Manuel enter the crowd, they wager, they keep drinking. But the chatter here too lacks direction. Their engagements with the crowd and the dramatic opportunity of onstage public spectacle both disappoint. Conventionally, an entrance or an exit can change everything—*enter a messenger* or *exit, pursued by a bear*—but here the French scenes are a series of beer refills and bathroom trips. At one point an unnamed "blonde" walks across stage while Buck is talking about other things, both pretentious and pedestrian: "Yeah—How long do these rebirths go on? When are you gonna lend me that book?" (72). Milo responds, "Just as long as there's somethin like that walking around . . ." (73)—the banter then returns to rebirths and bets. The woman's stage cross is an uncomfortable if familiar misogynist moment in Kerouac, but here it is made more conspicuous as it serves so little dramatic purpose.

By Act 3, the characters along with Kerouac seem to have run out of steam, to have lost interest in their own dialogue. As the assembled await the bishop's arrival, Kerouac introduces a new character, Paul. He enters for a single line, "Got television Milo?" (89). He is told that there is a set in the back room, and he prefers this offstage entertainment. Milo follows Paul offstage, saying as he goes, "Ah no more poetry for me" (90). Eventually the disinterest in the talk turns into collective fatigue, and the play ends with most of the characters falling asleep:

> PAUL. Well I guess I'll sleep.
> IRWIN. We gotta sleep sometime.
> PAUL. That's right Irwin my boy, I'm going to sleep now.
> IRWIN. Milo's already asleep, I can hear him snoring. (119)

As they drift off, flute music lingers, apparently played offstage by Buck. This rare sound cue is an odd rhyme with the end of Arthur Miller's *Death of a Salesman*, but while Linda Loman's sobs are drowned out by the non-diegetic sound—which opens the play as well—the music in *Beat Generation* is just a nuisance for characters who'd rather not be awake.

This is, of course, not the only mid-century play in which nothing much happens, in which boredom or claustrophobia is rendered onstage. *Waiting for Godot* opened in Paris in 1953 and had its American debut in Coconut Grove, Florida in 1956. Kerouac wrote *Beat Generation* in 1957 at his sometimes-home in Orlando, a mere three-and-a-half-hour drive from that debut—and maybe less, if Neal Cassady were driving. And while there is certainly more action in *The Glass Menagerie* (1944) or *Death of a Salesman* (1949), Tennessee Williams and Miller had firmly established a poetics of sententious claustrophobia on the domestic stage.

The play ends with stillness and a listening for what is on- and off-stage. Kerouac is a clumsy stagehand in terms of action, setting, and the development of character, but *Beat Generation* may show more promise as something worth *listening* to. Its "pretty fine spontaneous speeches," when spoken well, may provide one way to shift attention away from the play's dramatic shortcomings.[4] When discussing the play's appeal, Betsy Steve of Thunder's Mouth Press highlights the play's aurality: *Beat Generation* "reads like a jazz song, with switching rhythms" (ctd. in Glaister). When the Merrimack Repertory Theatre (MRT) staged the play's world premiere in Kerouac's hometown of Lowell, Massachusetts, they presented it as a staged reading. The choice to do a reading rather than a full production may have had less to do with practical considerations (as it often does) than with the MRT's recognition of the script's dramatic limitations but its spoken appeal. In their reading, the "centerpiece of the 2012 Jack Kerouac Literary Festival," the MRT focused on the spontaneous speeches that sound like a jazz song ("'Beat Generation' to be Staged").

It is indeed in some of the longer speeches that the reader/listener may find that loose big-idea lyricism that sometimes makes Kerouac's prose pop: "How many sands are there, to be removed from the Pacific Ocean, each time

4 There seems to be a quiet consensus on the play's weakness. In an interview, even the publisher's representative was modest in describing its merits: "It might not be Jack's best but it definitely highlights something of his work, it's part of the canon" (Steve ctd. in Glaister). Theater companies have not pursued the script for production. Other than the MRT reading and the public reading of an excerpt (featuring Ethan Hawke) in New York, *Beat Generation* has yet to be staged on a significant scale.

you pour a million gallons of joy juice into the emptiness of all space, and does it even matter. [DRINKS]" (42). At the races, Manuel gets going for three pages, scored with italics and exclamation marks:

> Let's go back to the sweet city! I keep getting the feeling that as Milo wins he really loses and as he loses he really wins, it's all ephemeral, it can't be grabbed by the hand, it's *hurt*! The *money* can be grabbed by the hand, I wanted to buy myself a new typewriter with the money I put in but look! there's no patience in eternity! eternity! means more than all time and beyond all that little crap and forever! (75)

In the longest speeches, Kerouac falls into his signature performance-typing rhythm. Truman Capote famously quipped that Kerouac's work wasn't writing but typing, and this slight—from a different perspective—may actually highlight this work's dramatic distinction and its virtues. Kerouac's own renowned scenes of composition, those manic typing sessions, might provide one way to approach Kerouac's dramatic imagination. To think of the typing of the text as one of several linked performances allows the reader to listen to punctuation and italics more as physical traces or as stage directions than as the grammatical scaffoldings of the text.[5]

This print-dramatic sensibility is informed by Kerouac's own sense of his writing process. Kerouac self-consciously framed his writing/typing as a performance, and he took pride in his technique. His father had been a printer and Jack grew up "in a world of type, galleys, and proofs" (Theado 12). The craft of writing was a physical challenge for Kerouac as much as an artistic, spiritual, or intellectual one. Matt Theado has suggested that Kerouac associated his typing with the same kind of athleticism that took him to Columbia University to play football, a combination of "physical speed, strength, and recklessness" (13). By reading these reckless scenes of typing, Theado and

5 Tim Hunt also turns to the Capote line as a way to establish the "performative quality" of Kerouac's writing (182). His argument very much resonates with my own, but he locates the performative quality in live jazz and in the immediacy of the second-person address, without considering the broader framework of theater or drama.

other critics have connected Kerouac with a new kind of literary theatricality, reframing his composition sessions as durational performances.[6] Kerouac famously typed for three drug-laced and sleep-deprived weeks to produce the continuous 120-foot scroll of *On the Road*. The manuscript is now a touring art object in galleries and libraries, and its display is more a memorial to the spatiotemporal event of its production than to the mass-produced novel it makes possible.

With this richer sense of the setting for Kerouac's writing, *Beat Generation*'s spontaneous speeches are perhaps lent a more prominent performance element. The text rediscovers percussive rhythms in its course and "a syncopation that could be enacted by a jazz musician or sounded on a typewriter" (Theado 14). Especially in the longer monologues, Kerouac finds characteristic verve, adding, clarifying, and exclaiming, choreographing ideas in something like live improvisation. It is as if Kerouac forgets there are other actors onstage—in a good way. He returns to that precarious, singular voice that is trying to hold everything together while knowing that it all falls apart. He just keeps typing.

In "Belief & Technique," Kerouac provides glimpses of this aspiration, of straining to type expansive stories in a singular voice: "Telling the true story of the world in interior monolog." This way of fitting the whole world into monologue salutes a familiar literary ancestor, that is, Walt Whitman and his own inclusive pronoun play. In a related spirit, Joyce Johnson named her recent Kerouac biography—one of the many—*The Voice Is All*. This title too draws attention to that one typed voice, that exteriorized-interior that tries to tell the true story of the world. Johnson attributes the phrase to Kerouac himself and positions it as the early-career breakthrough that made all his work possible (6). In the novels, "the voice is all" and it becomes something to listen to and to mouth the words along to. Listening to *Beat Generation*, it seems there may have been too many voices for Kerouac to make them different or keep them straight. Kerouac's prose strives to contain multitudes in sheeted steel, but it remains monologically singular and this resists being effectively thrown onstage.

6 Hunt and the poet Kenneth Goldsmith have both recently explored this relation.

Performing the Novel

In recent considerations of Kerouac's work, there are consistent invitations to view him in a different light, whether as a cultural icon, a novelist, a musician, a photographer, a filmmaker, or even a painter.[7] In one sense, *Beat Generation* adds another line to Kerouac's growing resume. More broadly and more importantly, the play provides the dramatic imagination and the precedent for considering Kerouac's many engagements within a single artistic framework. In the Duluoz Legend, Kerouac's varied work is unified into something like a scripted *Gesamtkunstwerk*, where the bookplay can figuratively synthesize all of the other arts. It is in these novels that Kerouac consistently draws on a much wider *dramatic* palette: he involves the reader in a heightened immediacy of reading; he continually blends and bends sensory imagery; and he suggests that this legend is not the document of a historical performance so much as scripted directions for stories still to come.

At the end of *Tristessa* (1960), for example, the voice calls for an ambitious—almost impossible—dramatic synthesis; it repositions the novel as a future-looking script, or a bookmovie to keep listening to. In the final pages of this novella about a junkie, religion, and love in Mexico City, Jack feels out of place. His romances with both the place and Tristessa have faded. Heroin has addled and rattled his friends, Old Bull Gaines and Tristessa "both bags of bones" (96). Kerouac, character and performance typist, gets going: "I'd leave them be and go on my way . . . and drink aperitif with coffee muggers on the card street—O movie—A movie by God, showing us him—him,—and us showing him." It might be Kerouac's favorite movie, so he cashes out:

> I'll go light candles to the Madonna, I'll paint the Madonna, and eat ice cream, benny and bread . . . I'll go to the south of Sicily in the winter, and paint memories of Arles—I'll buy a piano and Mozart

7 Nearly simultaneously with the rediscovery of *Beat Generation*, Ed Adler collected and published Kerouac's "lost" drawings and paintings in *Departed Angels* (2004). Kerouac's work is surprisingly varied and accomplished, and Adler suggests that Kerouac was "decidedly an 'insider'" in the New York art world of his day (142). Especially during the late 1950s—coincident with *Beat Generation* and "Belief & Technique"—Kerouac was steadily making art and was in close contact with a number of eminent artists, including Willem de Kooning.

> me that—I'll write long sad tales about people in the legend of my life—This part is my part of the movie, let's hear yours (96)

This prose is scattered with props, lit by candlelight coming off a painting that's yet to come. As Jack schemes, fueled by next-round cocktails of Benzedrine and ice cream, he imagines memories of a place he has yet to go, and Mozart is a verb. This type of playful and future-oriented talk is a long way from *Beat Generation*'s ending, in which the characters fall asleep. The end of *Tristessa* is the bookmovie-you-listen-to of the people in Kerouac's life. And he leaves it open to do some listening of his own; he wants to hear your part of the movie—there's no full stop.

Much of the criticism on Kerouac, notably that of Tim Hunt and Regina Weinreich, strives to recover Kerouac as a literary writer, to counter, complicate, and complement his more prominent reputation as a cultural icon. One of the principal strategies in this reassessment is to interpolate Kerouac into an American novel tradition, to place him in line after the likes of Melville, Twain, and Fitzgerald. Critical narratives on influence are of course rarely fixed or linear; the beat generation only hazily follows the lost generation, despite the resemblance of the names. Even so, Kerouac's bookmovie prose seems especially resistant to canonization, and its radical differences to other writing more than its resemblances reframe Kerouac's critical and popular legacies in a *dramatically* new way.

When Fitzgerald's Nick Carraway is swept into his first party at Gatsby's—to stage one scene of Kerouac's distinction—the sentences become long and effusive, perhaps even tipsy: "Laughter is easier minute by minute, spilled with prodigality, tipped out at a cheerful word. The groups change more swiftly, swell with new arrivals, dissolve and form in the same breath" (40-41). Carraway tries to keep up with the band, in which "[a] celebrated tenor had sung in Italian, and a notorious contralto had sung in jazz" (46). He riffs on "spilled" and "tipped" and he marks the sounds of swift swells; he rhymes Italian and jazz, to transpose jazz into the language it already was. His tactics here are excellent examples of the matching of form and content and of conflating—and naming—the musicality of the language and of the mood.

Tristessa's prose, scored by dashes, does not exactly display a match of form and content, and it is hard to reconcile with even its most comparable stylistic forebears. With its oddity to the eye and the ear, this modern prose calls on the reader to rehearse or recite in order to gloss the text's elusive sense. The isolated gestures and images in the writing may correspond to literary terms and devices—synesthesia here, ekphrasis there—but this vocabulary seems to mostly miss the point. Kerouac's is a denser, less strictly literary text that continuously leads elsewhere. The composition leaves the reader no choice but "to cross conceptual wires," as the anthropologist Clifford Geertz puts it in his broader reading of cultural practices (445). Geertz's methodology—which incidentally is embraced by many performance studies scholars—is in more comfortable step with Kerouac than a close literary reading or a search for canonical affiliations would be. Kerouac's writing is the scripted element of a broader and denser social text, about which Geertz writes: "the established conjunctions between objects and their qualities are altered, and phenomena . . . are clothed in signifiers which normally point to other referents." Kerouac Mozarts Mexico City, Sicily, and wherever he is typing into a kind of stage space littered with pills and unfinished paintings, a space where anything can happen depending on the lighting or the next entrance. It is culture, performance, or perhaps a "flow of feeling unimpeded." The novel is only one part of the movie.

In *On the Road*—the work that needs the least introduction but perhaps the most rehabilitation—Kerouac alters these conjunctions and redresses these signifiers to develop an unprecedentedly rich dramaturgy of highway-crossed America. The characters rant and revel and ramble, as they do in *Beat Generation* and elsewhere, but *On the Road* takes more time to design the space, refine the details, and rehearse heartbreak across three years of fieldwork and three furious weeks of typing. He works, like a director, from notebooks and scripts. Dean Moriarty's voice is all, but so is Sal Paradise's listening, and Kerouac's typing, and the car and the road that hold them all together. The world takes shape around the talk.

In a characteristic episode, Sal and Dean drive from New York City to

Virginia and back in a single night. Dean launches onto the Interstate and into the conversation, and the talk and the drive seem to converge in the typing, "Now this is the first time we've been alone and in a position to talk for years" (119). He indicates to Sal and the reader that these ideas have been distilling, decanting, and they now pour forth. Sal interrupts for a moment with the explanatory stage direction, "And he talked all night." In the relayed all-night talk there are the same abstractions, the same potentially pretentious effusions as in *Beat Generation*, but here Kerouac more artfully performs theatrical sleights-of-hand, directing the eye and the ear to the constructed spaces that fall between the words and hold them up. Kerouac splices speech with gestures and images; he designs and directs. And Dean keeps talking:

> "Everything is fine, God exists, we know time. Everything since the Greeks has been predicated wrong. You can't make it with geometry and geometrical systems of thinking. It's all *this!*" He wrapped his finger in his fist; the car hugged the line straight and true. (120)

Sal draws our attention to how Dean wraps his finger in his fist, like *this*, and "the car hugged the line straight and true." With that gesture, rendered in the conventional italics of stage directions, the reader is asked not only to see it but to make it happen again, to witness and re-enact *that* finger in *that* fist.

As the talk resumes and that gesture transforms into a grip on the wheel, the *this*-ness somehow pulses through the car to produce the road and the guiding line down its center, "straight and true." This concatenated metonymy functions as what Roland Barthes calls the "reality effect," wherein a seemingly inconsequential thing comes to unexpectedly signify "nothing but this: *we are the real*" (148). This effect holds for novelistic discourse—Barthes's chief example is a barometer in Flaubert—but it has a clear corollary in theater. Carol Martin leans on Barthes's term to describe her "theatre of the real," how a physical "citation . . . confers the status of legitimacy upon the artwork with the concomitant sense that what is represented is real" (5). And Andrew

Sofer makes similar moves in *The Stage Life of Props*, suggesting how a well-placed scenic detail works as "*visual shorthand*" for a broader scene, a concrete synecdoche for the dramatic imagination. In *On the Road*, the world takes shape around the touch of Dean's hand on the steering wheel. Later on the same page, that same world is expanded with a pack of cigarettes and a Groucho Marx-walk "with the coattails flying, except that [Dean] had no coattails" (120). Sometimes the stage directions even show us something that isn't there.

The road is a stage, in fiction as in theater. For Franco Moretti, the road marks "the very beginning of the modern European novel" (48), but it is also older and newer, a real place, and an especially theatrical one. It is at a crossroads that Oedipus kills his father. It is at a crime scene on the roadside that *Rashōmon* produces conflicting tellings (whether as a fifteenth-century Noh drama, a 1915 story, or a 1950 film). Closer to *Beat Generation*, of course, Estragon and Vladimir continue to wait by a road that might be in 1950s Florida; they may be the hitchhikers that Dean is going too fast to stop for. Roads produce, combine, and collide stories, and in theater like in fiction (following the work of Moretti and Mikhail Bakhtin) the space produces the work. Bert States, in his phenomenology for the theater, suggests that a diegetic place determines the stories told, that in the theater "Space is destiny" (69). In Kerouac, the gestures and the cigarettes and this Groucho Marx and that Mozart pepper the landscape, like improbable stage properties that produce the world as a specific destiny, straight and true.

Exit Stage-West

Beat Generation strangely illuminates the dramaturgy that informs Kerouac's novelistic discourse, underscoring the way in which his work's distinctiveness and its persistent appeal do not reside strictly in its literary qualities. The novels—like all good novels—invite something else, a kind of present voicing, a space for rehearsal. This strange effect of openness, the unconscious structuring of this literary world—to defer to Eric Hayot's recent theorization—leads to the most important way in which the dramatic imagination informs and infuses the novels. Reading Kerouac's road novels as both documentation of past performance *and* scripts to-be-performed serves to mediate the tension in Kerouac's legacy between his seemingly distinct—and sometimes at-odds—castings as a literary and a popular author. Reading the novels as scripts suggests how these two roles might be interdependent.

Kerouac's newly recognized involvement in a number of art movements reveals his artistic ambitions and provides a clearer sense of him as a cultural producer, rather than as a heavy drinker, a fast driver, and—as The Gap's 1993 ad would highlight—a khakis-wearer. And while his engagements with film, theater, and visual art in the late 1950s might not make him a significant filmmaker, playwright, or painter, they do inform our critical vocabulary for reckoning with his primary form, the novel (or that new form: a "flow of feeling unimpeded"). The novels remain Kerouac's most impressive work, but his practice with brushstrokes, storyboarding, and dramatizing provide an avenue for recovery of his reputation from its critically-damaging popularity.

While *On the Road* is a fixture in most takes on a mid-century American canon, its enduring popularity seems to also make literary critics dismissive of it; its treatment is not unlike that of J. D. Salinger's *Catcher in the Rye*. With a veritable beat industry to match the popular market—at the Beat Museum in San Francisco, for example, one can find Kerouac's name, words, and image on t-shirts, bags, and other collectibles—the majority of publications on Kerouac are pitched to a "fan" readership; there are many more books about his life and his milieu than about his work. According to a review of the most recent biography, there are "about a dozen biographies . . . not to mention memoirs, an oral history—the excellent 'Jack's book' (1978)—and wider surveys of the Beat Generation" (Campbell). Each new work is driven by interest in a different biographical angle, and that attention seems to inversely produce a disinterest in the novels *as* literature. As with *Catcher in the Rye*, most critics are satisfied to have read *On the Road* only—in school, or as a young rebellion *against* school. *The Guardian* recently corroborated this demographic marketing, with a piece about the book's enduring appeal on their website. Tara, the first-name-only contributor to the Teen Books section, writes: "Surpassing the boundaries of physical geography, the novel typifies what it is to be a teenager." Despite the fact that the novel follows two twenty-something men, the parts always seem open for play or adaptation, by female British teenagers, or most anyone else. There is something in the texts themselves, in the unconscious of its road-trip chronotope, that produces this persistent feeling that it is a script to be acted out—and *this* textual effect may help flip the script on the novel's sometimes-infantilized treatment.

Tara concludes her article by saying, "To those who haven't [yet read it]—grab a copy, fill your tank with petrol and buckle up. You won't regret it." The book continues to be read as somewhere between a novel and a set of lengthy, personalized stage directions. The Kerouac-inspired road trip has become a staple in the popular imagination, whether that takes the form of broad cultural influence (as Rowland Sherrill suggests in *Road-Book America*), of celebrity reenactments (as in the Kerouac-styled trips of Russell Brand and Katy Perry), or of a teenager writing for other teens on a blog. The world that Kerouac constructs through his typed performance crosses both real highways and conceptual wires. It reads as a flexible set of directions, lit alternately by street, reading, and stage lights. The novels insist on a cumulative openness while promising what always feels like a personal invitation; they are scriptive things.[8] They remain works-in-progress to be revised and synthesized later—that always-later which might be now. The Duluoz Legend is therefore a performance text composed of the written traces in notebooks, the memories of conversations, long-typed scrolls, and the tattered copies circulating among traveling friends. The details keep changing, just like the characters' names and the routes we might next drive. This open and playful quality, emerging from Kerouac's bookmovie stagecraft, shows one way in which celebrity and literary style may be related—dramatically—and need not be pitted against each other: the novel's popularity is in part due to its inviting theatricality. The effect of the novels' complex constructions is an enduring popular fandom, while its cause is a system of beliefs and techniques that are not quite accounted for by literary terms and traditions.

8 In her work, Robin Bernstein theorizes "scriptive things" as material objects that inspire and guide particular sets of embodied behaviors.

Kerouac's writing is still ongoing, still becoming the Duluoz Legend in its revival, reception, and reenactment. Its open and reiterative legacy rhymes with a theater script's, as a performance history is shaped by both archival materials and their present and future stagings. As this Kerouac drama proceeds, Sal Paradise might come to admit that he's really Jack Duluoz, who might also be Jack Kerouac, typing away or playing a part. And through all the performance-typing, at least one of the characters still seems to be saying, to teenagers and critics alike, "This is my part of the movie, let's hear yours"

WORKS CITED

Barthes, Roland. "The Reality Effect." *The Rustle of Language*. Trans. Richard Howard. Berkeley: U of California P, 1989. 141-8. Print.

"'Beat Generation' to be Staged in Literary Icon's Hometown." U of Massachusetts Lowell, 12 Mar. 2012. Web. 22 Aug. 2014.

Beckett, Samuel. *The Complete Dramatic Works*. London: Faber and Faber, 1986. Print.

Bernstein, Robin. *Racial Innocence: Performing American Childhood from Slavery to Civil Rights*. New York: New York UP, 2011. Print.

Brown, Joel. "Jack Kerouac's 'Beat Generation' comes to the stage." *The Boston Globe*. 6 Oct. 2012. Web. 14 Aug. 2014.

Campbell, James. "Road Ready." Rev. of *The Voice Is All*, Joyce Johnson. *New York Times*. 18 Jan. 2013. Web. 20 Aug. 2014.

Fitzgerald, F. Scott. *The Great Gatsby*. 1925. New York: Scribner, 2004. Print.

Frank, Robert. *The Americans*. Intro. Jack Kerouac. New York: Grove P, 1959. Print.

Glaister, Dan. "'Lost' Kerouac play resurfaces after 50 years." *Guardian*. 20 May 2005. Web. 14 Aug. 2014.

Goldsmith, Kenneth. "Uncreative Writing." *Harriet: A Poetry Blog*. The Poetry Foundation. 23 Jan. 2007. Web. 22 Aug. 2014.

Hayot, Eric. *On Literary Worlds*. Oxford: Oxford UP, 2012. Print.

Hunt, Jim. *Jack Kerouac's Crooked Road: The Development of a Fiction*. 1981. Berkeley: U of California P, 1996. Print.

—. "Kerouac and the Subversion of Modern Print Textuality." *Tim Hunt: Poetry, Textual Theory, Modern American Lit.* 2013. Web. 22 Aug. 2014.

—. "Typetalking: Voice and Performance in *On the Road*," *What's Your Road Man? Critical Essays on Jack Kerouac's* On the Road. Ed. Hillary Holladay and Robert Holton. Carbondale: Southern Illinois UP, 2009. 169-186. Print.

Johnson, Joyce. *The Voice Is All: The Lonely Victory of Jack Kerouac.* New York: Viking, 2012. Print.

Kerouac, Jack. *Beat Generation.* New York: Thunder's Mouth Press, 2005. Print.

—. "Belief & Technique in Modern Prose." *Evergreen Review* 2.8 (1959): 57. Print.

—. *Departed Angels: The Lost Paintings.* Ed. Ed Adler. Boston: De Capo P., 2004. Print.

—. *On the Road.* 1957. New York: Penguin, 1991. Print.

—. *Tristessa.* 1960. New York: Penguin, 1992. Print.

Miller, Arthur. *Death of a Salesman.* 1949. New York: Penguin, 1988. Print.

Martin, Carol. *Theatre of the Real.* New York: Palgrave Macmillan, 2012. Print.

McGrath, Charles. "Visions of Kerouac at an Un-Beat Symposium." *New York Times.* 26 Oct. 2005. Web. 14 Aug. 2014.

Moretti, Franco. *Atlas of the European Novel, 1800-1900.* London: Verso, 1999. Print.

Sargeant, Jack. *Naked Lens: Beat Cinema.* London: Creation Books, 1997. Print.

Shakespeare, William. *As You Like It. The Riverside Shakespeare.* 2nd ed. Ed. G. Blakemore Evans and J. J. M. Tobin. Boston: Houghton Mifflin, 1996. 403-34. Print.

Sherrill, Rowland A. *Road-Book America: Contemporary Culture and the New Picaresque.* Urbana-Champaign: U of Illinois P, 2000. Print.

Sofer, Andrew. *The Stage Life of Props.* Ann Arbor: U of Michigan P, 2003. Print.

States, Bert. *Great Reckonings in Little Rooms: On the Phenomenology of Theater.* Berkeley: U of California P, 1987. Print.

Tara. "The magic of Kerouac: On the Road and teenage experience." *theguardian.com.* 6 Jul. 2012. Web. 18 Aug. 2014.

Taxidou, Olga. *The Mask: A Periodical Performance by Edward Gordon Craig.* Oxon: Routledge, 1998. Print.

Theado, Matt. "Revisions of Kerouac: The Long, Strange Trip of the *On the Road* Typescripts." *What's Your Road Man? Critical Essays on Jack Kerouac's* On the Road. Ed. Hillary Holladay and Robert Holton. Carbondale: Southern Illinois UP, 2009. 8-34. Print.

Weinreich, Regina. *Kerouac's Spontaneous Poetics: A Study of the Fiction.* New York: Thunder's Mouth P, 2002. Print.

Worthen, W. B. *Print and the Poetics of Modern Drama.* Cambridge: Cambridge UP, 2009. Print.

W. MICHELLE WANG

WRITING FOR THE EAR: ALASDAIR GRAY THE PLAYWRIGHT

Though Alasdair Gray is best known as an artist and a novelist—a large part of his literary corpus was published in the eighties and nineties following the success of his Scottish epic *Lanark* (1981)—it was his dramatic work in radio and television a decade or two earlier that first familiarized Scottish audiences with Gray's work. The recognition of his importance as a playwright re-emerged six years ago when Luath Press, based in Scotland, published a collection of Gray's plays for stage, radio, and television, produced between 1956 and 2009. In light of this special edition of novel-writing playwrights and playwriting novelists, Gray merits especial interest given the ease and deliberateness with which he transcends boundaries and mixes mediums. Through a comparative analysis of the play and prose versions of *Quiet People* (play 1968; novel 1990) and *Near the Driver* (play 1975; short story 1993), I suggest that despite the adaptive nature of his work, Gray is highly attuned to medium specificity. By pointing to elements such as performative directions in the play script and the synthesis of its thematic and aesthetic qualities, I explain how Gray writes specifically for the ear by creating effects that aren't quite replicable in the short story and how the stories remain, at heart, plays for voices.

Gray's plays are worthy of critical attention not least because they have been the genus for so much of his later work in prose fiction. At least four of his plays have been re-written as novels: *A History Maker* (play 1965; novel 1994), *The Fall of Kelvin Walker* (play 1966; staged 1967; adapted for television 1968; novel 1985), *McGrotty and Ludmilla* (written as a television play 1973; first appeared as a radio play 1975; staged 1987; novel 1990), and *Mavis Belfrage* (commissioned for television 1968; broadcast 1973; staged 1975; published in 1996 alongside two other adapted plays and subtitled *A Romantic Novel with Five Shorter Tales*). Two collections of short stories, *Lean Tales* (1985) and *Ten Tales Tall & True*, include various re-written stage, radio, and television plays. Gray's propensity for playing with medium boundaries is further evident in *Something Leather* (1990), which hovers the uncertain border between a novel and a collection of short stories, whereby six of its fourteen chapters were originally written as stage/radio/television plays.[1]

The bulk of Gray's dramatic output occurred in the sixties and seventies, and often "reflect the political mood of the time they were written" (Gray, *Play Book* 10). Gray's summary of how his dramatic work reflects "the body and pressure of their times" is worth quoting at length: *The Fall of Kelvin Walker*, "[m]y sexual comedies and *Mavis Belfrage*," for instance, evince the "widespread sense of liberation" amongst young Britons and imaginatively explore the experience of living in London at a time when "British fashions in dress, pop music and cinema [were] widely known abroad" (334). On the other hand,

> *The Man Who Knew About Electricity* shows real poverty returning to Britain as building programmes and new motorways destroy old districts and communities. Public scandals showed many civil servants and politicians were being bribed by industries they were starting to privatize—see *McGrotty and Ludmilla* . . . Despite trade union resistance, British heavy industries were asset stripped and destroyed, as reflected in my *Rumpus Room*. Later plays, including *Fleck* which I am certain is my best, show a world of governments whose only aim is monetary power got by using laws and police forces. (334)

Working simultaneously on *Lanark* in the sixties, some of Gray's most crucial themes—likewise common to his novels—such as dystopia, the threat of corporatization, and the dynamics of sexual power are already evident in early plays such as *Near the Driver* (1975), *Quiet People* (1968), and *The Loss of the Golden Silence* (1973).

Though *A Gray Play Book* (2009) lauds Gray as "one of Scotland's greatest

1 The preceding list in this paragraph was assembled using Stephen Bernstein's appendix of "Alasdair Gray's Fiction Based on His Plays" in his critical volume *Alasdair Gray* (pp.161-62) and information taken from Alasdair Gray's official website, http://alasdairgray.info/.

playwright[s],"[2] there has been a regrettable deficit of academic scholarship pertaining to his work as a dramatist. Apart from Gray's own headnotes within the play book, to my knowledge, only four other critical pieces address Gray's work as a playwright. The most recent is Jean Berton's "A Subversive View of Scotland in the 'Now Plays'" in *Alasdair Gray: Ink for Worlds* (2014), focusing on his recent dramatic work written between 2006 and 2008.[3] Stephen Bernstein closely examines texts such as *The Fall of Kelvin Walker*, *McGrotty and Ludmilla*, *Something Leather*, *A History Maker*, and *Mavis Belfrage*, rightly noting that they all have their genesis in plays. Bernstein, however, analyzes these texts in their fictional rather than dramatic mode.

Rodge Glass's *Alasdair Gray: A Secretary's Biography* (2008) traces Gray's career as a dramatist in piecemeal fashion, providing important contextual information about the commissioning of plays against the backdrop of Gray's life and career up to 2008. More pertinently, Glass comments critically on plays such as *Goodbye Jimmy* (2006), noting that

> Alasdair's plays have been criticized for being weaker than his fiction. His characters are two-dimensional, some say—mere mouthpieces for Gray's opinions, who cannot be believed by intelligent audiences. It is harsh to generalize all his drama, the best of which contains perfectly rounded characters, but in this case it is a relevant point. *Goodbye Jimmy* doesn't always feel like it needs to be a play: the story might work equally well, if not better, on the page. (284-5)

David Hutchison likewise observes that in the dramatic version of *McGrotty and Ludmilla*, "characters are one-dimensional, and the shafts of wit about political opportunism do not develop into a coherent comic version. The novel version . . . is much more effective, because the dialogue is framed by Gray's narrative persona, and that persona offers a sustained ironic commentary which the dialogue by itself does not carry" (154). Hutchison traces the

2 http://www.luath.co.uk/a-gray-play-book-deluxe-edition.html. Accessed 1 May 2014.

3 At the time of writing, this volume of critical work *Alasdair Gray: Ink for Worlds* had yet to be released.

trajectory of Gray's dramatic output against the landscape of Scottish dramatic production and notes that "[a]s a dramatist, Alasdair Gray is less given to experiment than he is in his fiction," since most of his work tends to be "naturalistic in form and there is nothing to compare with the interpenetration of the real and the imagined to be found in *Lanark*" (150).

Glass and Hutchison make a similar point about one important weakness in some of Gray's plays: despite the adaptability of his work across mediums, the writing is at its weakest when it fails to account for the particularities of its chosen medium, as evident in Glass's comment that *Goodbye Jimmy* works better as prose than play and Hutchison's analogous assessment of *McGrotty and Ludmilla*. Such weaknesses become particularly visible when both fictional and dramatic forms of the same work are readily available to audiences and critics for comparison. What this also offers from a scholarly point of view, however, is a valuable theoretical opportunity to understand processes of artistic creation via comparisons of Gray's work in its various forms, so as to gain insight about writing with medium specificity in mind and factors influencing successful transmedia writing.

Apart from creatively (and economically) re-working plays as prose, Gray's interest in playing with mixed mediums is further evident in the way he purposefully blends art with writing. One prominent way he achieves this is through the creative agency he exercises over the visual layout of his texts, which includes illustrating the designs of cover artworks, inset drawings, and author self-portraits. Gray's attentiveness to medium and visual presentation is also evident in his use of stylistic textual idiosyncrasies such as his hallmark "Goodbye" page/section across his literary works, running commentaries in the headers of particular texts, and *Lanark*'s famous "Index of Plagiarisms" tucked in the margins of the "Epilogue" section.[4]

Gray notes in the preface of *A Gray Playbook* that "[r]eaders of my novels and stories will find them here in their earliest form, though not in immature or clumsier forms" (9). Notwithstanding the evident creative economy of rechanneling his early dramatic work into prose fiction, such continuous,

4 The "Index of Plagiarisms" came about as a result of "a typesetter's miscalculation," Gray explains, that "gave me about a foot of blank column in the margin, which I filled" (White 69).

deliberate refashioning evinces not only Gray's sense of the continually evolving nature of his own literary art-form and artistic propensity for crossing mediums, but perhaps points also to critics' implicit neglect of these plays in scholarly critiques of his work—despite the fact that the plays fuel his fiction in direct and important ways. The trajectory of Gray's literary career would quite simply be an incomplete story without a critical examination of his work as a dramatist—a dearth that can now be rectified with readers' access to his early plays, which Gray definitively states are by no means less polished than the prose fiction into which they have been channeled.

I examine two of Gray's radio plays in this article and, taking the converse approach to some earlier critiques, focus on works that I consider to be *more* successful in dramatic form and explain why this is so through comparative analyses of the prose and play versions of *Quiet People* and *Near the Driver*. I suggest that Gray's plays are more successful when they are attentive to medium particularities and that in addition to the similarity of subject matter in his fictional and dramatic work—concerns with "structures of political, institutional and sexual power that present themselves as 'normal'" (Donaldson and Lee 155)—such attention to medium differences is a critical point of similarity between Gray the novelist and Gray the playwright.

As one of the "most efficient and cost-effective way[s] of reaching a huge audience"—especially with the move from analog to digital technology in the age of Internet radio with the advent of the world wide web—Tim Crook notes that "[r]adio drama and radio drama-documentary expression are undoubtedly the most understated creative, dramatic and literary art forms and seem to have suffered an element of cultural neglect in terms of the volume of critical publication," and are "under-explored [in] academic study compared with other dramatic media" (ix). My analysis of both Gray's first and last (widely) available radio plays works not only toward contributing to an understanding of his dramatic work, but is also an attempt to address the critical lack and underdevelopment that Crook identifies in the study of radio drama.

Quiet People was one of six broadcast radio plays Gray wrote between 1968 and 1977. Commissioned and produced by Scottish BBC Radio, it was later rewritten as an episode in *Something Leather* (1990; thereafter renamed *Glaswegians* [2012])—which the blurb on the inner flap of the book's dust jacket describes as "a series of vignettes that together provide a kaleidoscopic portrait" of the sexual and emotional lives of four women, Donalda, Senga, June, and Harry, from 1963 to 1990. The move from play to prose meant a significant revision not only in the style but content of *Quiet People*, as the episode had to cohere with the narrative thread of the larger novel. The play thus shifts from a focus on the dynamics between landlord and lodgers (the Mitchels and Browns respectively) to account for the episode's relationship to the rest of the novel by recasting the female lodger as one of the novel's four protagonists, Donalda. Another major difference between the two versions is that the play is a complete episode that begins with the Browns inquiring about the room, to their move into and eventual departure from the Mitchels' home, whereas the novel—which comprises fourteen chapters that describe discrete episodes at various points of the four female protagonists' lives—begins with the Liddels (previously known in the play as the Mitchels) renting their room out to a dubious stranger who leaves after one night, and later to Donalda and her family. The chapter concludes without a wholly satisfactory resolution to the tension between the Liddels and their lodgers.

A novel set in a cycle of short stories, *Something Leather* is widely considered to be one of Gray's weaker books. Part of the reason for this is that unlike most of his other plays-turned-prose, which tend to be transmedia adaptations of single works, "*Something Leather* draws on a mixed bag of half a dozen radio and television scripts originally written between 1968 and 1974" and has been "[d]ismissed as 'a shameless re-hash of sorry kitchen-sink dramas'" (Bernstein 99). The reworked dramatic chapters, however, are what Bernstein considers most worthy of interest in the novel, as he notes that the main problem with the book has less to do with the content of those chapters and more to do with "the poor thematic fit between them and the seven chapters written expressly for the novel. The main characters . . . are visible in the dramatic chapters, but too often it is clear that Gray has only sketched them in hastily to make the chapter's inclusion in the novel comprehensible" (99).

Gray explains the novel's composition in the final epilogue chapter:

> The chapters called "The Proposal," "The Man Who Knew about Electricity," "In the Boiler Room" and "A Free Man with a Pipe" stick so close to original plays that they contain nearly every word of the original dialogue. "Mr Lang and Ms Tain" uses half a play, "Quiet People" the start of one. If readers of "Quiet People" feel worried for the Liddels I can show them typed proof that the Liddels and their lodgers were good for each other, separating with friendship on both sides, though very suddenly. (*Something Leather* 251)

In the episodic novel, the Liddels are a retired, middle-aged couple who reluctantly rent their room to some rather shady lodgers on multiple occasions. No resolution in the relationship is achieved by the end of the chapter and the Liddels fall asleep wondering if their new lodgers are using the rented room as a brothel. In the earlier dramatic version of *Quiet People*, the Mitchels are a retired couple who rent a room to the Browns—here, they are dubiously engaged in the scrap business—and it is to this text that Gray refers, where readers find proof that the reluctant landlords and grateful lodgers separate "with friendship on both sides, though very suddenly," by the end of the play.

When Gray recasts Donalda—one of the novel's four protagonists—as the female lodger in *Quiet People*, this causes a fundamental shift in the dynamics of character relations since the play casts the Mitchels as the protagonists, while the chapter gives relatively equal attention to both sides in order to account for the coherence of the novel as a whole. The shift is a necessary move for the novel's narrative coherence that unfortunately ends up weakening the episode, since dramatic tension is sustained in the original play by restricting audience's access to the lodgers' minds and lives such that the interaction given in the dialogue becomes a crucial means of inferring the Browns' intentions and motivations. Gray thus keeps his (radio) audience hanging on to the dialogue—the medium's dominant channel of communication—by using focalization to great effect. This careful balance is disrupted when Donalda is cast in the role of the female lodger in the novel, effectively furnishing audiences with sufficient background context about the lodgers from preceding chapters, so as to dilute the dramatic tension hitherto present in the terse dialogues between the Mitchels and Browns.

The term *focalization* was coined by Gérard Genette to more precisely account for the way "perspective" or "point of view" is typically introduced in narratives. Focalization "may be defined as a selection or restriction of narrative information in relation to the experience and knowledge" of the narrator or characters in the storyworld (Niederhoff). While narratological concepts such as focalization have traditionally and dominantly been used in reference to prose narratives, scholars like Manfred Jahn have argued for narratology's applicability to plays. It is only "in recent times," Monika Fludernik notes, that the discipline "has started to focus on drama as a narrative genre—quite oddly so, since some of the key concepts of narratology derive from Aristotle's *Poetics*, whose prime example for elucidation of plot was the Athenian stage" (355). In turning to Gray's dramatic work, I thus hope not only to draw attention to his importance as a playwriting novelist/novel-writing playwright, but also to use my analysis to show how narratology can be fruitfully applied to dramatic analyses. Though narratologists like Brian Richardson have labored to build a narratology of drama by establishing a shared vocabulary of analytical tools that can be used to study both prose fiction and drama, Ansgar Nünning and Roy Sommer observe that, excepting film studies and Richardson's own work, dominant issues in narrative studies such as "unreliable narration" or "focalization in drama has received hardly any attention to date" (341-3). "Much work clearly needs to be done before a full-fledged narratology of drama emerges" (Fludernik 378). By showing how focalization functions as a result of Gray's attention to medium in my comparative analysis of *Quiet People*, I hope to likewise contribute to the growth of narratology in drama by showing its applicability to Gray's radio plays.

Gray himself notes in *A Gray Play Book* that despite the adaptive nature of his work, "*Quiet People* worked best as a radio play" (62)—an assessment I agree with—and I suggest that one crucial dimension of its success as a "play for voices," as Gray puts it, has to do with the way it sustains dramatic tension through the use of focalization. The dramatic version of *Quiet People* observes "Aristotle's golden rule of unity of action": every word, line, and scene "serves a dramatic purpose in terms of the play's characterisation and plot development," and does away with all redundancies or inconsistencies in "the development of the main character towards the main crisis and action" (Crook 172)—namely, (the outcome of) the Mitchels' experience with their lodgers, who are of a very different class and lifestyle, and what they learned and gained from the experience. The unexpected, eventual realization that the Mitchels / "Liddels and their lodgers were good for each other" (*Something Leather* 251) is very much the point of *Quiet People*.

The play's move from exposition to rising action and climax to denouement are well-paced and tautly written, such that every event serves a dramatic purpose of furthering plot or character development; all that is said is as important as that which has been left unsaid. Sandy Brown's seemingly innocuous and apparently generous act of giving Tom Mitchel the books he picks up during his removal work, for instance, is later revealed to be an occasion for Brown's manipulation. Dramatic tension is sustained by the audience's task of (and pleasure in) inferring what has been left unsaid, such as the gradual revelation of Sandy Brown as a manipulative opportunist. Brown first invites Mitchel for a drink on the pretext of getting to know him better (later shown to be a strategy for browbeating Mitchel into allowing Brown's brother-in-law to stay in their already overcrowded rented room); he later uses Mitchel to evict this brother-in-law, Jimmy (and thus gets out of paying Jimmy, who accuses Mitchel of cheating him); and, finally, when Brown wheedles two pounds out of Mitchel (for the aforementioned books) before going back on the run. The pleasure audiences derive in gradually inferring Brown's character is made possible by restricting information about the lodgers through focalization.

Crook observes that good radio plays depend on the mediation of narrative information: "[t]he creative radio drama producer knows too much information causes frustration and consternation and that too little information induces boredom. Radio drama is an art of striking a balance or equilibrium within in its directions of narrative" (95). Gray achieves this in *Quiet People* by focalizing the play largely through the Mitchels, such that listeners or readers are privy to private conversations between the couple, whilst restricting our access to the minds of the Browns, by keeping our knowledge of them to only what is said in conversation with the Mitchels; all other knowledge about the Browns has to be inferred from the dynamics of the interactions between the two families, or based on the Mitchels' reports of and reactions to events that occur "off-stage"—such as when Mitchel sees Jimmy eavesdropping on the Browns.

Focalization is also established through the use of spatialization, creating a sense of "panoramic perspective" for the ear that operates similarly to the camera's "long shot and close shot" in film (Crook 75). Gray's attention to this panoramic sound-perspective is apparent in his use of cues such as "*In the distance the chime of a doorbell*" and distinctions between "*distant*" and "*approaching*" sounds in his radio playscripts (*Play Book* 66-67). The reader/listener does not have to be told when the Mitchels are conversing in the privacy of their room (and out of their lodgers' earshot); this is established in the radio play through the closing of doors. Following Mitchel's angry outburst at the Browns, "*[a] door is opened and slammed. Quick footsteps. A door is opened and shut. Sounds of* Mitchel *breathing deeply*" followed by Mrs. Mitchel speaking creates a three-dimensional sense of their home for the ear, and establishes an intimacy between the listener/reader and the Mitchels by controlling the information and character thoughts we are privy to through the use of focalization. The spatialization created by Gray's performative directions in his radio plays (parallel to stage directions) fosters a sense of intimacy, as we "overhear" the Mitchels in conversation within the privacy of their bedroom.

As the play progresses toward its dramatic climax—when three policemen arrive at the Mitchels' home with Mr. Brown in tow[5]—Gray includes an increasing number of "off-stage" sound directions to create suspense and dramatic tension, as the audience waits with Mrs. Mitchel to find out what has

5 Mrs. Mitchel's reaction to this incident is instructive as it illustrates one of the play's key thematic concerns—the confrontation of two very different classes and lifestyles, and its impact on the Mitchels: "Tom, this is terrible. I've never had police in the house in my life. What will the neighbours say? We'll have to do something. It's like living with an unexploded bomb. We never know what's going to happen" (Gray, *Play Book* 67).

happened. The increasing number of sound directions as the play progresses works effectively in contrast to the story's title, *Quiet People*, to manifest not only the metaphorical but literal, auditory disruption to the Mitchels' initial quiet lives.

Most of these nuances in perspective and sound are lost in the transition from play to prose. In order to account for the overall coherence of the novel set in a cycle of short stories, *Something Leather* contains lengthy expositions explaining Donalda's past as a narrative thread to help tether the fourteen chapters together, such that the dramatic tension established between the two families (and by extension, the two classes) is lost in the move. The Mitchels' sense of apprehension and unease with regards to the Browns' dubious origins and circumstances—a main source of dramatic tension in the play—is thrown open or discharged in the novel, as Donalda explains to Mrs. Liddel her circumstances of being driven into prostitution. Not only is there a distinct sense of diminished dramatic tension that is substituted with an almost undisguised voyeurism into Donalda's life as a sex worker, by making the lodgers' circumstances so bare-faced and unequivocal in the prose version, the Liddels' motivations for allowing Donalda and her family to stay on—especially given Mr. Liddel's persistent, ominous sense that "Britain is getting worse" (Gray, *Something Leather* 114; 130)—are considerably weakened. The chapter ends with Mr. Liddel wondering if their rented room is "being used just now as a brothel? Yes, that seems possible . . . All a good landlord should expect of his tenants is quiet and orderly conduct . . . and his lodgers have been as quiet as possible, in the circumstances. Tomorrow he will give them a key. Having decided this, a relaxation which is almost happiness pervades Mr. Liddel" as he falls asleep (131). The plot's progression and the Liddels' actions and motivations appear to be inconsistent with the portrait that the reader has been offered thus far.

Focalized through the Mitchels, the play's ending implicitly suggests that the couple decide to continue renting the room out less from economic necessity (Mrs. Mitchel notes that "[w]ith care I could manage not too badly without those extra pounds" [Gray, *Play Book* 68]), but more importantly because their experience with the Browns has connected them with a very different class of Glaswegians than the solid middle-class existence they are used to. Furthermore, the Mitchels surprise themselves (and us) by learning at the end that they have not been averse to the experience and are quite ready for the next adventure with some new lodgers, as evident in their reflections on the Browns following their departure and the decisive change from their initial desire to rent the room to a single person to the eventual decision to leave out the line, "Single persons only need apply" (68). The immediate "threat" posed by the Browns in the play vanishes with their removal from the Mitchels' home, such that the Mitchels can reflect on the experience rather fondly and with some nostalgia.

> MRS MITCHEL. It's good to be alone isn't it Tommy? I never appreciated peace and quiet until they came.
> MITCHEL. Aye, it's good . . . What a way to live Jean! . . . Never a month in the one place. Getting your money chancily from day to day. And the police after you! . . . Mind you, I didn't dislike them, Jean . . . They were feckless, but there was life in them. (68)

However, this is not the case in the prose version, where the Liddels' home is now potentially a partial brothel. The conclusion of the chapter in *Something Leather* is inconsistent with the impression of the Liddels readers have been given up to this point; neither are the Liddels' motivations for continuing to rent the room out to Donalda particularly convincing. The pleasure the Mitchels derived from their experience of a lifestyle wholly unlike their own is effectively conveyed in part by focalizing the radio play largely through their consciousness, thus keeping their lodgers' lives shrouded in an uncertainty that listeners/readers have to infer on our own—a stylistic move that is largely absent in the novel.

Gray's attention to medium becomes even more apparent in *Near the Driver*, which he calls his "best and last radio play" (*Play Book* 147). Whereas *Quiet People* is an effective, "straightforward little piece of naturalism" that manifests "Gray's comic talent," *Near the Driver* is a "fantastic play about an impossible train journey" that ends horribly for its passengers (Hutchison 151; Gray, *Play Book* 184). Described as a "social parable" and "political allegory," the passengers of an automated high-speed train in *Near the Driver* find themselves powerless to prevent a head-on collision with another train (Böhnke 117).

> When the train is about to crash and kill everyone including the driver, he is more concerned to keep order even at the price of his life than allow damage to government property. Gray is satirising the rigidity of thought that verges on insanity where a government is so convinced of the primacy of profit that it will not interfere in 'the market' even when the country is on the verge of annihilation . . . Gray specifically links this play with the government attitude to nuclear power stations, in the wake of the Three Mile Island accident. (Charlton; ctd. in Böhnke 119)

As Gray explains in the short talk that accompanied the play's broadcast on Scottish BBC Schools Radio in 1989,[6] the terrifying, almost dystopic quality of *Near the Driver* is meant to resonate with his own concerns about the direction of Britain's nuclear ambitions (*Play Book* 183-4). Bernstein observes that *Near the Driver* is "rooted in late-twentieth century technological anxiety" and "addresses both the experience of an impersonally digitized near future and a sentimental nostalgia for the nineteenth century symbolized through its greatest British engineer, the towering figure of Isambard Kingdom Brunel" (116). By attending to the synthesis of these thematic qualities with its aesthetic qualities in its medium particularities as a radio play, I suggest that Gray creates effects in the play version that are not quite replicable in the short story.

Unlike *Quiet People*, there are fewer differences between the play and prose versions of *Near the Driver*. Only minor details were revised, while the progression and structure of the *fabula* remains largely identical in both ver-

6 Gray also notes that since its conception in 1975, *Near the Driver* was rejected by BBC London on no fewer than three separate occasions over the course of a decade (*Play Book* 147; 183).

sions. I agree with Gray's own assessment that *Near the Driver* works more effectively as a radio play than a short story, because his writing reveals a commitment to medium particularities that suggest he wrote this radio play specifically with the listening experience in mind. Gray's attention to a "panoramic perspective" (Crook 75) for the ear is evident not only in his use of spatialization—the cues accompanying Mr. and Mrs. Dear's dialogue ("*[distant]*") indicate their relative positions to the Fireman's and Teacher's seats on the train, and are dropped when Mr. Dear leans in to join their conversation—but also in the further texturing of sound in this radio play.

Crook explains that the "notion of texture is fundamental in sound drama" (78) and Gray attends to this texture by richly layering multiple audio channels together at critical moments. Unlike the straightforward naturalism in *Quiet People*, which consists mainly of dialogue and the sounds of everyday domestic life such as doorbell chimes and doors being opened, closed, or slammed shut, sound (direction) is much more textured in *Near the Driver*. Gray conscientiously differentiates between the driver's voice over the loudspeaker (which sometimes includes pre-recorded messages) and the driver's voice when he is in conversation with the passengers in their carriage. Another richly textured moment is when Noel Coward's "The Railways of Old England" is being broadcast over the train's loudspeaker in honor of the 150th anniversary of the construction of the "Grand Albert Royal Tennine Suspension Bridge" and Mr. Dear and the Fireman are heatedly arguing over the music about the privatization versus nationalization of BritRail (*Play Book* 150). Their respective shushing wife and daughter (futilely) attempt to break up the argument, by which time the music is over. The texturing of sound works not only to enhance the realism of the experience of being on public transportation with its lively mix of noises, but also creates a richer listening experience for the audience, which is brought to a dramatic climax with the double explosion at the end of the play.

One key reason as to why *Near the Driver* works more effectively as a radio play has much to do with Gray's inspiration for the play. Gray explains that when he was commuting from London to Glasgow in 1975,

> I came home by train and for the first time heard over a loudspeaker the voice of someone who claimed to be the driver. He told me where and when the train would arrive, some features of the landscape we were passing through, and the opening times of the restaurant and buffet cars. This was eighteen years before British Rail was privatized, yet it had begun imitating the little talks by which pilots of commercial airlines reassure flight passengers. I thought this very funny. Before reaching Glasgow I had imagined most of *Near the Driver*, my best and last radio play (*Play Book* 147).

Besides the effective use of spatialization and the rich texturing of sound, *Near the Driver* draws on a characteristic exclusive to radio (plays): the "disembodied communication of sound" (Crook 30). As a short story, "Near the Driver" loses much of its original thrust quite simply because the disembodiment of the driver's voice over the loudspeaker and its associative themes of the alienation and dehumanization that mark modern technological progress—key thematic elements of the story—lose their vitality in the shift of medium. Precisely because its process of composition and subject matter draw so significantly on the radio play's unique characteristic of the use of disembodied voices, the synthesis of its thematic and stylistic qualities (or the medium's particularities) are lost in the transition from play to prose.

Gray's attention to medium particularities is evident not only in his dramatic work but in his creative work across genres. Adam Mars-Jones notes that as an artist and designer of his own literary works, Gray celebrates "the bookness of his books, with illustrations and embellishments, and even the pageness of his pages; with pseudo-Victorian running titles on the right-hand leaves" (20). Likewise, in his radio plays, I suggest that Gray celebrates the "soundness of his sounds" with increasing sophistication, through techniques such as spatialization and the rich, layered texturing of sound. Gray's almost obsessive creative control is even evident in the choice of *Near the Driver*'s publication dates. The work imaginatively explores the deadly consequences of BritRail's privatization some eighteen years (1975) before its privatization became a reality in January 1993—which was the year Gray chose to re-publish the work as a short story in the collection *Ten Tales Tall & True*. Curiously, the publication of *Near the Driver* in its original dramatic form in Gray's *Play Book* in 2009 coincides with the date of incident in the story: the 150th anniversary of Isambard Kingdom Brunel's completion of the Royal Albert Bridge in 1859. Coincidence, or Gray's inside joke? Medium, I argue, is on Gray's mind *all* the time.

Despite the fluid, adaptive nature of Gray's literary output, I argue that his writing is most successful when it is driven by considerations of medium particularities. Perhaps it is precisely Gray's experience in working with mixed mediums—painting, fiction, drama, poetry—that has been particularly pertinent in honing his sensibilities to the singularities of his chosen genre. Notwithstanding the economic reasons that initially propelled Gray in the direction of radio playwriting,[7] there are other important reasons for attending to Gray's dramatic work and especially to his radio plays. While "popular cinema was almost certainly the biggest part of my dramatic education," Gray recalls, "even more important than that was BBC radio" (*Play Book* 12). The influence of radio plays on Gray's art of storytelling is evident in his own creative practice: when revising books one and two of *Lanark*, for instance, Gray explains that "the rewriting needed to make sentences sound easy on the ear. When the ear had no trouble with them I assumed they were as good as I could make them" (Gray and Axelrod 106). Examining Gray's own creative output in a medium that has had such a tremendous influence on his own literary technique is particularly instructive and can lead to further insights about how his dramatic work has shaped his novelistic practice.

By showing how form reinforces content in radio plays such as *Quiet People* and *Near the Driver*, I suggest that they work most effectively (as Gray intended) as plays for voices. Given the limited attention he has received as a playwright, the potential for future avenues of critical inquiry into Gray's importance as a cross- or trans-medium artist are expansive. Little has changed in the two decades following Hutchison's observation that Gray "had not achieved in drama the position of eminence he was to reach in prose diction; rather he was regarded as an interesting but minor playwright, pursuing

7 Hutchison traces a particularly "chequered history" of Scotland's dramatic landscape that in part explains how radio and television were important alternative markets for Scottish dramatists (148).

his own concerns outside the mainstream of Scottish drama" (146). Gray's reputation, in short, has been that of a playwriting novelist—a novelist who happens to also write plays. One hopes, however, that the ready availability of his plays to the public and a gradual increase in critical scholarly attention to his dramatic work, as undertaken in the present study, might mean that the tide is about to turn at last for Alasdair Gray, the novel-writing playwright.

WORKS CITED

Axelrod, Mark. "An Alasdair Gray Checklist." *Review of Contemporary Fiction* 15.2 (Summer 1995): 197-8. Web. 22 Jul. 2014.

Bernstein, Stephen. *Alasdair Gray.* London: Associated UP, 1999. Print.

Böhnke, Dietmar. *Shade of Gray: Science Fiction, History and the Problem of Postmodernism in the Work of Alasdair Gray.* Berlin and Madison: Galda and Wilch, 2004. Web. 25 Jul. 2014.

Bray, Christopher. "Pictures of people talking." Rev. of *Ten Tales Tall & True*, by Alasdair Gray. *Spectator* 30 Oct. 1993: 35. Web. 24 Apr. 2014.

Crook, Tim. *Radio Drama: Theory and Practice.* London and New York: Routledge, 1999. Print.

de Juan, Luis. *Postmodernist Strategies in Alasdair Gray's* Lanark: A Life in 4 Books. Frankfurt: Peter Lang, 2003. Print.

Diamond-Nigh, Lynne. Rev. of *Ten Tales Tall & True*, by Alasdair Gray. *Review of Contemporary Fiction* 14.3 (Fall 1994): 204-5. Web. 24 Apr. 2014.

Donaldson, George and Alison Lee. "Is eating people really wrong? Dining with Alasdair Gray." *Review of Contemporary Fiction* 15.2 (Summer 1995): 155. Web. 16 Sep. 2013.

Fludernik, Monika. "Narrative and Drama." *Theorizing Narrativity.* Ed. John Pier and José Ángel García Landa. Berlin and New York: Walter de Gruyter, 2008. 355-84. Print.

Glass, Rodge. *Alasdair Gray: A Secretary's Biography.* London: Bloomsbury Publishing, 2008. Print.

Gray, Alasdair. *A Gray Play Book.* Edinburgh: Luath Press, 2009. Print.

—. Interview by Anne Garrec. Alasdair Gray's official website, 2000. Web. 16 Jul. 2014.

—. Interview by editor of Why Writers Write. Alasdair Gray's official website, 1984. Web. 16 Jul. 2014.

—. Interview by Glenda Norquay and Carol Anderson. *Cencrastus*. Alasdair Gray's official website, 1983. Web. 16 Jul. 2014.

—. Interview by Kathy Acker. Alasdair Gray's official website, 1986. Web. 16 Jul. 2014.

—. Interview by Mark Axelrod. *Review of Contemporary Fiction* 15.2 (Summer 1995): 106. Web. 16 Sep. 2013.

—. *Lanark: A Life in Four Books*. Edinburgh: Canongate Press, 1981. Print.

—. *Something Leather*. New York: Random House, 1990. Print.

—. *Ten Tales Tall and True*. Orlando: Harcourt Brace & Co., 1993. Print.

Hutchison, David. "Gray the Dramatist." *The Arts of Alasdair Gray*. Ed. Robert Crawford and Thom Nairn. Edinburgh: Edinburgh UP, 1991. 146-55. Print.

Jahn, Manfred. "Narrative Voice and Agency in Drama: Aspects of a Narratology of Drama." *New Literary History* 32.3 (Summer 2001): 659-79. Web. 29 Apr. 2014.

Mars-Jones, Adam. "Transforming the given order." Rev. of *Ten Tales Tall & True*, by Alasdair Gray. *Times Literary Supplement* (1 Oct. 1993): 20. Web. 25 Apr. 2014.

Niederhoff, Burkhard. "Focalization." *the living handbook of narratology* 4 Aug. 2011. Hamburg: Hamburg UP, 2009. Web. 2 Aug. 2014.

Nünning, Ansgar and Roy Sommer. "Diegetic and Mimetic Narrativity: Some further Steps towards a Narratology of Drama." *Theorizing Narrativity*. Ed. John Pier and José Ángel García Landa. Berlin and New York: Walter de Gruyter, 2008. 331-54. Print.

Pattie, David. "The Lessons of Lanark: Iain Banks, Alasdair Gray and the Scottish Political Novel." *The Transgressive Iain Banks: Essays on a Writer Beyond Borders*. Ed. Martyn Colebrook and Katharine Cox. North Carolina: McFarland and Co., 2013. 9-27. Print.

Smethurst, Paul. *The Postmodern Chronotype: Reading Space and Time in Contemporary Fiction*. Amsterdam and Atlanta: Rodopi, 2000. Print.

White, Glyn. "The critic in the text: Footnotes and marginalia in the Epilogue to Alasdair Gray's *Lanark: A Life in Four Books*." *Ma(r)king the Text: The presentation of meaning on the literary page*. Ed. Joe Bray, Miriam Handley, and Anne C. Henry. English and Burlington: Ashgate, 2000. 55-70. Print.

MIKE WITCOMBE

GOODBYE, *GOODBYE, COLUMBUS*: EXPERIMENTAL IDENTITIES IN PHILIP ROTH'S EARLY DRAMATIC WORKS

"Under the circumstances, I would just as soon be Jewish."
(Philip Roth, "Buried Again")

The Jewish-American author Philip Roth celebrated his 80th birthday, his first since his retirement, in a lavish ceremony at the Newark Museum. He gave a reading from his own work, which was framed by laudatory speeches by several fellow writers—some of whom (like Jonathan Lethem) boasted claims of influence, and others (like Louise Erdrich) who could boast of a lasting friendship. One of the evening's more surreal moments came when Roth cut into a birthday cake that served as an improvised centerpiece for the post-speech celebrations. The cake was made to represent a selection of his novels, replete with a typewriter paused mid-sentence and a book splayed open to reveal a brief biography of the writer's career. If it was strange to watch Roth happily cut into his own "books," it was even stranger to watch as the motley crowd of authors, journalists and academics consumed his career in a startlingly literal manner.

On a less symbolic note, the decision to depict many of Roth's texts in the cake itself reminded the onlookers that he has achieved his authorial fame as a novelist. Most of his published works (and all of those commemorated in confectionery form) are novels or novellas, but Roth has developed his authorial career by utilizing different literary formats. He can thus boast a wide array of non-fiction essays on a variety of topics, published in a variety of publications. His career was initiated by writings in the short story format—and a collection of interviews with other writers, *Shop Talk*, demonstrates a collaborative aspect of his writing. These alternative writings have been extensively documented in critical work on Roth, yet his experiments in dramatic writing remain shrouded in obscurity. His birthday cake implicitly celebrated

Roth the Novelist, but the time is ripe for a consideration (if not an outright celebration) of Roth the Playwright.

Roth's Playwriting in Context

Roth has published only one novel in which dialogue is given primacy as a narrative technique: *Deception*. This text is constructed entirely through dialogues between a protagonist named "Philip Roth" and a series of women (and, in one instance, a man). As with many of Roth's other works, this forms part of a broader strategy of metafictional subversion. The "novel" ends with "Roth's" partner discovering the script of the text and accusing him of infidelity.[1] Insofar as the text uses dialogue, it does so in a deliberately understated manner, eschewing quotation marks and providing no narrative description outside of dialogue. Furthermore, it is split into untitled chapters, and provides no signals for the reader as to which character is speaking at any given time.

The text is thus neither a novel nor a dramatic work. Roth's reworking of dialogue enables him to develop the familiar idea that communication is always a fraught endeavor. The text's narrator declares himself to be "an ecouteur, an audiophiliac," a claim implicitly substantiated when one of his conversation partners accuses him of using seduction as a means to further conversation (42). The text's depictions of post-coital intimacy and erotic jealousy tread familiar yet unexpectedly intimate territory within Roth's body of work—the text thus emerges as a work of dramatic fiction grounded in his previous novelistic interests.

Deception is nonetheless granted much of its experimental character through authorial decisions regarding the use of dialogue. *Deception* features many of the more instrumental uses of dialogue seen in other Roth texts; depictions of disputation and pseudo-psychoanalytic pseudo-monologue being the most notable. What distinguishes the text from Roth's other works is that it demands that the reader construct their perceptions of the characters entirely through dialogue. In doing so, it demands that readers of Roth's work

1 Nor do the complications end there; the woman in question, Claire Bloom, would attack Roth's depiction of her in a biography *Leaving A Doll's House*, declaring that "I found the portrait nasty and insulting, and his use of my name completely unacceptable" (201).

reconsider his interest in dramatic writing itself.

Roth published *Deception* in 1990, a transitional era for his work which saw a wide range of experimental fiction being published—most notably, 1986's *The Counterlife*, which is still frequently cited as Roth's best novel.[2] David Brauner notes that Roth has tended to become readily categorized as a realist writer, a perspective which his monograph has challenged. Brauner argues that most scholars writing on Roth have discussed this experimental capacity as part of an ongoing interest in postmodernism, and he thus argues that Roth's combination of experimental narrative and more traditional realism has not been adequately covered.

Brauner's monograph successfully reroutes simplistic constructions of Roth's bibliography, building on the more intertextual and playful approach of scholars such as Debra Shostak. Following Brauner's example, it is possible to extend this perspective on Roth's experimental fiction even further, to incorporate aspects of Roth's oeuvre that have not yet been extensively analyzed in critical discussions. This may lead to a reconsideration of less canonical works: for example, his satirical works of the early 1970s, which incorporate the metafictional, generic, and stylistic tropes that Brauner highlights as hallmarks of Roth's experimental work. More unusually, it may also necessitate a consideration of Roth's explicitly dramatic writings.

Whilst Roth's dramatic works do not consistently evoke all of the tropes suggested by Brauner, they nonetheless collectively function to prove the diversity of Roth's literary talents; to develop the idea of Roth as an experimental writer. These works, ranging wildly in style, subject matter and setting, enable a reconsideration of certain of Roth's core themes. It is little surprise, then, that Roth would appear to have a renewed interest in playwriting during the phase of his career in which his writing is most commonly considered to be experimental; the mid-to-late 1980s. During this period, Roth would adapt both a play by Chekhov (*The Pregnant Wife*) and his own works—*The Ghost Writer* (produced) and *The Prague Orgy* (unproduced)—for television, fol-

2 A 2013 "Literary Caucus" of Roth's work by New York Magazine found that 13% of respondents rated *The Counterlife* as being Roth's best book, second only to *Sabbath's Theatre*'s 24%. Perhaps more surprisingly, *Deception* made the list as well—with 7% of respondents selecting it as being Roth's best book.

lowing on from stage adaptations that Roth wrote during the late 1970s. These texts remain obscure—although Roth was convinced enough of the merits of his adaptation of *The Prague Orgy* to include it in the Library of America edition of his collected works.

Roth's adaptations are fascinating in their own right, but they do not substantially develop or complicate an understanding of Roth's fiction as a whole. As experiments, they remain remarkably mannerly—even *Into the Whirlwind*, one of Roth's rare mid-career ventures into original playwriting, remains conventional in its form and style. In contrast, Roth's earlier dramatic work shows none of this restraint, and would, for the most part, represent a substantial challenge to any director intending to use them as a script for performance. These works are often brazen in their presentation, cynical in their humor and unapologetic in their eccentricity. This is all the more revealing considering the point at which they were written in Roth's career.

Perhaps most immediately notable about many of the early dramatic works preserved in the Philip Roth Papers is that they tend to be clustered around the early few years of Roth's career. This is given added complexity by the nature of his early literary success—he won widespread acclaim for his 1959 debut novella and short story collection *Goodbye, Columbus* and lasting notoriety for his 1969 novel *Portnoy's Complaint*. Between these two enduringly popular works, Roth released two less celebrated works, *Letting Go* (1962) and *When She Was Good* (1967).

These novels, despite featuring many of Roth's abiding themes, have attracted relatively little scholarly critique to date. Stephen Wade, one of few scholars to devote a sizable proportion of a monograph to the works, notes that "both novels concern entrapments in a failing American Dream" (35)—there is certainly little doubt of Roth's ambition in these bleak and tragic visions of human incompatibility in American culture. Whilst neither novel was the critical or commercial success that many expected of Roth, *Letting Go* and *When She Was Good* are more naturalistic than the works that immediately preceded and followed. The apparent reluctance on the part of scholars to engage with them in detail is perhaps as attributable to their distinctiveness as much as it is to any perceived lack of literary merit.

Wade traces a history of Roth's writing that links *Goodbye, Columbus* to *Portnoy's Complaint* by means of a consideration of the works that he wrote between them. Nonetheless, there is a sense that this form of conventional chronology is insufficient for the kinds of comparison that proximity may seem to indicate. When Wade concludes discussion of *When She Was Good* and begins his analysis of *Portnoy's Complaint*, the transition is abrupt: "Turning to *Portnoy's Complaint* the reader returns to the fictional locus of [*Goodbye, Columbus*] once more, but now the concentration is explicitly on a novel of the self/persona duality" (47). Wade thus exacerbates the connections between the two better-known novels in a way that serves to unite them in stylistic and thematic opposition to the other works. Tellingly, these other works do not recur in his subsequent discussion of *Portnoy's Complaint*.

Wade's dilemma stems from the observation that thematic similarities do not offer the sense of coherence amongst these four disparate texts as they would for most of Roth's other work. The notion of entrapment that Wade proposes does, however, remain potent, and can be traced in other critical considerations of this period in Roth's career. For example, David Gooblar argues that Roth's work prior to 1967 (when early chapters of *Portnoy's Complaint* emerged) is notable for its "serious" character—by which he is referring to Roth's propensity for evaluative, meditative writing. Gooblar cites the nonfiction essays that Roth published during the 1960s as evidence of his rejection of frivolity, an abiding commitment to a highbrow, high-stakes notion of cultural engagement. This places more emphasis on *Portnoy's Complaint* as a liminal text which initiates a more characteristic and less careful approach to writing on the part of Roth. Much like Wade, Gooblar observes continuities between *Goodbye, Columbus* and *Portnoy's Complaint*—perhaps most notably, the use of "vibrant, comic, Jewish speech" (44).

This "rift" has been considered in terms of biography, particularly given the lack of Jewish characters in *When She Was Good*. In her recent biography of Roth, Claudia Roth Pierpont argues that Roth's increasing preoccupation with his rapidly destabilizing marriage is partly to blame for his diminishing literary vibrancy. She quotes Roth as retrospectively describing himself "imaginatively paralyzed" by the failure of *Letting Go* and the increasing chaos of his personal life (44). Both Pierpont and Bernard Avishai complicate this perspective by noting that *Portnoy's Complaint* itself emerged from a gradual process by which Roth was exploring more confessional themes in his work—an abandoned novel entitled *The Jewboy* and a complete play entitled *The Nice Jewish Boy.*[3]

These different perspectives expose a fundamental critical uncertainty about the significance of this era in Roth's career. The approaches taken by Wade, Gooblar and Pierpont emphasize the atypical nature of the period in Roth's career between the publishing of *Goodbye, Columbus* and *Portnoy's Complaint*, and serve collectively to reinforce the liminal quality of works written within this period. In light of this, the casual reference to Roth's playwriting made by Pierpont and Avishai may seem excusable, yet it can also point towards a body of work that few critics have been willing or able to discuss thus far—one in which this sense of liminality is foregrounded within the body of texts themselves.

The Philip Roth Papers, based in the Library of Congress, remain a relatively untapped resource in Roth scholarship.[4] Recent monographs and journal articles have gone some way towards correcting this, but the archive has mostly been used by scholars to garner supporting evidence for pivotal ideas. Debra Shostak's monograph *Countertexts, Counterlives* is particularly notable in this regard, as it often develops arguments through selected examples from specific sources—most notably, an early draft of Roth's 1972 novel *The Breast.* With a few exceptions, however, critics have not included this material as a core part of their analyses.

For example, whilst several scholars have now substantiated their arguments through their use of The Philip Roth Papers, Steven Milowitz integrates more obscure Roth texts found in the archive into his overall thesis—with startling effect. He includes discussions of short stories that Roth wrote as a college student ("Armando and the Fraud"), and several early uncollected short stories that Roth published prior to his 1959 debut novella *Goodbye,*

3 Both authors also note the same tantalizing curio: a young and "undiscovered" Dustin Hoffman performed the lead role of this play during a reading at The American Place Theatre in 1964 (Avishai 44).

4 This may be partly attributable to the amount and range of material to be found, for all that it is elegantly categorized by the Library of Congress. The Philip Roth Papers include not only manuscripts from every drafting stage of most of his novels, but also a huge assortment of correspondence and miscellaneous research material.

Columbus. Most unusually (and effectively), Milowitz discusses *A Coffin in Egypt*, one of Roth's earliest unpublished experiments in playwriting. Dating from 1959, this complete play depicts the experiences of a Jewish collaborator in the Vilna Ghetto of 1941. Milowitz uses the play at a pivotal moment in the development of his overall argument that Roth's work remains deeply indebted to his interest in the Holocaust. The resultant monograph offers a tantalizing glimpse into Roth's playwriting past that Milowitz's thematic interests tend to override. This is similar to how Pierpont's biography of Roth only discusses the play *The Nice Jewish Boy* as a means of considering the genesis of *Portnoy's Complaint*; in both cases the plays themselves tend to be secondary to the overarching considerations that they gesture towards.

These plays are undervalued insofar as their ramifications for Roth's work as a whole are wide-ranging. For example, *A Coffin in Egypt*, despite its unique historical setting, bears strong thematic similarities to the works collected in *Goodbye, Columbus*; Roth's emphasis on conflict and tension within the Jewish community is a theme that resonates throughout many of his works and recurs in unexpected ways within the play itself. However, for all that *A Coffin in Egypt* is thematically ambitious (especially given the era of its publication), it is shackled by its lack of narrative adventurousness. The plays Roth would write following *A Coffin in Egypt* display more of a willingness to take risks—often with impressive results.

Whilst a full analysis of Roth's interest in performative writing during this era would include many other works, including a full-length play (*The Nice Jewish Boy*), a proposal for a television series (*A Woman in the House*) and a movie scenario (*Grimes Case*), it is Roth's short plays that are most intriguing. "The National Pastime," originally written as a short play entitled *The Penetrator*, featured on the cover of the May 1965 issue of *Cavalier*. It was subsequently republished as part of an anthology, which was intended to be a screenplay for a movie that was never produced.

In "The National Pastime," Al ("the strong-minded husband") and Isabel (the "hard-working wife") are relaxing in their suburban house after dinner (16). Gregory, "their sullen twelve-year old son," is waiting for a baseball game to start on television, when the program is interrupted by an unexpected broadcast, which is introduced by classical music (16). The program shows a man and a woman engaging in sexual intercourse, and the rest of the one-act play shows the family's panicked response to this pornographic intrusion. The play ends when the pornography stops, and a scientist appears on screen to explain that the program was intended to expose "what you most want, when you most want it" (56). Al responds by hurling the television set out of the window, with the curtain closing mid-flight.

The subversion of suburban value systems is also the primary theme of *The Fishwife*, a play in which a surreal attitude towards narrative consistency marks it as one of Roth's more outlandish creations. *The Fishwife* shows power dynamics to be in constant flux through a consistent interest in the structuring of sexual desire. The plot concerns the relationship between Howard and Gloria. Little information is provided other than their age difference (Howard being "in his middle forties" and Gloria "his young wife"). The possession implied in this description—Gloria as an aspect of Howard's existence— may even be the play's first joke. The couple's relationship slowly unravels as Gloria reveals that she is shortly to marry Juan, a young and vibrant tango dancer. The play then shows Howard eventually revealing his own lover—the titular fishwife. Howard and Gloria come to an arrangement to create an open marriage, but even this is subverted by the play's final lines, in which Gloria contemplates taking yet another lover.

These plays are experimental in nature, and limited context is provided within the archival material through which a reader can contextualize them. They support many critics' shared observation that the writing of *Portnoy's Complaint* was the result of a process of continual change in Roth's work during the 1960s, but the nature of this genesis remains obscure in terms of biographical detail. Collectively, these works expose a sense of narrative and rhetorical playfulness that remains indebted to Roth's more caustic work in *Goodbye, Columbus*—yet shows Roth employing more vibrant stylistic, thematic, and narrative strategies. These plays thus represent neither a radical break from *Goodbye, Columbus* nor a staid restatement of its ideas; rather, they serve to support the work of scholars and biographers that have already noted the unsettled character of Roth's writings during this period. Nowhere is this more visible than in his 1964 one-act play "Buried Again," a play in which reworking of themes found in an earlier short story may help initiate a new chronology of Roth's engagement with notions of Jewish identity.

"Buried Again" and Jewish Identity

"Buried Again" is distinctive in Roth's body of work as it develops a sense of theological playfulness rarely detectable elsewhere in his fiction.[5] The premise of the play is that Weingast, a Jewish salesman from New Jersey, has died suddenly in late middle-age. He finds himself facing a panel of celestial judges who offer him choices pertaining to reincarnation, but he insists on maintaining many of the characteristics of his previous life—in particular, his Jewish identity. The judges offer him a wide range of choices, which are increasingly narrowed as Weingast's desires become increasingly tied to those of his previous life. Weingast rejects the panel's suggestion that he become female, homosexual or Christian, pleading desperately for an exception to the rules that would prevent him from resuming a similar lifestyle to that which he had previously enjoyed. In a macabre ending to the play, the judges reject Weingast's pleas and cast him into oblivion instead.

The judges are flagrantly biased, openly displaying their preference for Weingast to create new markers of identity in his reincarnated form despite their assurances that he has his choice of destiny. Weingast himself, torn between a desire to please his interrogators (and thus ensure his re-entrance into the human world) and a desire to be true to his own preferences, ends up satisfying neither party. The "robust man," one of Weingast's panelists, cheerfully advocates for Weingast's becoming a Native American, and the other judges similarly list the virtues of certain choices. This places Weingast in a double bind—he can abandon his known identity or abandon life altogether. Weingast's falterings are not conventionally heroic, but Roth depicts bravery in his character's stubbornness nonetheless.

5 Due to the erratic nature of pagination amongst Roth's draft manuscripts, page references for quotes from the play will not be supplied in this essay.

Roth's religious themes are usually best read as subsidiary aspects of a broader investigation into Jewish identity. Jewishness as a form of religious identity is thus commonly detectable in his work in the symbolic usage of the paraphernalia or clothing of worship—most brazenly in the use of clothing as a theme in the early short story "Eli, the Fanatic," but also in his description of his father's prayer shawl in the non-fiction work *Patrimony* later in his career. Similarly, Roth's use of the Beyond in "Buried Again" is best understood along similar lines as the vision of Richard Nixon campaigning in Hell that concludes his 1971 satire *Our Gang*—an opportunistic appropriation in the service of exposing the hidden undercurrents in American culture.

Roth's use of setting is thus somewhat of a misdirection, a means of allowing him to pursue familiar themes relating to the interaction between Jewish culture and the broader American culture. As is the case in *Goodbye, Columbus*, this division is most frequently expressed in terms of Christian belief systems, and Catholicism in particular. Roth had used this comparison before for a similar sense of mutually-constructed confusion. In "Defender of the Faith," one of the stories collected in *Goodbye, Columbus*, a non-Jewish soldier tasked with promoting Sabbath services does so by referring to it as "the Jewish Mass" (127). However, Roth undercuts any suggestion that this is purely a mockery of Gentile ignorance by having previously had the comparison made by his well-intentioned Jewish protagonist. Similarly, "Buried Again" (which presents its protagonist with the option of being reborn as either a Protestant or a Catholic) is not just a polemic attack on a relentlessly assimilative and bigoted American value system, but a more complex contemplation of intercultural relations in mid-century America.

Roth's version of the Beyond is thus consciously liminal, a staging area from which destinies can be rewritten. The remorseless bureaucracy and denial of individual agency found in this hinterland suggest that it is more strongly influenced by the aimless menace faced by characters in many of Franz Kafka's works than it is reflective of an explicitly Christian religious tradition.

This signals one of the key dilemmas in Roth's text—Weingast is a character who is constantly trying to reframe his situation in terms of his Jewish identity, but he is blocked at every turn by an audience which claims that "mankind has had enough of Jews." "Buried Again" can thus be interpreted as a means by which Roth was deliberating over the extent to which Jewish themes would play a prominent role in his writing. Roth's writing would regain much of its vigor when he made the decision to engage more fully with his own Jewish upbringing in writings that would eventually become *Portnoy's Complaint*, and it is possible to interpret "Buried Again" as part of this process. He would use the trope of the trial frequently in his fiction for a wide variety of purposes.[6] Nonetheless, it is worth noting that, in this instance, the defensive tone of Weingast is difficult to separate from the defensive tone of Roth himself in the contemporaneous non-fiction essays which according to David Gooblar display Roth's sense of artistic seriousness at its most piqued.

The play has, after all, an acute and pervasive sense of persecution; Weingast may try to finagle his way back into a quiet life in Maplewood, New Jersey, but he is repeatedly rejected by a panel of judges which include a woman who "speaks with a heavy Germanic accent." The judges speak in their own language amongst themselves, a nonsense tongue of Roth's own invention that serves to build a further communicative barrier between the celestial judges and their trembling subject. The sense of macabre bureaucracy and the desire to encourage the erasure of Jewish identity on the part of the judges gives the play a historical consciousness, evoking the still-recent European genocide that Weingast, as an American citizen, would be presumed to have eluded. The "language barrier" inherent in the nonsense language of the judges recasts explicitly Christian tropes ("speaking in tongues") as part of a methodology of senseless persecution. It is also worth noting, however, that the "Germanic" accent of the judges ("it might be some Central European tongue, though it isn't") is not simply a reference to Nazi atrocities, but could also be interpreted as a reference to the Yiddish that was spoken by many Central European Jews prior to the Holocaust, and by many first-generation American Jewish immigrants. Yiddish thus represents part of Weingast's, as well as Roth's prehistory. The key subject of the play is thus immediately configured as being that of

6 See, for example, the game of "Reality Shift" in which Roth is obliged to defend himself from a lover pretending to accuse him of misogyny in *Deception*, the use of trials as a plot device in *Operation Shylock* and the sense of an absence of fair trial that motivates the Newark Trilogy's cultural malaise.

Jewish identity. In thematic terms, Roth is very much in familiar territory.

Miscommunication functions as a theme as well as a narrative device; Roth places a strong emphasis on power dynamics within his narrative, and this affects the manner in which he constructs his dialogue. The judges speak in tones of professorial pontification, sullen rage or officious disapproval respectively, and the intersection of these styles helps to distinguish Roth's characters whilst reinforcing their general tendency towards a willful disregard of Weingast. Weingast's rambling equivocation, together with his kvetching and his hand-wringing, act as a symbolically humanizing mode of speech. The energy of this form of communication unsettles the pre-established codes thrust upon it. This helps Roth to depict Weingast as an empathetic character and his interrogators as bland forces of censure.

Weingast's futile bid to unsettle divine authority is a Promethean narrative rewritten to place a schlemiel in the starring role. Roth's protagonist thus shirks traditional markers of heroism; he continually questions any firm decision he makes in the course of the text, has to be stopped from digressing to unrelated topics, and calls the authority of his celestial judges into question. Even Weingast's single moment of unequivocal chutzpah, his defense of his right to a Jewish life even at the cost of his eternal soul, is couched in the language of violent rejection. Weingast concludes his final speech to the judges with a burst of impassioned oratory, as he states that "I depose, I condemn the whole miserable goyische system!" The use of a legalistic term such as "depose" may be a malapropism for "despise," undermining the vigor of Weingast's fury. Nonetheless, in its associations with conscious rebellion, the term functions as an ironic and powerful affirmation of the gesture itself. Roth's ambivalence towards his protagonist is thus reaffirmed by the very words which he provides him.

Similarly, earlier in the play script, Weingast exposes a seemingly unintentional appropriateness. For example, he defends his desire to be reborn as a Jewish man "because really and truly, what's the big deal? I'm Jewish, the other guy ain't, what's the big deal that everybody is making such a big deal about, in the final analysis." Weingast's language is clumsy to the point of comic excess, comprised for the most part of cliché colloquialisms and repetitions of the phrase "big deal"—to the extent that his basic point is unnecessarily muddled. Despite this, there is a ring of truth to his choice of words; his repetition of the phrase "big deal" serves to remind the reader that the issue of cultural difference is the primary theme of the play as a whole. Even the meaningless conclusion "in the final analysis" gestures towards Weingast's current predicament, exposing an unexpected connection between everyday speech and divine justice. It is scarcely surprising that the deconstruction of Weingast's democratic idealism is accompanied by a transition towards an explicitly Jewish language of apostasy—not only is the system and its administration "goyische," but even God is chastised as "a schmuck of the first degree." Much like the protagonists in the *Goodbye, Columbus* stories, rebellion from both Jewish and American social norms creates unanswerable paradoxes.

Roth is acutely aware throughout "Buried Again" that his protagonist is carrying a burden of symbolic weight that is incommensurate with his ability to articulate it. Even Weingast's initial description is rife with the kind of paradoxes that Roth shows to be more intriguing than the hegemonic discourse of the divine judges: "His intelligence is strong, his education negligible. A decent enough man, selfish and good-natured. His voice is full and raspy, and his accent is not strong, but recognizably that of a man born and raised in a city: a city man, a businessman, a Jew." Weingast is both an everyman and a very specific kind of representative figure. Roth thus creates a character that embodies a range of Jewish stereotypes, but does so in a manner that places these tropes as fundamental aspects of the human condition. The terror of Weingast is reflective not simply of human frailty and an entirely justifiable fear of death, but of a perception of Jewish suffering that emerges as a direct consequence of the significance of the Holocaust in American culture. Weingast is fretful, trying to negotiate his way out of a binding eternal predicament in pursuit of a reclamation of his cultural affinities. Weingast's avid pursuit of a peculiarly American model of happiness exposes the limitations of this form of cultural assimilation; he becomes a stock figure, but one for whom Jewishness, more than any other marker of identity, becomes non-negotiable.

In order to link many of the paradoxes and ambiguities mentioned in relation to "Buried Again" to the work Roth had previously published in *Goodbye, Columbus*, a comparison of the play to the short story "The Conversion of the Jews" may provide evidence of Roth's thematic consistency. The story depicts a young boy in Hebrew school escaping his domineering rabbi and running to the top of the school building, at which point he attracts the attention of his classmates. Upon threatening to jump, he manages to make all present below confirm their belief in the possibility of the Immaculate Conception, and their opposition to coercion in religious instruction.

Ozzie, the protagonist of "The Conversion of the Jews," shares a great deal of similarities with Weingast despite the obvious difference in their ages and manner of existence. Like Weingast, Ozzie is an unintentional and unlikely rebel whose rejection of the religious strictures of his environment leads him to vocal volubility. His friend Itzie asks him, "What do you open your mouth all the time for?" (107). This relentless questioning is counterbalanced by Yakov Blotnik, an elderly custodian who is perceived by the children to be "an object of wonder, a foreigner, a relic" (110) with an "old comical voice" (120). Blotnik is portrayed as having reduced moral complexities to simple categories, "either good-for-the-Jews or no-good-for-the-Jews" (114). Ozzie's rebellion is an implicit denial of this particular form of binary thinking, part of a critical perspective on religious education that recurs throughout the story. Ozzie's engagement with religious power is similar to that of Weingast insofar as both characters are opposed to totalizing methodologies that deny subjectivity. Ozzie may be more successful in undermining these strictures, but it is only through Weingast that Roth is able to extend this rebellion into an active assertion of Jewish identity through a wallowing in its ambiguities, rather than the more passive strategies undertaken by characters in the *Goodbye, Columbus* stories.

Ozzie's rebellion, which ends with him jumping from the roof into the "overgrown halo" of a firefighter's net, has a similar trajectory to that of Weingast in "Buried Again"—a rejection of a form of religion perceived to be authoritarian, petty and vindictive (120). At the root of both texts is a denial of violent force, a refusal to acknowledge the power invested in certain characters as having intrinsic merit. In "The Conversion of the Jews," this is made particularly blatant in Roth's choice of names. Rabbi Binder's surname evokes the threat of violence in the biblical narrative of Isaac's binding, and Yakov Blotnik's surname reminds the reader of his position as a cultural outsider—a "blot" on the pristine surface of cultural assimilation, a visual reminder of Jewish difference. As such, Roth's story can feel somewhat didactic, to the extent that its validation of independence and inquisition enacts what David Gooblar refers to as "something of an artist's fantasy" (19).

"Buried Again" is anything but didactic, and insofar as it is an "artist's fantasy" it serves as the obverse of the more utopian vision seen in "The Conversion of the Jews." Roth maintains his theological skepticism, his rejection of an uncritical adherence to a violent exertion of power, but extends it to a broader, externalized notion of dominant religion. "Buried Again" is not an attack on either Christianity or Judaism, but a powerful assertion of the pliability of Jewish and American identity. As such, it adds nuance to Roth's scathing attitude towards suburban Jewish life in the *Goodbye, Columbus* stories, developing the ambiguity of the earlier texts in a manner that trades on Roth's increasing sense of cultural vulnerability.

In "Buried Again," Roth argues that the status of being Jewish-American is neither a strength nor a weakness, but nor is it something that Jews can ignore (as Weingast had arguably been trying to do in adopting a conventionally American suburban lifestyle). Roth suggests that Jewish identity is both immutable and a source of endless paradoxes—a theme pivotal to the stories in *Goodbye, Columbus* and one whose subsequent development in *Portnoy's Complaint* owes as much to early texts like "Buried Again" as it does to Roth's better-known movement towards a distinctively Jewish comic sensibility in the late 1960s.

Beyond the Beyond

"Buried Again" is a complex work, offering readers of Roth a unique insight into the development of his perspectives on Jewish identity within a dominant host culture. However, it is important to note that the play has inherent literary value even aside from its connections to Roth's work and career. "Buried

Again," like many of Roth's unpublished plays from this period, is extremely funny, and much of its text reflects Roth's skill in writing dialogue. Nonetheless, a knowledge of the context of the play transforms what could be seen as an amusing curio into a significant moment in Roth's career.

The 1960s was a transitional era in Roth's work, and the difficulty that those writing on Roth have faced when attempting to discuss works written by him during this time is to be expected. Any sense of connection posited between the disparate corpus of published and unpublished works has to pay heed to the absence of a definitive theoretical or thematic perspective. Roth's writing within this corpus is best characterized as being experimental and speculative, a means by which he was to "find his footing" as a novelist of note. Nonetheless, certain aspects of Roth's writing are more visibly developed than others when uncollected and unpublished material is afforded a primary position. It is precisely through these works that Roth refines his notion of Jewish-American identity, helping trace the complexities contained within that ever-problematic phrase into the contemplations that would later become the thematic cynosure of *Portnoy's Complaint.*

The study of plays such as "Buried Again" can extend our understanding of a significant author at a point in time when, following Roth's retirement, critics are beginning to evaluate his career as a whole, complicating notions of connections between his works. This play and its companion pieces deserve larger audiences and more thorough critical engagement—even if they may not be cast into the form of a cake any time soon.

WORKS CITED

Avishai, Bernard. *Promiscuous: "Portnoy's Complaint" and Our Doomed Pursuit of Happiness.* New Haven: Yale UP, 2012. Print.

Bloom, Claire. *Leaving a Doll's House.* London: Virago, 1996. Print.

Brauner, David. *Philip Roth.* Manchester: Manchester UP, 2007. Print.

Gooblar, David. *The Major Phases of Philip Roth.* London: Bloomsbury, 2011. Print.

Milowitz, Steven. *Philip Roth Considered: The Concentrationary Universe of the American Writer.* London: Garland Publishing, 2000. Print.

"Literary Caucus: Salman Rushdie, James Franco, and 28 More Notables Assess Philip Roth's Career." *New York Magazine* 4 May 2013. Web. 23 Feb. 2015.

Pierpont, Claudia Roth. *Roth Unbound: A Writer and His Books.* London: Jonathan Cape, 2014. Print.

Roth, Philip. "Buried Again." Box 248. The Philip Roth Papers. Library of Congress, Washington DC. 1 May 2012.

—. *Deception.* London: Vintage, 2006. Print.

—. *Goodbye, Columbus.* London: Vintage, 2006. Print.

—. *Portnoy's Complaint.* London: Vintage, 2005. Print.

—. "The Conversion of the Jews" in *Goodbye, Columbus.* 137-158.

—. *The Fishwife.* Box 250. Philip Roth Papers. Library of Congress, Washington DC. 1 May 2012.

—. "The National Pastime." *Cavalier* May 1965: 16-56. Print.

Shostak, Debra. *Philip Roth—Countertexts, Counterlives.* Columbia: University of South Carolina Press, 2004. Print.

Wade, Stephen. *The Imagination in Transit: The Fiction of Philip Roth.* Sheffield: Sheffield Academic Press, 1996. Print.

JOSEPH H. O'MEALY

LATE STYLE IN ALAN BENNETT'S NOVELLAS AND STORIES

In June, 2014, a few weeks after his eightieth birthday, Alan Bennett, the celebrated playwright and memoirist, published what he called a "sermon" in *The London Review of Books*. First delivered as a talk in an ecclesiastical setting (King's College Chapel, Cambridge), his sermon playfully recalled the persona that introduced and endeared him to the British public more than half a century ago as one of the original four members of *Beyond the Fringe*: "our Alan," the socially awkward northerner who had probably missed his vocation as a Church of England vicar. But half a century later Bennett's sermon was no longer based on some comically arcane passage in the Scripture. Now Bennett sermonized on the parlous state of British education, especially the trend to privatize the same free state schools that gave Bennett, whose father was a Yorkshire butcher, and countless other scholarship boys the chance to create lives different from their fathers' ("Fair Play").

At this point in Bennett's long career, careful observers are not surprised by his engagement with controversial public issues, especially readers of *The London Review of Books* (*LRB*), where Bennett publishes annual excerpts from his diary. While Bennett will probably always be viewed by some as a twee figure, once likened to a "national teddy bear" (Schiff 92), anyone who had been paying attention to his television and stage dramas has seen emerge a darker and more complicated side to Bennett's work. The first series of *Talking Heads* monologues (1988), to cite one example, broadcast into the British home the stories of closeted homosexuals and alcoholics, and the second series, a decade later, upped the ante to pedophiles and serial killers. This led one television critic to ask, "Alan, lad, whatever's up?" (Banks-Smith), a tidy combination in four words of an old familiarity with a new recognition that Bennett had disrupted his cozy apolitical image as the comic chronicler of the sadness, embarrassment, and loneliness of life outside the distant metropolis.

Since the start of the new millennium, Bennett has increased his commitment to a more public and political face, including writing about the heretofore hidden secrets of his own family (his mother's mental breakdowns, his own homosexuality), in memoirs like *Untold Stories* (2005), as well as taking stands on issues of national import like the Iraq War. Bennett's annual diaries in the *LRB* have traditionally been the place he has chosen to express his dissent. Over the decades he has mixed anodyne descriptions of his day-to-day routines with trenchant criticism of the government and the media. But he has often felt that his voice did not carry very far or have much impact. As early as the 1980s Bennett made unmistakable his opposition to all Thatcherite policies and practices, especially the Falklands War. His 2003 diary, which he titled "A Shameful Year," focused his scorn and disdain on Blair and Bush for their criminal guilt in forcing upon the British an Iraq war based on lies and intimidation. He even chastised Tom Stoppard for having lunch at 10 Downing Street with Blair and Bush while an anti-war march went by the door ("Diary" 21 November 2003). But partly because his dissent was more moral than ideological, the gatekeepers who guarded the honor roll of leftist British artists usually overlooked him. By 2007 Bennett found it necessary to publicly demur when he read in *The Guardian* that Terry Eagleton had said "of all the eminent writers and playwrights only Pinter continues radical and untainted by the Establishment." Bennett, in typically modest fashion, merely wrote "Ahem" to remind the reader that Pinter had company—himself ("Diary" 7 July 2007). It was a throat clearing that clearly signaled a deep frustration and disappointment. Perhaps an annual diary was not enough.

At the same time that Bennett was becoming more personally outspoken, if largely ignored, his reputation and celebrity as a playwright grew, especially with Nicholas Hytner as his director at the National Theatre, where they collaborated on three productions in less than a decade: *The History Boys* (2004), which won several awards for best new play in both London and New York, *The Habit of Art* (2009), and *People* (2012). The latter two did not win the favor that *The History Boys* did, which was voted in 2013 Britain's "Favourite Play" in a poll conducted by the English Touring Theatre, pushing *Hamlet* into third place (BBC 2013). But all three attempt to deal with subjects that Bennett was finding increasingly necessary to confront, what Michael Billington, long-time theatre critic of *The Guardian*, terms Bennett's central themes: "the matter of England and the nature of art." Nonetheless, the extraordinary popularity of *The History Boys* can be ascribed less to the debate between Hector and Irwin over the proper purpose of education and more to the wit of Bennett's presentation of the classroom antics of eight young men preparing for the entrance exams to Oxford and Cambridge. Likewise, the imagined meeting in old age between W. H. Auden and Benjamin Britten in *The Habit of Art*, which was meant to explore the relationships between the private and the public artist, had to share theatrical time with the play-within-a-play rehearsal structure as well as jokes about Auden's taste in rent boys and Britten's fears of being outed. Similarly, the symbolism of the decayed stately home in *People*, with its echoes of Bennett's first play, *Forty Years On*, about English heritage, was largely lost in the shouting from the National Trust who felt the play was an attack on them organized by the National Theatre (BBC 2012).

The intensely collaborative nature of the stage, with the diminished role for the playwright once rehearsals begin (in *The Habit of Art* the appearance of the playwright at rehearsal elicits groans from the actors and stage manager), has led Bennett to feel that something is usually lost in the transition from page to stage. Looking at the drafts and notes for *The Lady in the Van*, one of Bennett's earlier collaborations with Hytner, he found himself "feeling, as I often do when a play has been mounted, that it's slightly to the side of the play I wanted to write and that, now it's on, here among the cuts and alterations is the real play" ("Diary" 11 December 1999). Bennett does admit that there can be advantages to the collaborative aspect of plays, citing the example of his successful efforts to rewrite and deepen Russell Tovey's role as Rudge the jock in *The History Boys* to fit the particular gifts of that actor: "This is one of the pleasures of writing plays which I can't see writing novels or poems ever providing" (*Untold Stories* 345). True enough.

Yet Bennett has not eschewed trying his hand at prose fiction. (Poetry is apparently a completely different story.) Between the ages of sixty-two and seventy-seven Bennett published three original novellas, "The Clothes They Stood Up In" (1996), "The Laying on of Hands" (2001), *The Uncommon Reader* (2007), and two long short stories, "The Greening of Mrs. Donaldson" (2010), and "The Shielding of Mrs. Forbes," collected in the volume *Smut* (2011). These prose works reveal that he seems to have increasingly found in prose fiction an advantage different from and equal to the stage. Bennett's focalized overview of the characters' thoughts and motives through the use of a traditional third-person narrator gives him the opportunity to be more present than the playwright would be in a stage production. No longer are we viewing a play written by Alan Bennett, directed by Nicholas Hytner, interpreted by a dozen actors, a costumier, a set designer, etc. It's Alan Bennett's voice, or at least the implied Alan Bennett's voice, that the reader encounters controlling all the other voices in the story, the kind of voice that allows him to clarify and express more personally, and take possession of, some of the issues and feelings that he had once stood "slightly to the side of."

Edward Said, borrowing from Theodor Adorno's study of Beethoven's late compositions, has noted a special difference in the nature of a mature artist's work. He calls this "Late Style," and he analyzes it in the final works of canonical writers like Cavafy and Lampedusa. When Bennett wrote his "Introduction" to the published text of *The Habit of Art*, he credited Said's theory of "Late Style" as a possible influence on the play's "stylistic oddities . . . rhyming furniture, neighbourly wrinkles, and words and music comparing notes—[which] may just be an attempt to smuggle something not altogether factual past the literalist probation officer who's had me in his charge for longer than I like to think and who I would have hoped might have retired by now" (xiii). Bennett often resorts to a self-deprecating joke in order to dissociate his own work from what might be deemed pretension, so his suggesting that Said's "Late Style" may only be "a permit for aging practitioners to kick their heels up"(xiii) should not throw the reader off the scent. The differences between the relatively inconclusive shapes of *The Habit of Art* (2009) and *People* (2012) and the tidy plotting of *The History Boys* (2004) may be just one example of the stylistic differences in Bennett's late plays.

However, for the purposes of this essay, Said's observations about "Late Style" are equally relevant to Bennett's late prose writings as they are to his latest plays, despite Bennett's attempts to evade and deflect. In the later stages of his career, he now says there is no subject he would not write about, even though he once worried what people would think: "I just wouldn't have wanted people to know too much about me. But I am so old it makes no difference now, does it? I have been around so long. And I also think people don't care now in quite the same way" (Crompton). Bennett's newly found indifference to public displeasure is balanced by his rationalization that no one artist's idiosyncrasies matter all that much to the public anyway. It is this tension, this decision to let the unreconcilable remain unreconciled, that Said emphasizes as key to his idea of late style and that captures so well the tone and substance of Bennett's late novellas and short stories:

> This is the prerogative of late style: it has the power to render disenchantment and pleasure without resolving the contradictions between them. What holds them in tension, as equal forces straining in opposite directions, is the artist's mature subjectivity, stripped of hubris and pomposity, unashamed either of its fallibility or of the modest assurance it has gained as a result of age and exile. (Said 7)

All of these late prose works take satirical pokes at contemporary British life and culture, sometimes with an apparent *carpe diem* theme. Yet none of them ends with a resolution that signals either comic triumph or tragic dissolution. Instead there reigns an air of contradiction, of the mixture of new pleasure in the liberating discovery of sexual and political outspokenness and familiar disenchantment with his limited capacity for actually changing the world.

****

Bennett's attraction to prose fiction as a medium for self-expression began fairly early in his career, with the creation in 1982 of a prose version of his television drama, *Intensive Care*. It stayed in his desk drawer until, nearly two decades later, he “dusted it off” and published it in *LRB* in 1999 with a new title, “Father! Father! Burning Bright.” His motives for attempting to tell the same story in two genres are revealing. Bennett says he began this second version when he was cast, much to his surprise, as the main character, Midgley. “It was in the hope of finding more to the character [than he had provided in the screenplay] that I decided, before the shooting started, to write the story up in prose. When I'd finished I showed it to the director [Gavin Millar] in the hope that it might help him to appreciate what the screenplay was about. He received it politely enough and in due course gave me it back, I suspect without having read it” (“Father! Father!” 164). Bennett's turn to prose fiction for another crack at the same story may have failed in one of its aims (Gavin Millar probably finding it superfluous and/or presumptuous), but in his attempt to help him see “more to the character” of Midgley it served its purpose. The parent-child conflict, foregrounded by the Blakean allusion in the title, affects more characters than just Midgley and the sexual underpinnings of many of the characters' motivations are more fully developed, making Midgley in the story more of an Everyman than Midgley in the play, who seems just a lost soul.

Three years earlier Bennett had published his first standalone novella, “The Clothes They Stood Up In” (1996). In this moral fable Bennett literally strips his middle-class couple, Mr. and Mrs. Ransome, of everything they own, except of course the clothes on their backs. Returning one night from Covent Garden, where they have attended a performance of *Così Fan Tutte,* they discover that everything in their flat has disappeared, everything— not just the stereo and the jewelry, but also all the carpets, furniture, kitchen appliances and fixtures, including the casserole simmering in the oven—“all the apparatus of that life which the Ransomes had the complete equipment for but had never managed to lead” (“Clothes” 115). In the months that follow, the Ransomes must rebuild their lives from scratch, but it's only Mrs. Ransome who truly uses this second chance to live even a little differently. Shopping at the local Asian grocery instead of only at Marks and Spencer's is one of those changes: “once she popped in and bought a mango for her lunch and another time a pawpaw; small adventures, it's true, but departures nevertheless, timorous voyages of discovery which she knew her husband well enough to keep to herself" ("Clothes" 99). She also begins to learn from Dusty, the counselor assigned to help her recover from the "trauma," and from daytime talk shows, the therapeutic language of self-actualization and "caring." Mr. Ransome, who prefers the company of Mozart's music to his wife, on the other hand, rebuilds his walled-in world, thanks to the top of the line stereo set and headphones he buys with the insurance settlement.

Sex enters their sexless lives when a bill arrives at the Ransomes' for storage charges on their missing household effects. Whoever had burgled them had arranged for all their property to be reassembled in an Aylesbury storage unit in an exact reproduction of the layout of their London flat. The status quo ante has been brilliantly recreated, with one small exception—the Ransomes discover an audiotape that has recorded the sexual activities of Martin, the storage unit manager, and his girlfriend, Cleo. The Ransomes are alternately shocked and titillated: "At one point the microphone was moved closer to catch a sound that was so moist and wet it hardly seemed human. "'It sounds,' said Mrs. Ransome, 'like custard boiling,' though she knew that it wasn't" ("Clothes" 138). The husband now spends many evenings surreptitiously listening to the tape on his headphones, having told his wife he had erased it and recorded Mozart over it. Though he is amazed to think that "two human beings could give themselves up so utterly and unreservedly to one another" ("Clothes" 140), he never is able to bring himself to translate that knowledge into his daily life with Mrs. Ransome, who of course knows that he listens to the tape. He dies of a stroke one day, the narrator sitting in final judgment: "When you come down to it, what he is being condemned for here is not having got out of his shell" ("Clothes" 155). Mrs. Ransome's eventual uncovering of the mystery behind the dispossession of their property seems almost incidental. It was a practical joke intended for a tenant with a similar name residing on a different floor in their block of flats. She tells herself that "the burglary and everything that has happened since has been a kind of apprenticeship. Now, she thinks, I can start" ("Clothes" 160).

This seems a hopeful ending, one of the two Ransomes coming out of their shells, yet questions remain unanswered—an apprenticeship to what? Start where? We cannot overlook Bennett's satirical attitude toward the jargon of self-actualization that Mrs. Ransome has picked up from Dusty and Oprah and made the touchstone of her new attitude toward life. As her husband lies dying, befuddled and frightened, she "begins to whisper to him in that language which she can see now she was meant to acquire for just this sort of eventuality. "'I find it hard to verbalize with you, Maurice,' she begins . . . 'but we are going to learn, I promise . . .' She talks about perspectives and sex and how it can go on joyful and unrestrained until the very brink of the grave" ("Clothes" 156-7). These no doubt caring, but dubious, assertions and plans are short circuited when she inadvertently turns up the volume on her husband's headphones so high that the grotesquely over-amplified voice of Kiri te Kanawa is the last thing Mr. Ransome ever hears. His devotion to Mozart has killed him, but Mrs. Ransome had her hand in it too.

Bennett satirizes a broader range of targets in "The Laying on of Hands" (2001): the God-Lite theology on offer in most Anglican churches, the public/private divide in English sexual behavior, the anodizing language of the therapeutic movement, the invasive presence of tabloid talk in everyday discourse, and the contemporary cult of celebrity. This is the story of a gathering of celebrity mourners at the memorial service for a thirty-four-year-old bisexual masseur. The celebrities, from actors in the Royal Shakespeare Company and TV news presenters to internationally famous architects and the Oxford Waynflete Professor of Moral Philosophy, have no idea what killed Clive, just that he died in Peru on holiday. Nor do they know yet that their connection with him is shared by so many recognizable others. Bennett's recollection of the 1980 memorial service for Kenneth Tynan, the drama critic, probably served as the springboard for this novella. Then, Bennett had been amused by the outpouring of mourners at Tynan's service from many corners of the English theatre world, their comic ineptness as speakers, and the chubby vicar's apologetic attempts to make these non-believers feel not too put off by the Christian rituals he had to perform (*Writing Home* 107).

Beginning with the double-entendre in the title, "The Laying on of Hands" with its conflation of religious ceremony (the Confirmation ritual) and therapy (in this case massage plus sexual healing of a sort), irony is Bennett's chosen weapon. It is no accident that the clergyman who will conduct the memorial service, Geoffrey Jolliffe, identifies irony as God's preferred mode of dealing with humans: "The truth was it was God that Geoffrey didn't trust. Irony was always the deity's strong point and to afflict a transgressor as timid as Geoffrey with such a disproportionate penalty [AIDS] might appeal to the Almighty's sense of cosmic fun" ("Hands" 31). Bennett is of course the deity in charge here, and his fun is of a more terrestrial nature, but not without some hints of, if not omniscience, then the omnipresence of the prose narrator.

At first we get the perspective of Treacher, an archdeacon and canon, who attends the service not because he cares anything about the deceased but because he wants to evaluate the performance of the young celebrant for future advancement in the hierarchy. Bennett introduces Treacher to us as a traditionalist, a strict, but not totally unsympathetic, critic. He would certainly prefer to see Geoffrey succeed in a difficult task: "So far, Treacher was bound to admit, Jolliffe was not doing too badly. Even the news of the priest's friendship with the dead man had scarcely counted against him, as the Archdeacon had all along assumed Jolliffe to be homosexual, though without seeing this as a cause for censure or even a necessary obstacle to promotion." Bennett makes sure we also see the more illiberal side of Treacher by telling us his views on the roles of women in the Church of England: "In Treacher's church there was a place for she, running the jumble sale, or doing the altar flowers; a she could even take the plate round or read the lesson. But there was no place for she at the altar or in the pulpit. So, give Jolliffe his due: he was not a she" ("Hands" 28). At the end of the story the narrator tells us, as Treacher "now passes out of this narrative," that "he is not entirely to be deplored, standing in this story for dignity, formality, and self-restraint" ("Hands" 61).

These are of course the very qualities that Geoffrey could use more of. Blinded by pride in his smooth handling of the proceedings so far, and trusting in his belief that "a congregation is first and foremost an audience. And I am the stand-up" ("Hands" 17), he judges that he has won them over. Now he can deviate from the script with some improvisational bits. So rather than tie things up with a final prayer, he announces that anyone in the congregation "with cherished memories of Clive which they would like to share should now feel free to do so" ("Hands" 33). Even without a trace of Treacher's prejudice in favor of unemotional ritual, the veteran reader of Bennett should recognize that two of Geoffrey's words in that brief statement— "cherished" and "share"—can lead only to a muddle. The language of "caring," whether in the hypocritical jargon of the Tories or in the tone deaf officialese of social workers has ever been for Bennett a linguistic symptom of an uncaring culture that prefers not to think for itself. The media may be the most egregious offenders in Bennett's view, and he adopts their language here and there in the novella. For example, among the congregants are a "prominent actor," a "leading international architect," a "high official in the Treasury," a soap opera "hunk," etc. One of Bennett's better jokes against the media involves the reporter from the *Daily Telegraph* who leaves early for lunch at the Design Museum, assuming this service will be like all the others she's covered. She files a story that bears no relation to what actually happened when the sharing began, "so she got the sack. But it was a nice lunch" ("Hands" 14).

Those who wish to share their cherished memories are legion, and as the ceremony drags on the sentimental recollections give way to a startling frankness. The spokesman for what appears to be a radical gay group, Carl, challenges the audience to talk about what Clive was like in bed, and insists categorically that Clive was gay, which is met with loud demurrals by several women in the congregation, and shock when he announces that Clive died of AIDS. The consternation among the crowd is overwhelming. What had begun as a meaningless social outing has now devolved into a *memento mori*. For a while they sit there, "stunned, their own fates prefigured, this memorial service a rehearsal for their own" ("Hands" 44). In time, other voices are heard as the debate heats up. First an awkward young man, Hopkins, who claims to have been a witness to Clive's death in Peru from an insect bite, speaks up, and then Clive's doctor, who insists Clive was not HIV-positive and thus could not have died of AIDS. The tide of relief is overwhelming: "the whole church was on its feet clapping . . . They cried for Clive, it is true, but they cried for themselves without Clive, particularly now that his clean and uncomplicated death meant that he had thankfully left them with nothing to remember him by" ("Hands" 52-3).

The final irony may seem to be that once the immediate threat of infection from Clive's healing services has passed, the congregants now return to their own thoughtless carnality: "some, to put it plainly, could scarcely wait to get home in order to have a fuck"; others don't wait and go at it amid the dustbins in the church alcove ("Hands" 58). Life, at least in this limited sense, has triumphed over death, and the comedy can end. But not in Bennett's ironic world. For there is one small detail—Clive had left in Hopkins' possession his account book, which contains coded information about his clients. Father Geoffrey, from a mixture of motives, some noble, some prurient, some defensive, manages to frighten Hopkins into giving up the book by making a pass at him. But the ironic deity/author turns the table on Geoffrey when many months later Hopkins returns, ready now, after some mature reflection, to take Geoffrey up on his insincere offer.

Bennett's non-judgmental (even amused) treatment of all varieties of sexual behavior in his late works has upset some of the more conservative commentators in the Tory media (Moore, Murray). Since he came out publicly as gay in the late '90s, Bennett seems to them to be making up for lost time, even though his treatment of sexuality is deeply ambivalent, usually wry, and sometimes broadly comic in the tradition of the English sex farce. Bennett's choice of *Smut* (2012) as the title of the volume that collects "The Greening of Mrs. Donaldson" and "The Shielding of Mrs. Forbes" demonstrates a level of mischief-making that is fairly new in his relationship with his readers. It seems almost designed to cause some embarrassment among the fans, with whispered questions to bookshop clerks such as "Do you have *Smut* here?" leading inevitably to even more embarrassment. And the stories are frank, though not explicit, in their treatment of sex.

Mrs. Donaldson, widowed, and a surprisingly gifted performer in training scenes designed to improve medical students' diagnostic skills and bedside manners, allows her young lodgers to pay their rent by having sex in front of her. She finds in voyeurism a pleasure that actual participation has not given her, though when asked one day by the young man to have sex with him while his girlfriend is away, she agrees, but only after she's finished the chapter of the book she's reading. Her sole troubling moment comes when she suspects that her lodgers have told the other students about their arrangement, and fears she has been outed as a species of brothel keeper or bawd. But she decides to put on "a bold face" (*Smut* 65) and brazens her way through it, performing indifference so well that no one lets on they know what they know.

The characters in "Mrs. Forbes" lead secret sex lives too, but they come from the world of a sex farce not all that different on the surface from Bennett's 1973 play *Habeas Corpus*. But those heterosexual adulteries with the usual supporting cast of the randy vicar and the sex-starved spinster have now metamorphosed in this story into homosexual, bisexual, and incestuous relationships. Since secrets are prized much more than candor, no one lets on that the bourgeois lives they apparently lead are so irregular. The couplings, which resemble a Yorkshire *La ronde*, are carried on calmly, without the slamming doors of the stage. The erotic permutations include Graham + Betty, Graham + Kevin, Betty + Mr. Forbes, and Kevin + Mrs. Forbes. Mrs. Forbes doesn't need to be shielded from the news that her son is gay; she has always suspected it and is pleased to find out she has been right again, as usual. What we are told part way through "Mrs. Donaldson" holds true for "Mrs. Forbes" too: "readers wanting a moral ending should probably stop here" because this will not be a "cautionary tale" (*Smut* 64). For the man who was once called the "poet of embarrassment" (Schiff), Bennett's decision to put on a "bold face" constitutes a large turnaround. It is now the reader's turn to blush.

Bennett's views on national politics, unlike his greater candor about sex, take a more oblique shape in his fiction. There is no story, for example, about meetings at Number 10 or the wars in the Mideast. But in his novella *The Uncommon Reader* (2007), a political fable about how Queen Elizabeth's life changes when she develops the habit of reading literature as a prelude to becoming a writer herself, he asserts the nature of reading and writing as political actions. He had used the Queen once before as a character in his stage play *A Question of Attribution* (1988), which was reportedly the first time a living monarch had been portrayed on the English stage. Given the discreet title of HMQ, she discusses her art collection with Sir Anthony Blunt, then the Keeper of the Queen's Pictures. In addition to being a highly respected art historian, Sir Anthony had also been a Soviet spy and his day of reckoning was coming soon. As he and the Queen discuss the nature of forgery, misattribution, and fakery, the viewer wonders whether she is asking questions about her paintings or about Blunt himself? Is this a cat and mouse game the Queen is playing? Is she much sharper and subtler than she is usually given credit for? Bennett leaves the audience guessing.

In his novella, on the other hand, Bennett takes the novelist's prerogative and tells us what the Queen is thinking. What he sees is a woman approaching eighty years of age who, much to her own surprise and by some happenstance, borrows a book from a mobile library, just to be polite, and finds herself growing more interested in reading literature than in performing her ceremonial duties, which, after more than fifty years on the throne, have become numbingly routine. While riding in the state carriage, for example, and waving to the crowds with one hand, she now holds on her lap a copy, say, of an Anita Brookner novel, and surreptitiously glances down at the page at every chance. Her less than total focus on her duties upsets the royal household staff, who begin to wonder if she is displaying the first signs of dementia. The narrator's comments, "thus it was that the dawn of sensibility was mistaken for the onset of senility . . . like any change of behaviour in the elderly it was readily put down to decay" (*Uncommon* 80-81), are also Bennett's reporting on his own situation as a long established writer breaking into unfamiliar territory in his old age, to the undisguised hostility of some of his former fans (Moore, Murray).

The Queen describes her pleasure in reading as a "late-flowering enthusiasm . . . At her age, people thought, why bother? To her, though, nothing could have been more serious, and she felt about reading what some writers felt about writing: that it was impossible not to do it and that at this late stage of her life she had been chosen to read as others were chosen to write" (*Uncommon* 46-47). As she masters texts more demanding than Anita Brookner's, the novels of Hardy, Dickens, Austen, Dostoevsky etc., she begins to take notes about her reading and then to scribble observations about the people she sees and the situations she encounters. She notices that her version of events is usually very different from the tabloid reports: "When some scandalous report about the royal family appeared in the newspapers, the real facts went into her notebook. When some scandal escaped public notice, that too went down, and all of them told in that sensible, down-to-earth tone of voice she was coming to recognise and even relish as her own style" (*Uncommon* 72-73). That voice is also of course her late style. When she is searching for the precise word to describe herself, after she has given the title of "amanuensis" to the young man who advises her on books and writers, she comes up with "opsimath: one who learns only late in life" (*Uncommon* 48).

Through reading, the Queen has started along a path that has led her to writing because "reading was not doing, that had always been the trouble. And old though she was, she was still a doer" (*Uncommon* 100). So at the party for her eightieth birthday she announces to the gathered elite that she will become a writer, but not the memoirist they cozily expect: "I was thinking of something more radical. More . . . challenging." Citing Proust's decision to "redeem" his life through "analysis and reflection," the Queen indicates that her own analysis and reflection will delve into the public and the political. "What about those ten prime ministers," who have served during her long reign, she asks. "There is much to reflect on there . . . I have at the instance of my various governments been forced to participate if only passively in decisions I consider ill-advised and often shameful" (*Uncommon* 115-116). The echo of Bennett's own description of the launch of the Iraq War in 2003 as the most egregious act of "a shameful year" ("Diary," 8 January 2004) is unmistakable here, and since Tony Blair was still Prime Minister when *The Uncommon Reader* was published, readers know that he would have been in that room when the Queen made her fictional but politically pointed remarks. Score one small point for Bennett.

Bennett's version of the monarch is surely almost entirely imaginary. But by having her decide to do something radical and challenging by becoming a writer and an honest witness to her own experiences, in her own voice and style, Bennett reminds us that political action is not limited to governmental acts. Sometimes it is necessary to step away from them, as the Queen does when she abdicates the throne in the final sentence to devote herself to the kind of analysis and reflection that only a dedicated writer with the habit of art can achieve. She says her book will be a "roundabout book" and quotes E. M. Forster, or is it Emily Dickinson? She is not sure: "Tell all the truth but tell it slant—success in circuit lies" (*Uncommon* 118).

Edward Said speaks of "the artist who is fully in command of his medium [and] nevertheless abandons communication with the established social order of which he is a part and achieves a contradictory, alienated relationship with it." For him or her, the works produced at this late stage "are a form of exile from his milieu" (Said 3). Bennett's exile in these late prose fictions is more figurative than the Queen's exit from the throne, but he still has embarked in his prose fictions on a different way of expressing both new pleasure and old disenchantment, without trying to reconcile the contradictions. No longer the collaborative playwright, he has taken on the mantle of the all-knowing and all-controlling narrator, so we can rest assured he knows that Emily Dickinson wrote those lines and understands how central they are to his own late style too.

WORKS CITED

Banks-Smith, Nancy. "TV Listings." *Guardian* 28 Oct. 1998: G2, 19. Print.

Bennett, Alan. "Diary: A Shameful Year." *London Review of Books* 8 Jan. 2004: 3-8. Print.

—. "Diary: What I Did in 1999." *London Review of Books* 20 Jan. 2000: 3-8. Print.

—. "Diary: What I Didn't Do in 2007." *London Review of Books* 3 Jan. 2008: 3-8. Print.

—. "Fair Play." *London Review of Books* 19 Jun. 2014: 29-30. Print.

—. "Father! Father! Burning Bright." *Four Stories.* London: Profile Books, 2006: 161-223. Print.

—. *Smut.* New York: Picador, 2012. Print.

—. "The Clothes They Stood Up In." *Four Stories.* London: Profile Books, 2006: 79-160. Print.

—. *The Habit of Art.* London: Faber and Faber, 2009. Print.

—. "The Lady in the Van." *Four Stories.* London: Profile Books, 2006: 225-282. Print.

—. "The Laying on of Hands." *Four Stories.* London: Profile Books, 2006: 1-77. Print.

—. *The Uncommon Reader.* New York: Farrar, Straus and Giroux, 2007. Print.

—. *Untold Stories.* New York: Farrar, Straus and Giroux, 2005. Print.

—. *Writing Home.* London: Faber and Faber. 1994. Print.

Billington, Michael. "Alan Bennett: A Quiet Radical." *Guardian* 12 Oct. 2012. Web. 10 Feb. 2015.

Crompton, Sarah. "People Shouldn't Think I'm Cosy." *Daily Telegraph* 30 Nov. 2012. Web. 10 Feb. 2015.

Masters, Tim. "Alan Bennett play *People* 'gives National Trust a bloody nose.'" *BBC News/Entertainment and Arts.* BBC, 8 Nov. 2012. Web. 10 Feb. 2015.

Moore, Charles. "Sex Has Dulled Alan Bennett's Satirical Edge." *Daily Telegraph* 24 Apr. 2011. Web. 10 Feb. 2015.

Murray, Douglas. "Beyond a Joke: The Decline of Alan Bennett." *Spectator* 10 Nov. 2012: 27. Print.

Said, Edward. "Thoughts on Late Style." *London Review of Books* 5 Aug. 2004: 3-7. Print.

Schiff, Stephen. "The Poet of Embarrassment." *New Yorker* 6 Sep. 1993: 92-101. Print.

"*The History Boys* named UK's favourite play." *BBC News/Entertainment and Arts.* BBC, 11 Dec. 2013. Web. 10 Feb. 2015.

DANIEL K. JERNIGAN

TOM STOPPARD'S FICTION: FINDING HIS FORM

The 1964 collection *Introduction 2: Stories by New Writers* contains three short stories by Tom Stoppard. Published some two years before the near simultaneous publication of his only novel, *Lord Malquist and Mr. Moon* (*Malquist and Moon*), and the initial production of what would eventually become his most famous play, *Rosencrantz and Guildenstern are Dead* (*RosGuil*), the stories provide a good place to begin investigating the question of how well-suited Stoppard's various aesthetic and philosophical interests are to novel-writing and playwriting respectively. Moreover, as the latter two stories from *Introduction 2*, "Life, Times: Fragments" and "Story," are concerned with journalism, they also contain thematic connections to the later plays, including *Night and Day* (1978) but also to the historiographical considerations of *Arcadia* (1993), *Indian Ink* (1995), and *The Invention of Love* (1997). However, as we will see, only in the first story, "Reunion," do we begin to see Stoppard addressing postmodern doubt in a way that truly prefigures the greater epistemological playfulness found in the novel and in the bulk of his plays.

"Life, Times: Fragments" and "Story" are more backward looking to his previous career as a journalist than forward looking to his eventual career as a playwright, as they both involve journalists trying to escape their profession. In any case, while neither story has any formal aesthetic connection to the plays, there are some compelling resonances all the same. "Life, Times: Fragments" is a collection of anecdotes stretching out over the career of a Journalist, each of which expresses some level of anxiety on the part of the narrator about being trapped in journalism as a career. In the first fragment we find that the narrator "killed off some woman in the first week" (126) when he misunderstood a call from the police about a woman they had identified. He felt sick about it at the time, but in the final sentence of the fragment we are informed that this was "before I became too good for Journalism" (126). In the next anecdote, he flubs an interview for a job he is not even sure he wants (he fails to name the Foreign Secretary) which would have taken him from the provinces to the *Evening Standard* in London. This anecdote ends with the narrator saying "I'll have a shot at a novel . . . Then I can make the Foreign Secretary anybody I bloody well like" (127). Several anecdotes later he is "The oldest sub" at a "daily" in London. Meanwhile, after receiving his "one-hundred-twenty-seventh consecutive rejection slip" from publishers for his novel, he finally decides to give himself over to god, crying out "Dear Lord, I have seen the light . . . and offer myself, Dear Lord, wholly to your service" (129). This provides for the only joke in the volume that is truly worthy of the later playwright, as god sends an angel to tell him "The Lord thanks you for your contribution but regrets that it is not quite suitable for the Kingdom of Heaven." Moreover, the play concludes with a swipe at literary critics which would be familiar to any reader of Stoppard's plays; the dead writer's body is eventually found by a literary agent who goes on to make a living off of the stories left behind by this undiscovered "vision of Kafkacetera etcetera."

The other short story in the collection, simply titled "Story," tells of a Journalist who, against his better judgment, decides to write up an article about a schoolmaster who is convicted of indecency for fondling a girl he was teaching to swim. After the article goes on to appear in newspapers across the country, the schoolmaster commits suicide by jumping in front of a train. While its title and content are suggestive of metanarrative treatment, in its spare realism the work is more suggestive of a short story by James Joyce (whom Stoppard deeply admires) than it is of the later Stoppard. The story is ultimately quite critical of the profession, as it concludes by suggesting that the money received for the article is a poor balance to the man's life: "I don't know what I spent it on. It got mixed up with my other money and at the end of the month I was broke as usual" (136). Notably, *Night and Day* was also critical of this aspect of the press; Milne, for instance (hardly the hero of the story), speaks somewhat fondly of "waiting to grab a bereaved husband or footballer's runaway wife who might be good for one front page" (61). "Life, Times: Fragments" and "Story" were written by a man desperate to escape a career in journalism. However, they are not the work of an author who is committed to using the structure of the medium to raise philosophical questions about the nature of reality and humanity's relationship with it.

"Reunion" is the increasingly foreboding tale of a man making an unannounced visit to what we assume to be his former lover, on the apparent condition that he can only stay a minute: "You agreed a minute, you promised" (121). The foreboding turns towards the uncanny as the man begins to describe how a word shouted in a crowded room might change the shouter's reality such that "all things that just miss will click just right, and the mind that heaves and pops like boiling porridge will level off, secretly" (123). Almost as if under the spell of this concept, and after having spent much of the story trying to talk the man through what has the appearance of an imminent anxiety attack, it is relatively strange that the woman seems genuinely receptive to this line of thinking: "'It's an idea,' she said, almost amused, and he felt it go away" (123).

He asks for faith on her part, and for a suggestion as to what he might do with this line of thought. Her response—"Fire!"—in addition to coming as something of a non sequitur (is this perhaps the word which, if "shouted in a crowded room," might change everything?), also, oddly enough, contains the only exclamation mark in the whole story, despite the work's ominous tone and content. Even when the man in the story had been so bold as to touch her against her wishes in an earlier scene, her reaction is explicitly described as quite composed: "'Don't,' not weary or terse or soft but a simple directive, don't as in don't cross the road without looking" (122).

Stoppard would later use this same one word line to compelling theatrical effect in *RosGuil*. One of the central thematic conceits of *RosGuil* is that Rosencrantz (ROS) and Guildenstern (GUIL) are quite literally confined to the strict parameters of the logic of the stage—and to the content of Shakespeare's original script. When Ros finally decides to test these parameters, however, we get the following exchange:

> *ROS leaps up and bellows at the audience.*
> ROS. Fire!
> *GUIL jumps up.*
> GUIL. Where?
> ROS. It's all right—I'm demonstrating the misuse of free speech. To prove that it exists. (*He regards the audience, that is the direction,*

> *with contempt—and other directions, then front again.*) Not a move. They should burn to death in their shoes. (60)

In this instance, the theatrical context makes the implications of the line quite explicit, alluding as it does to a famous argument within political theory which suggests that an individual's right to free speech should never be given such free rein as to allow for the shouting of "fire" in a crowded theatre. Indeed, a live audience is fundamental to the argument, for this limit to free speech depends on the realization that, upon yelling "fire" in a crowded theatre, the audience might panic, resulting in a dangerous stampede towards the exits.

It is to be sure a prototypically metatheatrical moment in Stoppard, which highlights the artificiality of ROS and GUIL's environment. By contrast, even while the shouting of "Fire" in "Reunion" can be read as a surreptitious cry for help, it is comparatively quite pedestrian given that it is not the most fortuitous environment for such a cry. For even if "fire" does happen to be "shouted at the right pitch" it is much less likely to "nudge the universe into gear" (123) when one is alone with one's ex-lover in an apartment, than if one is shouting the same in a crowded theatre. Of course the fact that ROS also fails to nudge the universe in any meaningful way only speaks to an even deeper metatheatrical point—that the logic of live theatre is such that it is one crowded venue in which the dictum against shouting "fire" can be broken, and in turn indicating that ROS and GUIL exist on a different ontological plane than the audience (which is, of course, their tragic theatrical reality). The transition from page to stage brings the conceptual point Stoppard is striving for into full flower.

There is, moreover, both a verbosity and movement to "Reunion" that seems far more suited to theatrical production than to the printed page, as the man responds to the woman's shouting of "Fire!" with unrestrained delight:

> Laughing, suddenly free of it, he circled the kitchen—"It may not be English at all. [. . .] It might very well be Chinese or Gaelic. One would have to avoid a billion permutations of phonetics and chance unawares on the one sound which is the Word. Pafflid," he

> said, as happy as he had ever been in his whole life, "brilge, culp, matrap, drinnop, quelp, trid, crik, Christ." (123)

The Man is increasingly trapped by his own anxiety and private yearnings. He is more trapped than The Woman, who eventually tells him to shut up when he goes too far. His explosion is ultimately spent by putting space between the two of them, finally getting ahold of himself "stairs and streets later" (125). In its focus on the tortured spaces which arise out of and between spent relationships, "Reunion" is perhaps most reminiscent of Stoppard's *The Real Thing*, where the space between one spent relationship and the next is manifest in so many imbedded metatheatrical narratives. In turn the imbedded narratives of *The Real Thing* serve as metaphors for Stoppard's own escape into writing in response to his own troubled relationships. I would argue, moreover, that the metanarrative resonance of such an "escape" is much more pronounced in theatre than it ever could be in fiction, suggesting one more way in which Stoppard has found his form in drama.

The story of the gentlemen, Malquist, and his less than capable Boswell, Moon, *Malquist and Moon* provides for an even more compelling examination of Stoppard's relative abilities in fiction and drama than do the short stories. Like Stoppard's plays, the novel was crafted in accordance with many of the same philosophical questions about the nature of reality and humanity's relationship with it—most notably, the fallibility of historiography, as Lord Malquist eventually proves much too large a topic for Mr. Moon's limited talents to capture on page. That Moon is simultaneously writing a history of the world only adds to the epistemological doubt which pervades the novel.

There has been very little written about *Malquist and Moon*, and the majority of what has been written treats the novel fairly perfunctorily before moving on to the more famous plays. Providing one of the only sustained critiques of the novel, Peter Rabinowitz argues that the work failed to reach a wider audience largely because it "falls slightly short of its target both emotionally and philosophically" (57). Rabinowitz's central point is that, unlike the more balanced *RosGuil*, the novel "unwittingly, I believe . . . becomes an intellectual puzzle rather than the wrenching emotional experience its terrifying subject matter might lead one to expect" (60). However, while Rabinowitz looks to what he sees as narrative weaknesses in the novel to make his case, the current essay is more interested in how Stoppard eventually turned these same "weaknesses" into strengths by going on to work in a medium that was quite simply a more natural environment for Stoppard to engage in the sorts of intellectual puzzles which so fascinated him.

In turn, this essay serves as something of a rebuttal of Rabinowitz's belief that "In terms of audience dynamics, narrative is more complex than drama" (59), as well as the corollary implication that Stoppard need not even have improved as a writer in order to succeed as a playwright. For while I am perfectly willing to admit that much of Stoppard's eventual success came about as the result of having found and settled into the medium which best suited his philosophical and aesthetic interests, I see no reason to discount this success because his path was somehow simpler for having chosen to work in theatre. Aristotle, for instance, preferred the tragedy of Sophocles to the epics of Homer on the grounds that there was a tightness and completeness to the dramatic form that cannot be replicated in an epic narrative wherein "Such length implies some loss of unity, if, I mean, the poem is constructed out of several actions, like the Iliad and the Odyssey, which have many such parts, each with a certain magnitude of its own" (111). This is what I see in Stoppard's plays. A decidedly complex tightness and completeness that, unlike the novelistic bagginess of *Lord Malquist and Mr. Moon*, better serves the complex theatrical puzzles Stoppard is prone to building.

As chance would have it Stoppard's *Malquist and Moon* was to go on sale in bookstores during the same week *Rosguil* premiered in Edinburgh. And while Stoppard apparently had more confidence that the novel would make his career than the play (Nadel, 129), it also appears he was prepared to take up whichever path proved more successful.[1] Be that as it may, the novel is quite clearly the work of an author fully invested in the theatre, as is most evident in the various chapter titles, including "One: Dramatis Personae and other Coincidences," and "Two: A Couple of Deaths and Exits."

1 As John Fleming explains it, Stoppard offered contradictory stories over the years about his initial preferences in this regard (262).

In keeping with the *Dramatis Personae* section of a play script, Chapter One begins by briefly introducing the reader to all of the major characters, each in their own subsection (albeit with the exception that Malquist and Moon are introduced simultaneously, in the first subsection). Indeed, at times the very language used in the descriptions recalls the *dramatis personae* section of a play. For instance, when Moon praises one of Malquist's witticisms, the narrator is quite clear as to the fact that this is a character trait to be noted: "'Very good, Lord Malquist!'—hearty friend of the nobility Moon" (4). A few lines later we are reminded that Moon in turn is subject to Malquist's continual suggestions to "Write it down" as he responds: "'Very good, Lord Malquist!'—Boswellian Knows-his-station Moon." Similar references to play scripts extend throughout the novel, especially as servants and messengers *Enter* and *Exit* as if characters in a play (132, 173, 174). Eventually, Moon gets the full dramatic treatment: "MOON (*falling to his knees and feverishly kissing Lady Malquist's hands*): My dear Lady Malquist . . ." Indeed, these features of the novel mirror Stoppard's later tendency to extend his *dramatis personae* into the very body of his plays, perhaps most intriguingly accomplished with Ms. Drudge in *The Real Inspector Hound* (*Inspector Hound*, 1968) who speaks throughout the play in a way that is all too reminiscent of the stage directions for a play: "[answering a telephone] Hello, the drawing room of Lady Muldoon's country residence one morning in early spring?" (11). In any case, while Stoppard may well have been willing to pursue a career as a novelist had *Malquist and Moon* been a success, the fact that the novel itself contains many theatrical elements gives us some reason to be skeptical of this notion.

Moreover, Malquist himself proves to be quite the performative dandy whose aesthetic ideals as well as his wit owe much to Oscar Wilde: "I find crowds extraordinarily lacking . . . Taken as a whole they have no sense of form or colour. I long to impose some aesthetic discipline on them, rearrange them into art" (10). Stoppard, of course, would later be compared to Wilde, not only for his wit but for a similar preference for aesthetics over politics. Malquist goes on to provide a "descriptive note" of himself to Moon: "My hat is of a colour described by my hatter as pearl black. My pearl pinned to my lapel is of a colour described by my jeweler in literal translation from his native Chinese as sunkissed dewdrop on earlobe of bathing-in-pool maiden." This continues apace for several more sentences, at the end of which we find that Moon's "hand wrote as far as *pink as pearl in ear of Chinese bathing beauty*, at which point its memory gave out" (11). Aside from the tellingly theatrical "descriptive note," this passage is also compelling for how it recalls Stoppard's ongoing fascination with the dilemmas of representation. For just as ROS and GUIL's tragic situation in *RosGuil* comes about as a consequence of their having been underrepresented by Shakespeare, next to the charismatic Malquist, Moon suffers perhaps something of a similar tragedy (indeed, the section introducing both Malquist and Moon might rather be seen as focusing on Malquist, meaning that unlike the rest of the characters in the novel, Moon never gets a proper introduction).

Much of the novel's fixation on the difficulty of representation comes into view through the work's various repetitive descriptions, which ultimately provide little comfort to our faith in representative discourse. For instance, we get our first anonymous glimpse of Lord Malquist's wife, Laura, as she is being stalked by a lion: "From behind the scrub of thorn the lion watched her. He was not sure yet and the wind was wrong. He lay flattened and nothing of him moved except the very end of his tail which flicked in the grass" (8). Moon has no presence in this or the rest of the brief scene, and we are led to believe that, having witnessed her "falling until the earth smacked her flatly from ankle to cheek" the Lion now only waits "for her to move" before attacking. In an extended treatment of the same material later in the next section, Malquist provides much of the necessary context for identifying his wife's situation as he and Moon pass her in the coach:

> Ahead of them a woman staggered out of the colonnade of the Ritz and swerved through the gate into Green Park, almost falling.
>
> "Laura!" shouted the ninth earl. "Pull yourself together and go home!" adding, "I can't stop now," and pulled his head back into the coach.
>
> Moon saw the woman fall down a few yards into the park. From

> behind a bush a long yellow animal like a mountain lion padded towards her and put down its great cat-head to sniff at her hair. Several people were watching the scene. The lion suddenly turned and ran off across the park. (20)

And so we learn that the Lion is Malquist's own escaped pet and that, perhaps rather than stalking "Laura," the Lion has, rather, been interrupted in his wanderings by a familiar human face, which we definitively learn is Malquist's wife in the following exchange: "'Was that your wife?' Lord Malquist responds. 'I certainly don't know anyone else who could be thrown out of the Ritz before eight o'clock without feeling rather *passé*'" (20). So only when the scene repeats are we able to fill in the narrative gaps in the original description. Laura has fallen by the side of the road because she is drunk. The Lion is her husband's pet. Malquist treats his wife with the same level of disregard that Moon's wife treats Moon.

Moreover, the same scene is re-presented three more times before the end of the novel. Part Three, Chapter One, "Chronicler of the Time" contains Moon's attempt to record the day's events. Of this scene, he writes: "By chance Lady Malquist was leaving the Ritz as we were approaching but she did not see us and we were unable to stop. We saw her turn into Green Park and there—the second of two remarkable coincidences—we caught a glimpse of Rollo" (100). Not only is this written without his notes of the day (which Moon had negligently destroyed in a fire), in the following chapter we are also told that they are much edited: "Moon decided not to mention his bomb or Marie's death or the general" (104). Still later, we get another summary (in this case, presumably, the stream of consciousness reflections of an increasingly discomfited Moon): "To sum up: Muffins with Malquist, into coach, knock down woman, horses bolt, see Laura drunk outside Ritz" (150). Only moments later Moon re-thinks the same scene in reverse: "To sum up (backwards): "I returned home in the coach after a ride—during which were encountered The Risen Christ, Laura (Lady) Malquist, (drunk, in park, shoe-losing), and Rollo and woman in Pall Mall—after having muffins with Ninth Earl." Indeed, what hope does even a competent and earnest Boswell have in writing down the truth of such an extravagant and whimsical subject as Lord Malquist, let alone the incompetent, bumbling, hyper self-conscious Prufrockian Moon. Moon is an unreliable narrator, unreliably narrated, whose most notable characteristic is that he can be defined by all that he is not—that is, he is *not* having sex with his wife, *not* writing a history of the world, *not* writing a bio of Malquist.

Indeed, just about the only motive-driven characteristic we can attribute to Moon is that he has taken to carrying a bomb in his pocket wherever he goes, which he intends to use to "shock people into calling a halt" to the "sheer volume and numbers of things we're filling up with" (18). Increasingly afraid that he might well never be able to enumerate and record all of society's quickly accumulating detritus, Moon keeps his bomb close to hand as his final editorial response to the madness. This characteristic of the novel perhaps finds its most compelling dramatic compliment in Stoppard's one-act play, "After Magritte" (1970), which, modeled as it is on the René Magritte painting *L'Assassin menacé*, begins by introducing such an odd collage of items to the audience that it can easily be interpreted as rejecting traditional understandings of theatre as mimetic. As the curtains rise we find Mother lying on an ironing board, one foot propped up against the iron. She is wearing a black rubber bathing cap, and a black bowler hat sits on her stomach. Thelma Harris is on her hands and knees, expensively dressed in a full-length gown, while Reginald Harris is standing on a chair, bare to the waist, wearing fishing waders over his dress trousers. A lamp hangs from the ceiling, complexly counterbalanced by a basket of fruit. A police constable stares through the rear stage window.

Our first impression of such a scene would undoubtedly be confusion. However, just as Lord Malquist's perspective on Laura helps to explain the gaps in Moon's initial picture of Laura Malquist, so too as *After Magritte* moves beyond its opening tableau the anti-representative tensions quickly dissolve. For we soon discover that Thelma and Reginald have been preparing for a professional dancing competition (which explains their fancy dress), that Reginald is wearing waders in order to change the lightbulb above the water-filled bathtub, and that Mother is lying on the ironing board so that Thelma, who must give Mother her daily massage, can more easily accomplish her task (15). In Stoppard's world, it would seem, there is "a place for everything, and everything in its place." It is also worth noting, moreover, that because perspective itself has a significant spatial-temporal element to it, these issues can be explored on a three-dimensional stage and in real time in ways that they could never be considered in fiction.

Perspectivism aside, however, there can be no doubt that the world Moon lives in presents an extremely difficult subject for Moon to capture on the page, and, moreover, that Stoppard has created such a complex collage at least in part to exacerbate Moon's epistolary predicament. Perhaps partly aware of the difficulty he faces in chronicling Malquist's eccentricities, Moon's obsession with the cultural complexity which surrounds him comes into starker focus. Indeed, the world for Moon involves such a complex structural chain of contingent parts and events that it seems in danger of imminent collapse, whether he eventually decides to detonate his ever-present bomb or not:

> It was starting up again and he tried to concentrate on the tins but it got away from him. There was a pig and butchers and knives (who made the knives? The butcher's apron?) and a packing factory, packing millions of tins and a printing works for the labels printing millions of labels, with machine minders and foremen, all of whom lived in houses and travelled by bus and bicycle made by other people (and who looks after the coolies on the rubber plantations for the tyres?) and they all got given money and had children (and who makes the bricks for the schools and suppose they couldn't find anyone and it all just stopped?). (42-43)

It is just this sort of paranoia that Fredric Jameson some twenty years later would go on to attribute to the postmodern era's late-stage capitalism, where "conspiracy theory (and its garish narrative manifestations) must be seen as a degraded attempt—through the figuration of advanced technology—to think the impossible totality of the contemporary world system" (Jameson, 38). Not known as an especially politically oriented writer, if there is one Stoppard work which does seem consistent with Jameson's thinking on the difficulty of representation in the postmodern world it would be *Malquist and Moon*. To be sure, the very complexity described in Moon's fantasies is also suggestive of Jameson's conception of postmodern conspiracy narratives which are to be seen as "a degraded attempt—through the figuration of advanced technology—to think the impossible totality of the contemporary world system" (38).

Moon's predicament is not all that dissimilar from Oedipa Maas's in Thomas Pynchon's *The Crying of Lot 49*, who has her own difficulty understanding the complexity of postmodern multinational business culture, which for Oedipa is manifest in the California suburban highway system rather than in London traffic jams:

> [Oedipa] looked down a slope, needing to squint for the sunlight, onto a vast sprawl of houses which had grown up all together . . . and she thought of the time she'd opened a transistor radio to replace a battery and seen her first printed circuit. The ordered swirl of houses and streets, from this high angle, sprang at her now with the same unexpected, astonishing clarity as the circuit card had. Though she knew even less about radios than about Southern Californians, there were to both outward patterns a hieroglyphic sense of concealed meaning, of an intent to communicate. There'd seemed no limit to what the printed circuit could have told her (if she had tried to find out); so in her first minute of San Narciso, a revelation also trembled just past the threshold of her understanding. (14)

Moon's socio-cultural anxiety is similarly triggered by witnessing technological complexity: "the sight of a power station or traffic jam or a skyscraper . . . gutted him like a herring. The technical and human complexity of the machine shook on the edge of disintegration, held together only by everyone else's unawareness of the fact" (43-44). More prone in his drama to investigating logical, philosophical, and mathematical complexity than the sociopolitical complexity which Jameson sees as having given rise to the postmodern conspiracy thriller, this characteristic of *Malquist and Moon* stands out as something of an anomaly in Stoppard's work, and one which may very well be attributed to the greater loquaciousness which comes with the novel format.

It is little wonder then that Moon can't bring himself to put even the first sentence of his planned history of the world to paper: "Moon, who had experimented on a number of variations of a first sentence . . . found the vastness of his chosen field reassuring rather than daunting, but it did cramp his style: he could not put down a word without suspecting that it might be the wrong one" (29). This stands as the natural complement to how in the face of the ever-shifting conundrum which is Pierce Inverarity's estate, Oedipa is finally left wondering "whether, at the end of this (if it were supposed to end), she too might not be left with only compiled memories of clues, announcements, intimations, but never the central truth itself, which must somehow each time be too bright for her memory to hold" (Pynchon, 66).

While in plays such as *Travesties*, *Arcadia*, and *Indian Ink*, Stoppard would continue to satirize academics who are as incompetent as Moon, he would never again look to postmodern socio-political complexity as the cause. Instead, an image which graces a can of pork and beans becomes a much more pronounced metaphor for the sort of metatheatrical trickery which would come to dominate Stoppard's theatrical oeuvre: "On the table was a jumbled pyramid of tins identically labelled with a picture of a cowboy holding a tin with a picture of a cowboy holding a tin with a picture of a cowboy." In *Postmodernist Fiction*, Brian McHale refers to such recursive structures as "Chinese box worlds," and argues that they are common technique in both modernist ("Here recursive structure serves as a tool for exploring issues of narrative authority, reliability, and unreliability, the circulation of knowledge and so forth" [113]) and postmodernist fiction ("one such strategy, the simplest of all, involves frequency: interrupting the primary diegesis not once or twice but often with secondary, hypodiegetic worlds, representations within representation" [113]). In his plays, Stoppard would go on to use such recursive structures to raise philosophical questions about reality and representation in new and surprising ways, most notably in *Inspector Hound*—where one of two critics who appear to be sitting with the audience eventually ascends the stage to answer a ringing telephone—and *The Real Thing* (1982)—where the first scene closes to the realization that it is a fictional-dramatic construct written by a character in the second scene.

And while the image on the can of beans is suggestive of the possibility that there are perhaps recursive Chinese box worlds at play in *Malquist and Moon*, what we find in the novel pales in comparison to the way Stoppard employed such effects in his stage plays. For while the can itself is being held by a cowboy—who is himself in costume because he has a role in an advertisement for these same beans—this is as far as the recursive structure goes in this case. Later still, we find Moon catching a reflection of himself in a mirror just right so as to witness a similar recursive structure: "When he leaned forward between the hinged mirror-leaves he caught the reflection of that, and of that, and he saw himself multiplied and diminished between the mirrors to the flat edges of a flat earth" (87). Presumably, this is a metaphor for Moon's role as Boswell to Lord Malquist since in addition to the complications of perspective, there is the issue of whether or not Moon should (recursively) write himself into the narrative as well.

However, these items work to fairly limited effect as compared to the full visual resonance achieved by Stoppard in *Inspector Hound* (where the names Moon and Birdboot themselves are recycled for the play's central characters—two critics, viewing the play from the audience). The play's climax has Moon mounting the stage to answer a ringing phone, which, apparently, is for Birdboot, and Moon calls him to the stage: "Birdboot gets up. He approaches cautiously. Moon gives him the phone and moves back to his seat. Birdboot watches him go. He looks round and smiles weakly, expiating himself" (32). At this point the entire play begins to repeat itself with rather surprising results, as Birdboot finds himself standing in for one of the play's characters, Simon. And just as Simon had been secretly involved in a love triangle with both the mistress of the manor, Lady Cynthia Muldoon, and her houseguest, Felicity Kimball (whom he wishes to dump for Cynthia), so too Birdboot is secretly involved with the actress who is playing Felicity and, in turn, is immediately smitten with the actress playing Cynthia (causing him to want to dump the actress playing Felicity). Thus, when thrust onto the stage, Birdboot finds himself responding to the characters (or is it to their actor-counterparts?) in precisely the same way that the fictional Simon had in the previous scene. Moreover, just as Simon feels compelled to explain his mysterious appearance at Muldoon Manor in Act 1, Birdboot feels similarly compelled to explain his own (perhaps, more mysterious) appearance within the play:

> FELICITY. What are you doing here?!
> BIRDBOOT. Well, I . . .
> FELICITY. Honestly, darling, you really are extraordinary—
> BIRDBOOT. Yes, well here I am. (*He looks round sheepishly.*)
> FELICITY. You must have been desperate to see me—I mean, I'm flattered, but couldn't it wait till I got back? (33).

Much of the dialogue comes word for word from a similar scene in Act 1. Yet this isn't just a case of a man stumbling onto a stage where he doesn't belong, since all of the other actors accept Birdboot into Simon's role without hesitation. To be sure, the recursive structure of the play is all the more compelling for the fact that the audience physically experiences the event along with the characters on stage, especially given that one of their own has ostensibly jointed that structure as it plays itself out to its full comedic effect.

While recursive elements are much more reserved in *Lord Malquist* than they are in Stoppard's plays, the whole second half of the novel does involve a recursive structure of sorts. For instead of continuing on in his role of the ostensible serial cuckold that he plays in the first half of the novel, Moon himself becomes cuckolder of none other than Lord Malquist himself. What Laura Malquist sees in Moon is hard to say, although we find out even as Laura does that apparently both Moon (no surprise) and his wife are virgins.

Narrative inversion (peripeteia, if you will) is as old as Greek theatre, where the definitive example is Oedipus learning that the murderer he seeks is himself, and that he has killed his own father and married his mother. Stoppard would go on to make inversions of one sort or another central to his own dramatic aesthetic identity, from casting the minor characters of Hamlet as major characters in his own *Rosguil*, to having the murdered man in *Hound* turn out to be the same theatre critic that has gone absent at the beginning of the play.

Indeed, as indicated briefly above, such inversions are perhaps most pronounced in *The Real Thing* (1982), where one scene after another inverts the reality of the scene that came before. This is most explicit in the first two scenes. In Scene 1 Charlotte returns from a "business trip" to find that Max has proof that she has been elsewhere (his discovery of Charlotte's passport—she is meant to have been in Geneva). While this scene ends with Charlotte storming off, in the very next scene we meet Charlotte again, only now she is married to Henry, a playwright, and while our first impression is that she may be remarried, it soon becomes clear that the earlier scene was, in fact, merely a re-enactment of one of Henry's plays, with Charlotte in a starring role.

To say that Stoppard himself finds his most successful form with drama isn't meant to suggest that novelists haven't also used recursive structures in aesthetically intriguing and philosophically compelling ways as well. Indeed, Brian McHale describes numerous novels which accomplish just that. Rather, what I mean to suggest is that there is a visual (and even tactile) element to real world manifestations of these recursive structures (such as the endlessly reflecting mirror) which Stoppard as playwright can and does reproduce in a way that Stoppard the novelist did not—and (perhaps) could not.

Returning to Rabinowitz, we find that in addition to implying that Stoppard's success was the result of having embraced a simpler form, he also takes a shot at laying out "two intellectual strands" which he claims run through Stoppard's work: "an apparent relativism or skepticism growing out of his belief that intellectual inquiry leads to infinite regress" (61) and "the belief that one can discover truths behind the superficially absurd by finding the right vantage point" (62). I am largely sympathetic to this interpretation of Stoppard's philosophical agenda, as I am with Ira Nadel's argument that "No matter how outlandish, the novel suggests that 'there is an explanation for everything,' implausible as things might first seem, an idea Stoppard would develop in his plays" (168). Indeed, elsewhere I have argued that in adopting such an approach Stoppard increasingly rejects postmodern perspectives[2]—a reading of Stoppard perhaps best summed up by Michael Vanden Heuvel, who writes "Stoppard does not, then, fully inhabit the postmodern terrain, but he often travels there and traverses it, speaking the language of the region faultlessly even as he stops occasionally to arraign it with deadpan irony or wit" (213).

However, that Moon himself is the mouthpiece for such anti-postmodern sentiments problematizes coming away from the novel with any degree of certainty concerning Stoppard's philosophical commitments at this point in his career. Consider, for instance, how Moon likes arranging things "into sequences, and categories" with the hopes of eventually discovering "the grand design, find out if there is one, or if it's all random" (139). In dialogue with Laura Malquist, Moon fails miserably in an attempt to flesh out this perspective:

> [Laura] "But what difference does it make?"
> [Moon] "What?"
> [Laura] "Whether it is all random or inevitable?"
> Moon wished he had not exposed himself to examination. He floundered—"Well, you want to know that there is something going on besides a lot of accidents."
> [Laura] "But that's all there *is* going on."
> He almost accepted it but rallied.
> [Moon] "But if it's all random, what's the point."
> [Laura] "What's the point if it's all inevitable."

To my way of thinking, this is prototypically Stoppardian: "put a position, rebut it, refute the rebuttal, and rebut the refutation" (Gussow, 3). More-

2 See my *Tom Stoppard: Bucking the Postmodern*. Jefferson, NC: McFarland and Company, 2012.

over, it speaks to an ongoing philosophical issue that Stoppard would pursue throughout his career, from *Jumpers*, to *Arcadia*, to *The Coast of Utopia*. Temperamentally, I think Stoppard wants there to be answers to the hard questions (*The Hard Question* is the name of Stoppard's latest play, which deals with whether there is more to consciousness than matter and mechanics); indeed, I think Stoppard wants very much to believe that reality is not just random—that we are not all made up of bits of matter bumping against themselves. But as wanting does not make it so, Stoppard makes these very debates one of the central aesthetic conceits in his work—such that the comedy of the endless contradictions of these debates eventually trumps the need to find a final answer. Or, to quote Lord Malquist's response when Moon informs him that the details of his biography on Malquist are inaccurate: "Technicalities, dear fellow. The secret of biography is to let your imagination flourish in key with your subject's. In this way you will achieve a poetic truth that is the jewel for which facts are merely the setting" (187). For while Stoppard may well want to discover "the truth" through his works, I expect that he is happy enough to espouse a poetic truth instead. And, moreover, that these verbal exchanges—these "Socratic Dialogues," if you will—work better on stage than they do on the page should go without saying.

WORKS CITED

Aristotle. *The Poetics of Aristotle.* Trans. H. S. Butcher. London: Macmillan, 1902.

Fleming, John. *Stoppard's Theatre: Finding Order Amid Chaos.* Austin: The University of Texas Press, 2001. Print.

Gussow, Mel. *Conversations with Stoppard.* London: Nick Hern Books, 1995. Print.

Nadel, Ira. *Double Act: A Life of Tom Stoppard.* London: Methuen, 2002. Print.

Pynchon, Thomas. *The Crying of Lot 49.* London: Vintage, 2000. Print.

Rabinowitz, Peter. "Narrative Difficulties in *Lord Malquist and Mr Moon.*" *The Cambridge Companion to Tom Stoppard.* Ed. Katherine E. Kelly, Cambridge: Cambridge UP, 2001, 55-67. Print.

Stoppard, Tom. *After Magritte.* New York: Samuel French, 1994. Print
—. *Arcadia.* London: Faber and Faber, 1993. Print.
—. *Indian Ink.* London: Faber and Faber, 1995. Print.
—. *Jumpers.* New York: Grove Press, 1972. Print.
—. "Life, Times: Fragments." *Introduction 2: Stories by New Writers.* London: Faber and Faber, 1964, 126-30. Print.
—. *Lord Malquist and Mr. Moon.* London: Faber and Faber, 1980. Print.
—. *Night and Day.* New York: Grove Press, 1979. Print.
—. "Reunion." *Introduction 2: Stories by New Writers.* London: Faber and Faber, 1964, 121-5. Print.
—. *Rosencrantz and Guildenstern are Dead.* New York: Grove Press, 1967. Print.
—. "The Story." *Introduction 2: Stories by New Writers.* London: Faber and Faber, 1964, 131-6. Print.
—. *The Coast of Utopia.* New York: Grove Press, 2002. Print.
—. *The Invention of Love.* London: Faber and Faber, 1997. Print.
—. *The Real Thing.* Winchester, MA: Faber and Faber, 1984. Print.
—. *The Real Inspector Hound.* Tom Stoppard: Plays One. London: Faber and Faber, 1993. Print.
—. *Travesties.* New York: Grove Press, 1975. Print.
Vanden Heuvel, Michael. "'Is Postmodernism?': Stoppard among/against the Post-modern." *The Cambridge Companion to Tom Stoppard.* Ed. Katherine E. Kelly. Cambridge: Cambridge UP, 2001. 213-28. Print.

JANE WONG YEANG CHUI

DESIRE, CONTEMPT, AND THE FEMALE UNDERTOW IN HAROLD PINTER'S *THE DWARFS: A NOVEL*

The adjective "Pinteresque," first used in 1960, describes a wide variety of recurring themes in Pinter's plays having to do with "implications of threat and strong feeling produced through colloquial language, apparent triviality, and long pauses" (*OED*). Theatre critics and audiences easily associate the adjective with a sense of impending menace, some with despair and the breakdown of human communication, and others with Pinter's famous non-sequiturs and gnomic speeches. What has largely been overlooked when we think of what is "Pinteresque" is the essence of *where* the "implications of threat" and menace arise from and *how* they have become so entrenched in Pinter's drama. Interestingly, it is not Pinter's plays but his sole novel that sheds the most insight into this inquiry.

Pinter wrote *The Dwarfs* in the 1950s but the novel was not published until 1990. Though a number of poems precede the novel, *The Dwarfs* is the first full-length work that deals with multiple characters, each with distinct characteristics and flaws that are fully developed. Yet the novel, like its play version (1963), has received scant attention. Both novel and play are notoriously difficult to understand for a number of reasons. In the first case, there are several versions of *The Dwarfs*, including an early unpublished prose work entitled "Queen of the Fairies."[1] Pinter scholars like Martin Esslin and Martin Quigley have, in not so many words, declared *The Dwarfs* to be unreadable, "disconcertingly opaque," and even "a partial failure" (130; 413). These critical responses are more often than not directed at the cryptic speeches of the characters, particularly Len, whose seemingly nonsensical dialogues are characterized by his relationship with a group of invisible dwarfs. There are no indi-

1 First staged in 1963, the play is based on an earlier 1960 radio play, which was revised twice; once in 1961 and again in 1968. Kerry Lee Crabbe adapted the novel into a film script in 1996 but it did not secure a buyer. More recently, Christopher Morahan staged a revised version of Crabbe's script; this was filmed and played at Pinterfest (BBC 4) (*Guardian* 2003). Detailed discussions of the radio and stage versions can be found in Mary Jane Miller's "Pinter as a Radio Dramatist," and Scott Giantvalley's "Toying with *The Dwarfs*."

cations as to whether the dwarfs are literal, allegorical, or a product of Len's seeming madness. More recently however, Michael Billington has pointed out that the novel "holds the key to all his later plays" (*Guardian* 2003). Billington's observation stems from his focus on Pinter's imagination, and how Pinter's "intellectual, as well as emotional and linguistic development" is informed by the playwright's "life and memory," the characters' Hackney banter, their preoccupations, and the novel's topography of 1950s London.

What is especially distinctive about the novel is the presence of a single female character, Virginia, who is later omitted in the play version. Both novel and play are set in Hackney, where three friends, Mark, Pete, and Len negotiate the terms of their friendship with each other through what can best be described as a kind of antagonistic male rivalry. The tensions in the play are generated among the three characters' cynical perceptions of each other; this is played out in an all-male sphere. Pinter's creative decision—removing Virginia from the dramatic rendition of the novel—plays an important part in trying to understand a work that has largely been deemed indecipherable. Pinter himself noted: "The play is quite abstract, mainly, I believe, because I omitted the essential character of Virginia from it" ("Author's Note"). This remark can be read as a reference to Len, who is portrayed as the "traitor" in the play (as he betrays Pete to Mark). The original "traitor" is, in fact, Virginia. The inclusion of Virginia does not change the storyline but it does change the way we interpret the dynamics of the men's friendship. In drawing attention to Virginia's depiction, from an object of desire, to a figure of contempt, then of contention (alongside the men's friendship), this essay traces Pinter's early concepts about the role that female sexuality plays in forming and unraveling ideas of trust and betrayal, issues at the heart of the Pinteresque landscape.

Pete, Mark, and Len

The three male characters in *The Dwarfs* propel the movement of the story, and the tensions among them create unspoken boundaries about what their friendship entails. Their strained relationships with each other revolve around ideas having to do with their social, professional, and sexual lives, or their lack thereof. In the opening section of the novel, Len and Pete are in Mark's apartment; the latter is an actor who is seldom in his flat. When Mark returns, it is Len and Pete who open the door for him to enter. Like many of the plays to follow, Pinter maps out spatial boundaries that determine the fate of his characters. Mark's return to his flat, already occupied by Len and Pete, underscores his vulnerability as a traveling actor. Len is first to point this out:

> [The rooms] change at their own will, he said. I would have no quarrel, I wouldn't grumble, you see, if these rooms would remain the same, would keep to some consistency. But they don't. And I can't see the boundaries, the limits which I've been led to believe are natural. That's the trouble. I'm all for the natural behavior of rooms, doors, staircases, the lot. But I can't rely on them. (11-12)

The notion of changing rooms is implicitly attributed to Mark's frequent absence and reappearance but it also highlights the instability of the friendship. Len asks Mark about his recent acting gig, wanting to know where he acted and what it is like when he acts: "Does it please you? Does it please anyone else?" (15).

The men's relentless judgment of each other's way of life is central to the novel in that it generates a sense of discontent that paradoxically becomes the centerpiece of their friendship. Mark finds himself having to defend his profession several times, to Len ("What's wrong with acting?"), and later to Pete, who judges him incapable of being a gigolo even if he wanted to be one: "But be frank. Have you ever done an honest day's work in your life?" (101). Mark thinks Pete considers him a "parasite" and a "ponce" simply because he is an actor but he insists that even if he were a ponce, he lives and operates in his own life (79).[2] Mark Taylor-Batty likens Mark's defense to Teddy's comment about his work in *The Homecoming* (1964). For Teddy, one can only *see* if there is a balance between operating on things and operating *in* things, but Mark takes on a slightly different view in *The Dwarfs*: "[I]n Mark's terms, by claiming that to operate 'on' things is to have real insight, the ability to see, and is in some way superior to those merely operating 'in things'" (Taylor-Batty 94).

2 British slang for "pimp."

Pete's profession and Len's lack of one further complicate the competition between the two men. While Pete works in the financial district in London (though we are not quite certain what he does), he is also an aspiring writer, though not a very good one. He resorts to writing love stories in women's magazines. Len on the other hand is depicted as an odd-job man; he has been a porter, worked at a pub, and considers becoming an insurance salesman, to which Pete mockingly remarks: "See if he can stick it" (17). Pete's criticism of Len becomes increasingly direct as the novel progresses; he calls Len a "rotten old shirt" and suggests that Len will be locked up in a matter of time if he does not buck up his ideas. But it is Len's response that cuts through the mockery; even fairly early on in the novel Len appears fully able to stave off Pete's damning assessment of his life:

> —A bloke like you, Mark, only get the next best, not the best.
> —What about a bloke like me? said Pete.
> —Why should you [Pete] get the best? I don't know anyone who gets the best. (17)

Despite repeated taunts toward Mark and Len and being similarly taunted himself, Pete is aware that their friendship relies on the effect this has on each of them. He believes that he is the maintainer and savior of the friendship:

> For upon consideration, taking all differences into account, he knew their friendship was valuable. In fact he was not sure whether they might not be said to constitute a church, of a kind. They were hardly one in dogma or direction, but there was common ground and there was a framework. At their best they formed a unit, and a unit which, in his terms, was entitled to be called a church; an alliance of the three of them for the common good, and a faith in that alliance. (56)

The friendship between the three men is essentially troubled because each man feeds on the anxieties and insecurities of the other. Furthermore, their different "dogma" and "direction" render them incapable of protecting themselves from each other's judgment. That the friendship is associated with the trinity of the church is especially significant because this description is immediately followed by a rather lengthy section on Pete's failed attempt to become a part of the Church of England.

As a contrast to his disillusionment with the Church of England, Pete's vision of the role he plays in the three-man friendship appears to be a substitute for what he is unable to achieve as a member of the Church. The messiah complex that arises from this view is supported by Pete's conviction that he is the only one who can preserve the friendship. Moreover, Pete's messiah complex also suggests that he may need the friendship more than Mark, who "operates on things" and "live[s] safely tucked up in a test tube," (79), and Len, who declares himself to be a "non-participator" (49). More significantly, when asked if he has been getting along with Christ, Len responds: "Christ? No, no. No. He's what he is and I'm what I'm not. I don't see how we can be related" (49). The recurrent biblical references further assert Pete's perception of his role as "savior" in the friendship; his dialogue with Len and Mark in a pub is worth noting as he tells the two men they should follow him: "I am the way and the truth. I am the resurrection and the life . . . It's gospel . . . I said I'd accept the job on two conditions" (135).[3] The first condition is that he should be able to deal with matters in his own time and with a "free hand"; the second, "a worthwhile Judas" though he hasn't found one who "was quite up to the mark" (135). This phrase is particularly difficult to interpret; Pete's desire to manipulate the dynamics of the friendship as and when he deems fit is associated with a sense of contempt and deception. In wanting to have a "worthwhile Judas," Pete expresses a desire for the ability to cause damage to the friendship, although he does not want to be held responsible should this come about. His delusions of playing savior and traitor to the friendship are also paradoxically ironic. Pete's troubled relationship with Virginia essentially negates his role as savior and traitor; her presence exposes the faults and flaws of the three men in ways that have never been immediately apparent to them,

3 For a commentary on select references to the biblical allusions in *The Dwarfs*, see Łukasz Borowiec's "More or Less on the Mark? Translating Harold Pinter's The Dwarfs: A Novel."

and in doing so, she accomplishes what Pete has always wanted to do: to "save" the men from each other's destructiveness. Virginia is Pete's Judas, but Pete has overlooked the biblical fact that Judas betrays the savior.

Virginia and the Female Space

Virginia's role in the three-man friendship opens up a new dimension in *The Dwarfs* especially if we consider Len's part in the betrayal of the friendship. In the play version, she is entirely absent, and as a result, the tensions between Pete, Len, and Mark are often attributed to Len's seeming madness and his visions of the dwarfs. Len's cryptic speeches are variously interpreted as "the rantings of a madman," a representation of institutional orders, and as a metaphorical rendering of the "miseries, jealousies, and ignobleness of the dissolving relationship" of the men (Gabbard 132-33). Len's perception of the dwarfs in the play is of fundamental importance; he is in fact the only one who is aware of the impending dissolution of the friendship. In an early draft, Pinter explicitly notes the relevance of the dwarfs in Len's speech. Following this line of interpretation, Len recognizes that the friendship is no longer sustainable: "Pete thinks you're a fool . . . He may be your Black Knight, you may be his Black Knight, but I'm cursed with the two of you with two Black Knights, that's friendship, that's this that I know" (*Plays 2* 100-101). As Penelope Prentice has suggested, the essential motivation behind this betrayal is in essence a selfish one; in dissolving the friendship, Len also "rids himself of his imagined dwarfs, but also possibly exiles himself to a sanitized reality of mundane order" (Prentice 103). This interpretation, however, has no place in the novel, where the motivations behind the betrayal are underscored by a power struggle in which characters jostle each other for a vantage point from which they can determine the direction the friendship will take.

The inclusion of Virginia in *Dwarfs* the novel undermines what Pete refers to as the "trinity" of the three-man friendship, and more particularly, Pete's conviction that he is the "savior" of the men's relationship with each other. Virginia's presence in the novel is, in Len's words, a "smoke signal" (*Plays 2* 90). Her name is first mentioned when Pete tries to ask Mark (apparently a "lovelark") for advice on how to write romance for women's magazines; he wants to know what it's like to be in love. Mark's response is instinctive: "Why don't you find out for yourself? . . . What's the position between you and Virginia?" (20). This section is immediately followed by a chapter that provides a general outline of the nature of the relationship between Pete and Virginia. Not surprisingly, the scene takes place in a room. Space and spatial boundaries are intrinsically dangerous in the Pinteresque world; when boundaries shift and are reconfigured, menace, in the form of the famous Pinter "intruder," threatens to disrupt the lives of the characters. Power struggles inevitably follow. Pinter's formulation of the intruder figure and his perception of its purpose is key to understanding the more subtle instances where the struggle for power in his works appears deceptively safe and intimate:

> For if the intention of the visitor is to strip the man of his delusion, and if this is successful, he may then clothe the man in one of his own, on the principle that delusions are adjustable and can be worn by anyone. You can wear mine. I can wear yours. All you have to do is give me time for a fitting. (*Various Voices* 14)[4]

It is precisely this fitting that undermines any of Pete's efforts to play savior to the friendship. Virginia does not appear with Pete and Len as they wait for Mark to return in the opening section of the book. Mark's flat is wholly a male space, and this space is soon "disrupted" when Virginia steps into the narrative, inevitably forcing the men to reconfigure the dynamics of their friendship around her presence *and* her absence.

Taking into account Pinter's comments about "the visitor," there is little doubt that Virginia is his chosen intruder in *The Dwarfs*. From the outset, her role as intruder is already clearly defined through the genre of the work itself. In Pinter's plays, the dialogues rarely include internal monologues (unless they were written as dramatic monologues). The economy of language, which Pinter emphasizes as an important quality in his writing, would not allow the characters to express their internal thoughts alongside the sparse and concise

4 Pinter's 1958 letter to the editor of The Play's the Thing entitled "On *The Birthday Party* II." On social, political, and sexual spaces, see Dilek Inan's "Public Consciousness Beyond Theatrical Space: Harold Pinter Interrogates Borders and Boundaries."

responses of those they are speaking to. In his prose, however, we are afforded a rare glimpse of these thoughts. As it turns out, they are immensely important in the case of Virginia because her internal thoughts reveal her awareness of her position and power in the novel; both are represented in her knowledge of how space and positioning can metaphorically determine power structures in a given room. Depicted first lying on a sofa in Pete's apartment, she realizes that when she stands up, "[t]he posture of the room changed. The sunlight jolted. The room settled. The sunlight re-formed. But, she thought, *I stand upright and the balance is disturbed. I have thrown a spanner in the works. I have done violence to normally imperturbable forces. I have inflicted a reverse* (my emphasis)" (23). This suggests that the "balance" in the room is determined by the fact that the space belongs to Pete, and by virtue of this advantage, any sense of power should be inclined to his advantage.

If in lying down Virginia takes her place as the "submissive" other and standing up entails a disturbance of this balance, then we already know that the space is open to possibilities of contention. Furthermore, Virginia's actions and awareness do not go unnoticed. Pete's desire to be the "leader" of the male pack parallels his desire to play the dominant male in his relationship with Virginia. In his flat, he offers Virginia a white summer dress which he has made for her. In the act of stripping and putting on the dress, Virginia accedes to Pete's dominance, albeit Pinter's caution is quite telling; the identity of the intruder is reassigned according to the desires of the more dominant character (Pete in this case): "the intention of the visitor is to strip the man of his delusion, and if this is successful, he may then clothe the man in one of his own." Virginia is right when she thinks to herself that she has "inflicted a reverse" as, rather than stripping Pete of his clothes and, metaphorically, his dominance, she is made to strip and put on Pete's clothes (literally a dress that he made). The result in this reversal highlights not only the precarious position that Pete has placed himself in, but it also exposes his own insecurities and anxieties about his place among Mark and Len.

The shifting power dynamics between Virginia and Pete spill over into Pete's friendship with Mark and they also intensify Pete's underlying insecurities as he attempts to assert his control over the three-man friendship. Michael

Billington astutely notes that Pete shares an "intellectual companionship of almost erotic intensity" with Mark (*Life and Work* 58). The dramatic work downplays this aspect of their friendship, which may be implicitly implied but never explicitly expressed. In the novel, Pete's relationship with Virginia highlights his feelings towards Mark. As Virginia models in the summer dress he made for her, Pete tells Virginia: "But you know what? he said, sitting down, in some ways you're more of a boy to me than a woman [. . .] you're a woman all right. But I like the way you conserve your mental energy [. . .] You're a true companion" (27). Mark, he claims, could never understand what true companionship means because "[a] woman is simply one thing to him and no more [. . .] Mark wants all his women to call him sir and salute him three times a day" (27). But when Virginia asks Pete if he "likes" Mark, Pete affirms this. Pete's affection for and protective attitude towards Mark is reciprocated; when Len expresses doubts about Pete, Mark jumps to the latter's defense:

> —Look here, Mark said.
> —What?
> —Why don't you leave Pete alone?
> —Leave him alone?
> —Why don't you give it a rest? He doesn't do you any good.
> —What did you say?
> —I'm the only one who can get on with him, Mark said.
> —You?
> —Yes. You've got to have a certain kind of—something—to get on with him. Anyway, I've got it and at the moment you haven't. What good does he do you? You should give it a rest [. . .] He doesn't take any liberties with me. He does with you. (70)

Pete and Mark are set apart from Len, the middleman who has neither money nor women but dabbles instead in obscure theories and philosophical ideas, but it is Pete who thinks he alone is responsible for the welfare of the men and their friendship. Len is alienated in the friendship, but it is precisely this alienation that magnifies the rivalry between Pete and Mark.

Pete's negative comments about Mark stem from jealousy, and this jealousy essentially comes from a sense of unfulfilled desire. Pete openly admits to Mark that he rarely makes love to Virginia. This admission subverts his dominance and places the two men on opposite ends of the spectrum: Mark is a "lovelark" and Pete is hardly intimate with his girlfriend. Pete's admission comes across as an attempt to place himself "above" Mark, who thinks that sex is the "answer to anything" (21). This may also be his way of asserting a kind of male solidarity with Mark by demonstrating that the female other has no place in the male sphere; outside of Pete and Virginia's relationship and in an all-male setting, Pete depicts Virginia as a sex object. Even as he tells Virginia that "[a] woman has potential in other spheres," he is clearly not referring to her place within the male sphere. Pete's views of Virginia tell us more about his anxieties among the men than about his relationship with Virginia. Gender psychologists have observed the social aspect of bragging about sexual conquests (or the lack thereof) and how it affects all-male friendships: "The link between young males' tendency to 'tell [sexual] stories about girls' and their lack of intimacy with girls and young women is an important one," but more importantly, men "commonly use sexually aggressive stories and jokes as a means of 'negotiating' the latent tension and aggression they feel toward each other" (Messner 352). Against this backdrop, Virginia functions as a character that threatens to expose the men's anxieties.

For Pete and Mark, Virginia then becomes an object against which they measure themselves and each other, as each compensates their "shortcomings" through sexual dominance. While Mark is a traveling actor and does not have a stable income, his sexual conquests put him "above" Pete, who works in the financial district but has little or no success with women. Virginia is quick to observe this when Pete tells her that he has told Mark about their lack of intimacy, which Pete thinks is nothing to "be ashamed of" (28). Virginia's sarcastic response—"but why don't we write out a joint statement and send it to him? [. . .] Of course, I could always send him a poison-pen letter, telling him to mind his own bloody business"—elicits an unexpected retort from Pete, who defends Mark. On top of this, Pete blames Virginia for misinterpreting what he has just said; she heard it "entirely out of context" (28). This early "betrayal" of Virginia as Pete takes Mark's side is heightened when he outright rejects her in a scene where he enters her flat and finds her fresh from a bath, dressed in an open bathrobe: "And for God's sake, he shouted, keep that robe done up! I don't want to see the hair on your crutch. What do you think I am? [. . .] You're being very disappointing, Virginia. You know what you're doing, don't you? You're behaving like any other little tart who must show herself off or cease to exist" (85). Pete's rejection of Virginia suggests his anxiety about his own inadequacies as her lover. He refers to Virginia's act of seduction as "a little effort to get out of this masturbatory rut" when it is he, not Virginia, who is in one. In associating her with her friend, Marie Saxon, whom he believes to be the ultimate tart (and Mark's former lover), Pete draws a line between those who derive their contentment from sexual encounters (like Mark) and those who regard such a lifestyle to be less than intellectual, and in turn, undeserving of his attention.

Virginia's "potential sphere" in the novel lies in her gender and sexuality, and her ability to negotiate the sphere that is the men's friendship lies in their "marginalization" of her as the other. It is essentially Pete who makes this very explicit distinction. Becoming subservient to Pete after he has chastised her for behaving like a tart, Virginia begs for his forgiveness, only to discover that his anger towards her is directed at an earlier comment that she made on *Hamlet*. His long diatribe runs almost three pages as he chastises her for her "extremely stupid" opinions about *Hamlet*:

> Did you realize that? You don't know anything about *Hamlet*, Ginny. Don't you understand that? [. . .] You made me look, in effect, a bloody fool [. . .] I've told you to leave him [Shakespeare] alone, I've told you you're not capable of expressing an opinion about him [. . .] What must Mark and Len think? [. . .] What did you hope to prove? That you could form your own opinions? To prove to Mark that you could read? Do you think that if you carried a book on Advanced Mathematics under your arm you would necessarily persuade Len you could add two and two? [. . .] Did you think you would be excused because you were a woman? (87)

Pete's rage at Virginia is fueled by desire, desire that stems from his own anxieties. On the one hand, he is angered that someone could come by and find Virginia in the nude. The notion that men could be seduced by her nudity suggests that Pete is well aware that he has not been an adequate lover for Virginia, yet he wants to have ownership over her body. His attraction to Virginia is in fact a latent desire to be more like Mark, whose sexual conquests affirm his attractiveness and his "manhood." On the other hand, Pete's attack on Virginia's intellectual ineptitude appears to be associated with his feelings of inferiority and his desire to be more like Len. Throughout the novel, Pete demonstrates a constant desire to be more "intelligent." In one instance, he flaunts the number of books in his hands, including one on Elizabethan surgeries, in the company of Mark, Len, and Virginia. When Mark fails to pay attention to his remark about how an Elizabethan woman gave birth to puppies, he flares up: "For Jesus Christ's fucking sake! Pete screamed, hurling the books at Virginia's feet, will you stop walking between those fucking paving stones? You're driving me mad!" (104). Later, in the pub with Mark and Len, Pete picks up a woman named Brenda and tells her that he is "doing literary research at Cambridge University for students," where he deals with old manuscripts and offers his "honest and respected opinion" (123).

Pete's seeming dissatisfaction with his professional and social life contributes to his feelings of inadequacy even when he, among the three men, has the most stable and successful career (in a conventional sense). Mark's acting gigs are random and unpredictable, Len is either unemployed or working at odd jobs. Yet, neither is particularly concerned about their unstable and unpredictable lives. Even though Pete has a more stable professional life, he is deeply dissatisfied; he wants recognition and approval, and above all, admiration. He finds none of these in his friendship with Mark and Len, and quiet resentment is further exacerbated at work. In a scene where he stands outside Valparaiso Bank on Threadneedle Street, apparently during a break from work, he runs into an old friend named Derek, who insists that he must keep in touch with mutual friends from the past. Regretfully, Pete tells Derek that he is on his way to see Mark ("You know how it is, Derek. You know these actors, eh?") depicting himself as someone who is needed and wanted

(61). This scene is immediately followed by one in which Pete is informed that he is unwanted. His boss, a Mr. Lynd, summons him to his office; Mr. Lynd expresses concerns about Pete's role in the company as a response to feedback from Pete's colleagues that he is inclined to be "far away" and perhaps not "keen" on his work:

> —Tell me, Mr. Cox.
> —Yes?
> —What exactly, if you don't, as it were, he laughed, mind my asking, is your ambition?
> Pete watched Mr. Lynd open the cigarbox, close it and look up candidly.
> —I'm afraid, he replied, stroking his chin, I can't say that I've ever really considered it, Mr. Lynd. (64-65)

Asked if he has "other interests," Pete tells Mr. Lynd that his interests are mostly "domestic." This inquiry into Pete's life unhinges him far more than he thinks, particularly when he finds himself lacking the courage that Mark seems to have. The latter argues that even though he is an actor, and "a liability on the world's bank's balance" he does not depend on institutional orders; he has nothing but "contempt for the till" (79). Mark refuses to live according to the standards of others: "They don't apply to me. I don't live with them"; Mark has still "got balls" (79). But what strikes Pete as even more poignant is Mark's attitude towards life: "What you don't understand about me, Mark said, it is this—I've got no ambition" (79). This proclamation is made with such pride, gusto, and a deep sense of conviction that Pete could never hope to emulate it. Damned by Mark and isolated by Len's "madness," Pete finally turns to Virginia.

Pete's treatment of Virginia changes according to circumstances; in the presence of Mark and Len, she is a sexual object, but in private, he considers her to be a friend, not unlike Mark and Len. This oscillation affects the homosocial ordering that shapes the three-man friendship. Virginia remains subservient only until she is humiliated in front of Mark and Len. Len pays no attention to Pete's humiliation of Virginia but Mark does and finds himself increasingly drawn to Virginia. The homosocial tensions in the novel reach new heights in Mark's newfound attraction towards Virginia. Eve Sedgwick's seminal work, *Between Men: English Literature and Male Homosocial Desire* (1985), posits that patriarchal heterosexuality and male bonds are often formed in response to the female other, and driven by desire (homosocial and heterosexual), and these relationships can create both negative and positive types of bonding. Pete's bonding with Mark and Len is marked by his insecurities and fear that he has been "left out" because of his relationship with Virginia:

> —You mustn't think, Pete said, that I don't know what you and Mark are. I do. I recognize you both.
> —Me? Mark? What do you mean? What are we?
> —I take it you are my friends [. . .] Why don't you ask me, Pete said, if I recognize Virginia?
> —Why should I ask you that?
> —If you want to know another thing, I'll tell you. Because I lack guts, I commit spite, I suffer under that bondage. I commit spite at all corners, and in the face of the image. (114)

Pete does not say whether he "recognizes" Virginia but associates his responses with his lack of guts and the spite that results from it. The Pete-Mark-Virginia triangle calls attention to the homosocial ordering of the all-male friendship. For instance, homosociality determines the heterosexual relationships of young men: male friendships are privileged above male-female relationships; in the case of Pete and Mark, "sexual activity is a key path to masculine states, and other men are the audience, always imagined, and sometimes real, for one's sexual activities" (Flood 342). Homosocial ordering becomes dysfunctional in the novel because Pete conflates Virginia's role into lover *and* friend. Mark, however, demonstrates that he is fully capable of holding the "key path to masculine states"; his sexual affairs are consistently subordinated and they do not interfere or disrupt his friendship with Pete and Len, that is, until he has an affair with Virginia.

Virginia's ability to deliver the final and fatal blow to the three-man friendship is in fact a reenactment of Pete's betrayal of Mark. Pete makes the mistake of regarding Virginia as his confidante fairly early on in the novel, and he reveals and criticizes Len and Mark's faults after what may have been a lovemaking session with Virginia. His commentary on Len is not nearly as damning as his assessment of Mark, who he believes is nothing but a "sexual mechanic . . . letting his potentialities slip" (54). Moreover, unlike Len who may be "open both to instruction and to assistance," Pete thinks Mark is a foolish man who does not respond to either. Pete's betrayal of Mark to Virginia "backfires" when Virginia decides to take some time off from Pete and ends up in bed with Mark. Virginia strips for a second time in the novel under Mark's direction, and she does so happily. What is especially significant in this second act of stripping is the notion that she is invited to do so because Mark is clearly seduced by her body whereas in the earlier scene in which she strips for Pete, she does so not because he wants to make love to her but because he wants to assert a sort of blind control over her; she is subsequently rejected by Pete when she appears exposed in a bathrobe. This humiliation is "repaid" in full as she lies in bed with Mark after having sex with him:

> —So he thinks I'm a fool? [. . .] But he has said to you that I am a fool?
> —He's said so many things.
> —No, but I want to know exactly.
> —Why?
> —Tell me [. . .] You've heard him say it?
> —From all he's ever said to me about you, she said, I don't think he respects you.
> —He doesn't respect me and he thinks I'm a fool. (161-62)

Virginia's affair with Mark is a betrayal of Pete, but it is her decision to expose Pete's hypocrisy to Mark that completes the cycle of contempt she has for him: "I'd like him to walk in and see us, she said. Naked. In each other's arms" (162).

Virginia's contempt for Pete serves to highlight the contempt that Pete and Mark have for each other. Even though the homosocial bonds between Pete and Mark are undermined by the presence of Virginia, she does not figure as the person responsible for the ugly showdown in the final confrontation scene. Mark attributes the breakdown of the friendship to Pete, and not to Virginia:

> You see, I can appreciate, Pete, that you reserve the right to bestow contempt [. . .] But it seems to me that when it comes down to it, you inhabit a stronghold of contempt from which you can't escape [. . .] You say friendships and whatnot have never been productive. Most of the time then, I was under a delusion. In truth you've never shared [. . .] You couldn't work your salvation on me as you might have done on Len and Virginia, so because I was outside your moral consideration association was permissible. (175-76)

Virginia's betrayal of the men traces the fault lines in their friendship, particularly the distrust and deception that appear to be apparent even before her sexual involvement with Mark. Her contempt for Pete is comparable to Pete's contempt for Mark and Len, and so are her desires, as they are repeatedly subjected to Pete's humiliation.

Pinter's decision to omit the character of Virginia from the play version of *The Dwarfs* is never explained, but in removing her from the play, Len is granted a much more central role in the three-man friendship. Virginia's presence in the novel detracts from Len's Joycean monologues, which I argue should be credited with more poetic value than what is reflected in the scant attention they have been given in Pinter studies. Virginia is Pinter's "Eve" before she discovers the shame of nudity and of desire. In the years following *Dwarfs* the novel, Pinter's female figure slowly morphs into Ruth in *The Homecoming* (1965). Considered by many to be the epitome of the Pinter female figure, Ruth turns the tables on all the men who undermine her sexuality and her intellect, and she does so with the kind of finesse and understated swiftness and brutality that only appears in Pinter's plays. In writing a novel with Virginia in it, Pinter has also stuck close to his biographical details as Billington informs readers that there was indeed a female figure among the "Hackney gang," which consisted of Pinter (portrayed as Mark), Ron Percival (Pete), and Michael Goldstein (Len). Virginia is modeled after Jennifer Mortimer: "They talked about and quoted Shakespeare all the time and *The Dwarfs* is absolutely how it was even to the moment when Ron flung a book at me for daring to quote from *Hamlet* . . . I might have been a catalyst in lots of ways, but the real fight was over the fact that Harold was that much more powerful as a person and Ron was fighting that because he wanted to be king" (ctd. in Billington 59). Pinter's omission of Virginia from the play may have been a later reflection and reconsideration of the factors that contributed to the dissolution of the friendship. Without Virginia, notions of desire and contempt are reshaped in the play; these elements, along with Pete's rage, are downplayed to a large degree, perhaps suggesting the culpability and accountability of the men in their own tragic making. In the end, the men are forced to face their own inadequacies, with or without a woman.

WORKS CITED

Billington, Michael. "Look back in Hackney." *Guardian*. Web. 2 Jul. 2014.

—. Billington, Michael. *The Life and Work of Harold Pinter.* London: Faber and Faber Limited, 1996. Print.

Borowiec, Łukasz. "More or Less on the Mark? Translating Harold Pinter's *The Dwarfs: A Novel.*" *English Language Overseas Perspectives and Enquiries* 9 (2012): 16-27. Print.

Esslin, Martin. *The Peopled Wound: The Work of Harold Pinter.* New York: Doubleday & Company, Inc., 1970. Print.

Flood, Michael. "How Bonds between Men Shape Their Sexual Relations with Women." *Men, Sex, and Homosociality* 10.3 (2008): 339-59. Print.

Gabbard, Lucina Paquet. *The Dream Structure of Pinter's Plays.* Cranbury, NJ: Associated University Presses, Inc., 1976. Print.

Giantvalley, Scott. "Toying with *The Dwarfs*: The Textual Problems with Pinter's 'Corrections.'" *Harold Pinter Critical Approaches.* Ed. Steven H. Gale. Cranbury, NJ: Associated University Presses, Inc., 1986. 72–81. Print.

Inan, Dilek. "Public Consciousness Beyond Theatrical Space: Harold Pinter Interrogates Borders and Boundaries." *Nebula* 2.2 (2005): 33-57. Print.

Messner, Michael A. "Like Family: Power, Intimacy, and Sexuality in Male Athletes' Friendships." *Toward a New Psychology of Gender: A Reader.* Eds. Mary M. Gergen, Sara N. Davi. Hoboken: Taylor and Francis, 2013. 341-62. Print.

Miller, Mary Jane. "Pinter as Radio Dramatist." *Modern Drama* 17 (1974): 403–12. Print.

Nietzsche, Friedrich. *Human, All Too Human.* Trans. R. J. Hollingdale. Cambridge, UK: Cambridge University Press, 1996. Print.

Pinter, Harold. *Plays 2.* London: Faber and Faber Limited, 1991. Print.

—. *The Dwarfs.* New York: Grove Weidenfeld, 1990. Print.

—. *Various Voices.* New York: Grove Press, 1998. Print.

"Pinteresque, adj." *Oxford English Dictionary Online.* 2014. Oxford University Press. Web. 2 Jul. 2014.

Prentice, Penelope. *The Pinter Ethic.* New York: Garland Publishing Inc., 2000. Print.

Quigley, Austin E. "*The Dwarfs*: A Study in Linguistic Dwarfism." *Modern Drama* 17 (1974): 413–422. Print.

Sedgwick, Eve Kosofsky. *Between Men: English Literature and Male Homosocial Desire.* New York: Columbia University Press, 1985. Print.

Taylor-Batty, Mark. *The Theatre of Harold Pinter.* London: Bloomsbury, 2014. Print.

JEFFREY SEVERS

"SAY YES": CONSENT, MARRIAGE, AND HISTORY IN THE DRAMA AND FICTION OF SUZAN-LORI PARKS

Acclaimed African-American playwright Suzan-Lori Parks is best known as the author of experimental and metatheatrical plays about history and the malleability of racial identity, including among others *The America Play* (1994), the Pulitzer Prize-winning *Topdog/Underdog* (2001), and, most recently, *Father Comes Home From the Wars (Parts 1, 2, & 3)* (2014). In 2003 Parks added a novel about an African-American family, abortion, and exhumation in 1960s rural Texas, *Getting Mother's Body*, to her multi-genre portfolio, which also includes essays, work as a film and TV writer, and even songwriting. In this essay I argue that one overlooked point of unity for this diverse oeuvre is Parks's preoccupation with acts of agreement and consent as they are varyingly depicted on stage and page. How many ways are there to signify agreement? For Parks, there seem to be dozens, each distinct in meaning. In a 1995 interview, for instance, explaining her use of "o.k.," she reveals her great attention to single phonemes of consent, even in the most casual rhetorical questions:

> [I]f someone says, "I'm going with you, 'k?" that's different from, "I'm going with you, o.k.?" . . . It's a recording of, not only the way words sound, [but] what that means. The difference between 'k' and 'o.k.' is not just what one might call black English versus standard English . . . I am trying to be very specific in what's going on emotionally with the character . . . If you jump on that word faster, . . . you're feeling something differently. (Kolin and Young 69)

In her 1994 essay "Elements of Style," a riposte to Strunk and White, she lists under the "foreign words and phrases" of her work the expression "*do in diddly dip didded thuh drop*." It is "[p]erhaps an elaborated confirmation, a fancy 'yes!' Although it could be used as a question such as 'Yeah?'" ("Elements" 17). Elsewhere, she mentions "'doo-a-diddly-dit-dit' . . . that one means 'yes.' Actually, that's more like 'yeah!' or, sometimes, 'yeah?'" (Drukman 68).

Far from transparent, simultaneously declarative, exclamatory, and interrogative, these fancy yeses can result in phrasings that encapsulate both Parks's jazz-based strategy of "Rep and Rev" (repetition and revision) and her persistent claim that history saturates the present ("Elements" 9). In *Imperceptible Mutabilities in the Third Kingdom* (1989), for instance, four characters reckon with the Middle Passage in a surreal scene of call-and-response and complex amens as they enact the fate of unknown millions of slaves lost to the sea: "[W]e are not in uh boat!" says one, to which another replies, "But we iz. Iz iz iz uh huhn. Iz uh huhn. Uh huhn iz" (40). Such interpenetration of present-tense being and "uh huhn" suggests that the ultimate object of consent in Parks's work may be history itself—or the "'new' historical events" ("Possession" 4-5) that she credits inventive theater about the black experience with being able to "'make'" (4).

In this essay I examine the varying ways Parks's "yes"—often coerced, but sometimes more freely given—interacts with black emotional life, legacies of slavery and marriage, and the understanding of history in her work. In the end, examining the wreckage of thwarted black women's consent and romantic love, I suggest that Parks's ethic of "making" history partially redeems her characters' traumas by transforming the present-tense act of *our* consent to her creations into the central issue: audiences' and readers' consent to, or belief in, this difficult history of consent becomes Parks's plea for a love across centuries and across races. While invoking a range of plays, I compare *Getting Mother's Body* (hereafter *GMB*) primarily to *Venus* (1996), Parks's controversial exploration of Saartjie Baartman, the Khoisan woman from southern Africa with a large posterior who was sold to freak shows and displayed in 1810's London and Paris as "the Venus Hottentot."[1] Upon her death, she was dissected by anatomist Georges Cuvier, with her remains exhibited in a French museum until the 1970s. Parks adds to a relatively scant historical record an extra-

1 Throughout, I refer to the historical figure as Baartman and the play character as "The Venus," as Parks's script does.

marital affair between The Venus and her final owner, modeled on Cuvier and called The Baron Docteur, who impregnates her twice, forces abortions on her, gives her syphilis, and dissects her after death. England has just outlawed the slave trade in 1807, but the play, like many others by Parks, finds that the essential subjugations of slavery are ongoing. In Parks's construction of nineteenth- and twentieth-century subjects, both The Venus and Billy Beede, the pregnant black sixteen-year-old in *GMB* who goes from planning a wedding to seeking an illegal abortion, deludedly seek marital love as a means to stabilize their penurious lives. I thus examine marital consent and the pageantry of weddings as indicators of the tenuous state into which black speech, especially women's, has been cast throughout history.

Reviewing minute and critically overlooked features of her art, I read these characters' yeses and romantic fantasies in both novel and plays as Parks's risky counters to what she calls an "insidious essentialism" that "reduce[s] [African-Americans] to only one way of being" rather than a "beautiful and infinitely powerful variety" ("Equation" 21-22). Parks's unexpected first step toward that infinite variety has been to resist providing contemporary audiences with historical models of black women, even in abject circumstances, saying only "no." In doing so Parks rejects those reductive narratives that enforce the notion that black historical lives do not really "exist without the presence of the White" world whose oppressions they are presumed at every turn to oppose ("Equation" 19).

Parks is and will remain primarily known, both popularly and academically, as a playwright; but several critics have noted the novel-likeness of her plays and the play-likeness of her novel, though without studying the overlaps in any systematic way. *GMB*, an array of interior first-person monologues and songs, is "more like a play than a novel," "engag[ing] in a continual call and response between various internal and external audiences," writes Laura Wright (140). Parks herself calls *GMB*, which mimics the structure and plot of Faulkner's *As I Lay Dying*, "a novel in voices" (Als). Writing on the genre in which she has been far more prolific, W. B. Worthen calls Parks's dramas both deeply performative and text-centered, pointing out her emphasis on puns and homophones that only a reader of the script can fully appreciate (4-5). Brandi Wilkins Catanese describes *Venus* as both "an object of print culture and . . . a roadmap for embodied performance" (54). While we usually insist that plays be primarily analyzed in performance, Parks adds layers to critics' obligation to (re-)read the printed text before, after, and alongside a production.

Surprisingly, the novel, not the play, is in several senses Parks's "first" genre. While every reader of *GMB* notes its major debt to Faulkner, modernist experimentation in the novel generally informs Parks's playwriting and her sense of what risks literature of all sorts should take. In "Tradition and the Individual Talent" (this time the white male authority targeted is T. S. Eliot), Parks encourages writers to "cross fertilize" or "cross-train": "novelists and those in the novel corner read the poets and the playwrights, playwrights and theater professionals read the novelists, and so on" (27). The best examples of Parks's own cross-training are her *In the Blood* plays, oblique "adaptations" of *The Scarlet Letter* from 1999 and 2000. But Parks's work has been cross-training from the very beginning: Shawn-Marie Garrett reports that Parks "began writing novels at the age of five" (22). In 1983, in a Mount Holyoke fiction workshop with (novelist-playwright) James Baldwin, Parks presented a story titled "The Wedding Pig" (hinting at her many wedding scenes to come). As she acted it out in the various characters' voices, Baldwin suggested she write plays. Taking up the new genre, Parks "had already learned from her favorite fiction writers"— Faulkner, Woolf, and Joyce—"that she could do anything she wanted with language" (Garrett 24). Indeed, Parks's fascination with female forms of "yes" clearly arises from Molly Bloom's dramatic, novel-ending reply to Leopold's marriage proposal: "yes I said yes I will Yes" (Joyce 642).[2] By writing all her variations on "yes," so repetitively that a tinge (or "Rev") of irony almost always creeps in, Parks also offers a feminist perspective on Ellison's *Invisible Man* and the grandfather's deathbed advice: "[O] vercome 'em with yeses, undermine 'em with grins, agree 'em to death and destruction" (16).

2 On Parks's other tributes to Joyce, see Geis (70-71).

Any actress playing The Venus must decide what slants, whether laced with Ellisonian irony or not, to give Reps of "yes," since they are so numerous. The Venus's utterances of consent occur in many forms and situations: they include "Yes" (90, 138), "(yes.)" (89), "Yes that's fine" (129), and "*Yes*" (138). The silences of Parks's trademark "spells," in which a speech attribution appears for a character but with no words, also interact with all the yes-saying; "*A Scene of Love (?)*" consists entirely of ten alternating spells between The Venus and The Baron Docteur, no dialogue (80). Parks signals that *Venus* will complicate a binary opposition in the first lines in the main plot: "So yll finance me? / Yes or no," says a white man to his brother, for whom Baartman is a servant in Africa (10). By the end of this scene, transferring his attention from his entrepreneurial scheme of animal exhibition to Baartman, her purchaser says, "Say yes and we'll go tomorrow!" (16). But rather than depict this as essentially a transaction of abject enslavement, Parks begins to construct The Venus as a willful, consenting figure motivated by money: promised "Gold!" and "A mint!," she immediately echoes the words back, a kind of agreement itself (16-17). Parks said at the play's premiere that her version of Baartman is "multifaceted. She's vain, beautiful, intelligent and yes, complicit" (Williams). "It's not the story of a black woman who's victimized," Parks says elsewhere (ctd. in Kolin and Young 14). Such characterizations call for more nuance than Deborah Geis provides when she writes that The Venus "participates" in her degradation because she "has no choice (she is asked whether she wants to leave Africa, but the choice is a sham . . .)" (85).[3]

At the same time, Parks also layers into the play's beginning the possibility of The Venus uttering a complex, overarching no. In the "Overture," as her various oppressors swarm around her, the first sounds we hear from her are self-identification ("The Venus Hottentot" (2)) and "Uhhhh!"—said twice, separated by a line from The Chorus (4). Her last lines in the overture are four repetitions, unbroken by other speeches, of "Uhhhh!" (8). Parks often plays with the duration of sounds and their echoes and gaps, and a director and performer could make an audience hear a dissenting "Uh-uh!" in these sounds,

3 For vehement criticism of Parks's play as a degrading "re-objectification" of Baartman, see Young, passim.

which seem in context to confirm the racist identification of The Venus with the subhuman. The opening lines' "Yes or no" (128) will later be revised by The Baron Docteur regarding abortions he wants and she does not: "A simple yes or no will do" (139). But throughout, all such mentions of "simple"—as in "We'll start with simple figure drawing," in an anatomy scene—signal actor and audience to seek the true complexity, the yes *and* no, in The Venus (112).

In the largely realistic *GMB*, Parks's language is more tame and conventionally novelistic; but portrayals of force and consent have clearly carried over from her stage work, along with a consistently vocalic effect in the interlocking monologues. As Billy worries about fitting into her wedding dress in spite of the mother's body she is "getting" (one hidden valence of the title), she urges her child not to grow: "The baby hears me. I can feel it hearing and listening to me, the mother, and saying yes. It's a good baby already" (61). Billy's later quest to rob her mother's grave to provide funds to abort her child, as her mother Willa Mae had planned to do with Billy, suggests that the baby "saying yes" in the womb is not the idyll Billy imagines. Since Parks herself was born in May 1963, this book functions as a sort of pre-autobiography: a meditation on the contingent context—and definitions of a "good" black child in a still regressive South—into which she was born. As Parks says, all her works revolve around the questions, "Who am I? . . . Who are we?" (Kolin and Young 42). *GMB* in essence explores the lack of autonomy in historical blacks by projecting its author into a prenatal state, a subtle act of intergenerational comparison that would inevitably take far more florid form on Parks's stage, where spectacle and pastiche make time inherently more malleable.

In pursuing those spectacles and her interest in consent, Parks invests in the pageantry and political meaning of weddings, where "I do" takes on the legal status of a performative speech act and becomes a marker of the liberal subject—but not, we are reminded, for the vast majority of black history in the Americas. Parks lists "ritual" among her major interests, and by staging weddings in her Rep & Rev forms she responds mightily to the history of prohibitions on slave acts of consent and contract (Kolin and Young 100). Tess Chakkalakal details the basic history: slaves in the U.S. "could not marry because they were legally incapable of giving consent" and "the slave had no status as a person before the law" (3), though flourishing marital relationships nevertheless "functioned as . . . passive resistance against . . . slavery" (4).[4] This history of legal status denied hovers over Parks's works: a racist asks Aretha in *Imperceptible Mutabilities*, "Were you legally wed[?] . . . Didn't—'jump the broom' or some such nonsense, eh?" (45). In such moments Parks strikes against slave history, but without sentimentalizing marriage as liberation, whatever the historical period: discussing *Devotees in the Garden of Love* (1992), featuring two women in wedding dresses witnessing a war from which one will pick a mate, Parks says, "I wanted to give black actresses a chance to wear pretty . . . wedding dresses"; she describes the actresses' "faces light[ing] up" upon examining a rack of potential costumes (Kolin and Young 95). But *Devotees*' ironizing of its courtly language and lavish costuming means that undermining love's mythologies—a garden here, the goddess of love in *Venus*—is Parks's ultimate goal. Toying with the *telos* of Shakespearean comedy, she establishes elaborate marital dreams that frequently end up dashed.

Larger allegories of personal and historical becoming are being worked out in these (non-)marriages. Parks suggests a central metaphor in her many unsteady couples: "[W]e, each individually, are a married whole of two halves. One side of us[,] very human, the side made of clay, is married to the other side made of spirit, and they are often in conflict" (Kolin and Young 147). If, as Jon Dietrick suggests, even the brothers Lincoln and Booth of the utterly polarized *Topdog/Underdog* can be seen acting out "traditional, nuclear-family roles of mother and father," it is clear that, for Parks, consenting to marriage stands for larger formations of selfhood, of acceding to full personhood (59). That marriages literal and figurative are so often full of strife in Parks's work indexes just how riven the black subject is for her—how much, as she depicts white-face Abraham Lincolns and such, blacks are subjected to DuBoisian double-consciousness.

Both *GMB* and *Venus* depict young black women set on clichéd romantic expectations in ways that grant this wider scope to marriage and consent. In

4 Considering Parks in terms of critical legal studies would bear much fruit. In addition to marital consent and the courtroom scene I examine later, other sites to consider would be the oath-taking and "histironical amendment" of *Imperceptible Mutabilities* (53).

GMB's first chapter, after having her head pushed into a car door during backseat sex with Clifford Snipes, father of her baby, Billy tries to incite in him the question to which she can clearly consent. "You gonna get down on yr knee and ask me?" she says, insistent on ceremony; when Snipes dissembles, she says, "[Y]ou gotta ask me to marry you on yr knees in front of [family] too" (8). Billy persists in her fantasies despite her mother—who passed as white, as Wright documents (141)— having died in a botched abortion of her child with a white man, who promised to leave his wife and marry her. While she does not have theatricality to work with in her novel, Parks nonetheless gives Billy a stage for her excitement: modeling her dress, she "pass[es] [her] hand slow down over the fabric," later "styl[ing] the shoes some, walking to and fro on the porch, holding her hand on her hip" (42-43).

In Parks's attention across genres to ritual theatrics, the marital often comes to be ironically aligned with the funereal. In *Venus*, with scene numbers counting down from 31 to 1, the specter of death is everywhere: the "Overture" pronounces The Venus dead as many voices, including the "Negro Resurrectionist," say repeatedly, "There wont be inny show tonite" (3). In *GMB*, readers sense a dramatic irony (long before Billy does) in her desire to marry Snipes, a custom coffin-maker who likes to anticipate which of his clients will die soon. In the second half, Parks turns Billy's objective from marriage altar to grave, suggesting a symmetry between them by making Willa Mae's "big diamond ring" (artifact of her engagement) the thing pursued (145). Parks also laces scenes with hints of *sati*: upon learning of Snipes' duplicity, Billy lights her dress on fire before stomping it out. When she requests a refund, Parks makes the connection to sacrificed wives by referring to "the burned dress offering" (82). Making Billy carry the mangled dress around constantly is the novelistic move of a playwright: a prop of sorts, it makes Billy physically perform the spectacle of marriage, even outside the ceremony.

Billy survives in *GMB* and does in the end get a wedding (to the safe, boring Laz Jackson). But Parks's carefully chosen setting suggests politicized historical consciousness might be a casualty of bridal distractions. In this novel, set in July 1963, there is skeptical discussion of locals going to Washington for Martin Luther King's August march, and the main cast ends up on a less noble pilgrimage in the opposite direction, toward a destination with ominous political resonances: La Junta, Arizona. As Billy boards the bus for Snipes's home with her unwieldy dress box, the white driver says, "I don't want no Freedom Riders, now," and Teddy immediately answers, "My niece is going to meet her husband," producing in the driver a "relax[ed]" expression (56). We notice, as Parks obliquely wonders "Who am I?" through art, that she shares a name with the most famous bus-rider of all, Rosa; there is significance, then, in Billy's greatest concern being whether her dress box will get its own seat—a talkative white woman with many thoughts on marriage takes that seat, sign of an integration different from that going on in Washington. As Brian Norman argues, *GMB* "tell[s] stories about those largely left out of the spoils of legislative victories" (134). But the funneling of attention toward Billy's wedding also makes marriage all the more potent a delusion for this apolitical young black woman. Meanwhile, the dire need for legal, accessible abortion lingers as a rights issue that Washington will not deal with for another decade, too late for Billy and Willa Mae. Parks's stage works are rife with satires of historical sites and reenactments; but working with the less theatrical materials of a historical novel in which characters do not transcend their times, she opts for an intimate tangent to the well-known events of civil rights history.

In *Venus*, the title character maintains romantic hopes far longer and in much grimmer terms than Billy does. The Venus never quite loses the identification with Cinderella created in the first scene, in which she is suddenly plucked from scrubbing floors. But the double life portended by marital love described earlier emerges primarily through Parks's favored trope of a play-within-a-play: *For the Love of the Venus* (invented by Parks but based on a historical French play) revisits *Devotees* through broad parody of a white "Bride-to-Be," the man she hopes to marry, and his terrible poetry. The fragmentary play turns on sexual exoticism and racial performance, which Parks shows still structure the reception of black female bodies. For example, The Baron Docteur anachronistically watches the play "almost as if he's watching TV" (25). The Bride-to-Be stimulates her passionless but Africa-obsessed intended by dressing up as the "Hottentot Venus" (132), the "something Wild" (48) he desires. The irony and artificiality are palpable for everyone except

The Baron Docteur (he applauds) and The Venus herself, who in the stage directions watches not the play itself but her spectating lover. Scene 7, bleakly titled "*She'll Make a Splendid Corpse*," comes on the heels of the appearance of the Bride-to-Be as the "Hottentot Venus" (note the mirror-reversal of the main character's stage name). The Venus nevertheless daydreams to herself, "[The Baron Docteur] will leave that wife for good and we'll get married / (we better or I'll make a scene) oh, we'll get married" (135). The Venus is a subject of history who—though a performer in an intense theater of race and sex—tragically fails to recognize the artifice that imprisons her.

Consent is, in ideal terms, a moment of question and answer, and questions—ubiquitous in *Venus*, from the casual to the profound—are never a neutral medium of curiosity or importuning for Parks, who often links questions' presumed objectivity to the history of "scientific" racism. The Baron Docteur, who spends the play's intermission sharing his findings from The Venus's horrific autopsy, builds on the character of the Naturalist in *Imperceptible Mutabilities*, who lectures in rhetorical questions that lead eventually to a genocidal plan. Freighted with this history of allegedly enlightened institutions, Parks's scenes often portray aggressive interrogation: in *Venus*, Scene 20 has the Kafka-inspired title "*The Venus Hottentot Before the Law*," and the questioning, to determine The Venus's consent to being exhibited, evokes the condemnation of Joseph K.[5]

> THE CHORUS OF THE COURT. We call the Venus Hottentot.
> THE VENUS. Im called the Venus Hottentot.
> THE CHORUS OF THE COURT. She speaks!!
> *(Rest.)*
> Simple questions first.
> Who are you?
> Where are you from?
> Any family?
> Are you happy?

5 As an article on Baartman's remains summarizes, the British "courts ruled that Baartman had entered into a contract of her own free will and the show went on. It is doubtful the Hottentot Venus ever saw a contract" (McGreal).

Are you a witch?
Were you ever beaten?
Did you like it was it good?
Do you wanna go home?
If so when?! If so when?!
Answer, come on, spit it out! (74)

Three "spells" for a silent Venus follow, before she says, "The Venus Hottentot / is unavailable for comment" (74). Clearly both these "[s]imple" (that word again!) questions and this "call[ing]," procedural gestures of the court, bear as much ideological weight as the degrading name The Venus answers to.

In novel form, without the velocity of stage dialogue or carnival pastiche, Parks constructs a plot driven by the question of whether anyone will give money to Billy, who keeps accounts of her progress toward the one hundred dollars she needs for an abortion. Billy is a supplicant throughout, requesting money for a dress, bus fare, and other needs. Switching tacks from wedding to abortion, she negotiates further transactions, selling her mother's jewelry and duping a man into buying her empty dress box. The name Beede, read as be-ed, resembles Parks's many idiosyncratic past-as-present verb-forms. In a story of jewels, Billy as "bead" is another resonance, while Melville's Billy Budd, unjustly sacrificed, places *GMB* in another white novelist's lineage. But Beede refers most pointedly to the medieval bedesmen, ascetics who were authorized by the Scottish king to roam the land begging in exchange for their prayers. Billy— "begging," supported by an aunt and uncle who run a gas station in an arrangement reminiscent of sharecropping—is indeed a supplicant, exemplary of the abject state of African-American women (111). As for virtue and prayer, this hellish story discounts any notion that Christian charity is viable: Billy is no Mary headed for a manger, and her mother's pearls—taken for fake, used as a down payment on an abortion—mock the parable on heaven as the "pearl of great price" (Matthew 13.46).

Outside of religious coding, Billy's perpetually poor family speaks to black class hierarchy and the way economic station, in the American understanding, calcifies as fate: people speak of "that Beede luck" (81) and being "born into" it (107), also of "Beedeism" (137). Parks is at root a chronicler of black poverty, often depicting contemporary economic situations that contain traces of chattel slavery's ownership structure. In *GMB*, amid deadly abortions, the economics of slavery survives in images of pig farming and its cycle of reproduction and slaughter. The connections between pigs and young black women are solidified when Billy and Dill look in on the latter's prize sow "Jez," short for Jezebel, clearly an association with Willa Mae, whom Dill was in love with (108). Jez gets to sleep in Dill's own bed after giving birth, calling up Dill's indelible memory of Willa Mae "dying in a bed of blood" (37) (alliterative phrasing foreshadowing a possible fate for "Billy Beede"). Such images give concreteness to Teddy's meditation on the "price" of black lives: "The life of a Negro man is cheap. The life of a Negro woman is cheaper" (124). Dill, who spitefully took Willa Mae's pearls before burial and has used their proceeds to finance the pig operation, manipulates Billy throughout, standing as Parks's complicated villain. In all these ways, Parks may be rewriting her unpublished college story, "The Wedding Pig," "about a school teacher in a small Texas town who attends a violent harvest ritual that goes dramatically awry" (Kolin and Young 100). In *GMB*, Billy's Texas wedding ritual goes momentarily awry—with symbolic violence visited upon her.

Victim of a violence far less symbolic, The Venus becomes a desperate supplicant as well, and her treatment as an animal, kept in a cage, is grounds for another essay entirely. As she sits in that cage, Parks employs her all-important word in Scene 17, when The Baron Docteur in effect restarts the plot by offering to buy her and take her to Paris. "Yll sleep with me," he says, as they negotiate her pay. "Say 'yes'" (88). Here Parks interweaves tropes of erotic desire, financial negotiation, and utter debasement through that single iconic word placed simultaneously in multiple contexts, audaciously trying to make it bear the complications of the horribly abused but "complicit" woman she seeks to portray. The notes say that parentheses signify "sotto voce," but there is also an opportunity for the actor to invest each "yes" with a different meaning, as The Venus considers the offer.

THE MOTHER-SHOWMAN. Hup Ho, Girl! Come on!

We got a crowd out there.
THE VENUS. (yes.)
THE MOTHER-SHOWMAN. Theyre fresh from the pubs and I hate to say it
But the stench of liquor on their collective breaths
THE VENUS. (yes.)

The Baron Docteur takes The Venus from her cage.
The Mother-Showman continues her rant.

THE MOTHER-SHOWMAN. is only matched by
the stench of yr shit in this pen, Girl! Jesus!
THE VENUS. (yes.)
THE MOTHER-SHOWMAN. Jesus! *Yr an animal!*
THE VENUS. Yes. (89)

Two more instances of "Yes" from The Venus follow lines from The Baron Docteur (90). Thus does The Venus become Parks's black Molly Bloom, herself likened to the goddess of love by her husband, who, in scenes Parks probably has in mind throughout *Venus*, admires a statue of "Venus Kallipyge" (Joyce 163) (i.e., Venus of the beautiful buttocks) and later kisses the "plump mellow yellow smellow melons" of Molly's "rump" (602). Molly's multiple ecstatic yeses are ironic, since the novel they conclude is all about her unfaithfulness to Leopold; but Parks's scene is shameful and incredibly difficult to bear. Why does Parks risk it, along with urging us to see The Venus's love for The Baron Docteur as genuine and passionate? This is among the most challenging examples of Parks's impulse to depict an "ugly" black history, full of betrayal, suicide, fratricide, embodied stereotype, and accepted degradation, seemingly in an effort to liberate that "infinite variety" of identities mentioned near the start. As noted by George C. Wolfe, director of many Parks plays, she offers a "demanding," "non-clichéd, not-easy-to-digest vision of American history [and] black culture" (ctd. in Als). In Parks's words, she "step[s] out of the [formula] 'I'm a black person, I'm oppressed, and when I represent myself on stage I'm going to represent an oppressed person'" (Kolin and Young 41).

But such provocations might become merely that—provocative. The greater ambition with The Venus's incantatory yeses seems to be for Parks to remind herself and the audience to consent to the history of consent itself—and thereby to love, if not marry, this historical subject. *Venus* has an epigraph from Woolf's *Between the Acts*, "'You don't believe in history,' said William," a line Parks keeps posted above her desk: "Because I really don't [believe in history]. I know that things happened in the past, but I do think that how they happened is more up for grabs than we are often led to believe" (Kolin and Young 56). Parks also says of the new history her theater "make[s]," "It is sort of the reverse of 'Don't believe everything you read.' I'd say: Believe it, because it is true," adding a link between such belief and the keyword I have examined: she wants viewers to say, "Oh yes, this is an account, not of what happened but of what was. Or an account of what is" (Kolin and Young 74-5). Such thinking replies to the playgoer or reader who dismisses the portrayal of Baartman falling in love with her owner as offensive—a viewer who assumes a late twentieth-century black woman writer must, in engaging a postmodern view of subjective history, choose to portray resistance. In *GMB*, such a reader might take exception to Parks focusing on a feuding black family while King prepares to argue for civil rights. Billy, digging up a history she is too young to remember, echoes Parks and The Venus in less theatrical terms when, expressing her own love of whiteness, she claims to remember holding Willa Mae's hand on her deathbed, "her husband-to-be, the richest man I ever seen," holding the other. "Believe what you please," Billy tells her aunt, "but I'm telling the truth" (161).

For Parks, believing in these invented and disturbing histories does not codify or harden them, or convert the believer into a dupe of the white power structure. Rather, in granting dimension to blacks' love of and assent to whites, she extends the project of her former teacher, Baldwin, who galvanized the civil rights movement with his *The Fire Next Time*, another intimate portrait of black families in 1963 that focused on the emotional dynamic on which political gains would have to be based: only love between the races, a love of "quest and daring and growth," can heal the nation—a love that "takes off the masks that we fear we cannot live without and know we cannot live within" (95). Baldwin had detailed such interracial love complexities in *Another Country* (1962), among other works. In Parks, interracial love is the reconciliation of polarized halves that her many difficult and denied marriages point to, from The Venus's affair to Willa Mae's. But the scope is far wider than personal emotions: the name Venus speaks to a mythological love greater than any single interracial relationship mimetically portrayed, and "Who are we?"—in the present tense of viewing and reading—remains the abiding question.

Parks ultimately rescues Baartman from lascivious objectification—and rescues Venus, archetype of love, from Venus Hottentot—through images of romantic love transcendent of race. Led into a refrain of "yes" at the play's midpoint, The Venus in the second half begins repeatedly asking The Baron Docteur, in this play of "simple questions," a most complex one: "Love me?" (103, 106, 107, 114, 127, 137, 138). Notably, he never says simply "yes" in reply. Parks strips the question down to make it both question and imperative but also, given The Venus's name, a self-exploration that a great performer can make audible: Love, me? Am I love embodied? Do I love myself? Can I love what Parks calls the "very human," "clay" side of myself? "Love me?" is ultimately a question for the audience (viewers of all races) to say yes to, regardless of how shameful The Venus may seem. Parks underscores the viewers' task in the play's final speech, called by The Negro Resurrectionist "A Scene of Love," which clearly offers a chance for playgoers themselves to redeem that earlier moment of silent "spells" titled "*A Scene of Love (?)*": "*Kiss* me *Kiss* me *Kiss* me *Kiss*," says The Venus in this final speech (162). Parks said succinctly in 1994, "I write plays because I love Black people" ("Equation" 21). She hopes viewers of her plays and readers of her novel—black, white, and otherwise—will as well.

WORKS CITED

Als, Hilton. "The Show-Woman." *The New Yorker*, 30 Oct. 2006. Web. 6 Mar. 2015.

Baldwin, James. *The Fire Next Time*. 1963. New York: Vintage, 2013. Print.

Catanese, Brandi Wilkins. *The Problem of the Color[blind]: Racial Transgression and the Politics of Black Performance.* Ann Arbor: University of Michigan Press, 2011. Print.

Chakkalakal, Tess. *Novel Bondage: Slavery, Marriage, and Freedom in Nineteenth-Century America.* Champaign-Urbana: University of Illinois Press, 2011. Print.

Dietrick, Jon. "Making it 'Real': Money and Mimesis in Suzan-Lori Parks's *Topdog/Underdog*." *American Drama* 16.1 (Winter 2007): 47-74. Print.

Drukman, Steven. "Suzan-Lori Parks and Liz Diamond Interview." *TDR* 39.3 (1995): 56-75. Print.

Ellison, Ralph. *Invisible Man*. 1952. New York: Vintage, 2010. Print.

Garrett, Shawn-Marie. "The Possession of Suzan-Lori Parks." *American Theater* 17.8 (October 2000): 22-26, 132-134. Print.

Geis, Deborah R. *Suzan-Lori Parks.* Ann Arbor: University of Michigan Press, 2008. Print.

Joyce, James. *Ulysses*. 1922. Eds. Hans Walter Gabler, Wolfhard Steppe, and Claus Melchior. New York: Vintage, 1986. Print.

Kolin, Philip C., and Harvey Young, eds. *Suzan-Lori Parks In Person: Interviews and Commentaries.* New York: Routledge, 2013. Print.

McGreal, Chris. "Coming Home." *Guardian*. Guardian News and Media, 21 Feb. 2002. Web. 6 Mar. 2015.

Norman, Brian. *Neo-Segregation Narratives: Jim Crow in Post-Civil Rights American Literature.* Athens: University of Georgia Press, 2010. Print.

Parks, Suzan-Lori. *The America Play and Other Works.* New York: Theatre Communications Group, 1995. Print.

—. "Elements of Style." In *The America Play*. 6-18.

—. "An Equation for Black People Onstage." In *The America Play*. 19-22.

— *Getting Mother's Body* New York: Random House, 2004. Print.

—. *Imperceptible Mutabilities in the Third Kingdom*. In *The America Play*. 23-71.

—. "Possession." In *The America Play*. 3-5.

—. "Tradition and the Individual Talent." *Theater* 29.2 (1999): 26-33. Print.

—. *Venus*. New York: Theatre Communications Group, 1997. Print.

Williams, Monte. "From a Planet Closer to the Sun." *New York Times*, 17 Apr. 1996.

Web. 6 Mar. 2015.

Worthen, W. B. "Citing History: Textuality and Performativity in the Plays of Suzan-Lori Parks." *Essays in Theatre/Etudes Theatrales* 18.1 (1999): 3-22. Print.

Wright, Laura. "Casting the Bones of Willa Mae Beede: Passing and Performativity in Suzan-Lori Parks's *Getting Mother's Body*." *Tulsa Studies in Women's Literature* 30.1 (Spring 2011): 141-157. Print.

Young, Jean. "The Re-objectification and Re-commodification of Saartjie Baartman in Suzan-Lori Parks's *Venus*." *African American Review* 31 (1997): 699-708.

H. L. MICHELLE CHIANG

TIME MADE FLESH: SAMUEL BECKETT'S DUAL DEPICTION OF TIME

In this essay, I compare the delineations of time in Samuel Beckett's novels *Malone Dies* and *The Unnamable* with his mimes *Act Without Words I* and *II* to postulate that Beckett's conception of time may be dual; that is, an external habitual continuum that is quantitatively perceived in space and an internal *durée* that is qualitatively intuited. As such, the focus of this essay is to demonstrate how the mimes seem to offer the playwriting novelist an opportunity to more directly express these two modes of time to his audience as an intuitive experience rather than as concepts that can only be derived discursively through textual inference.

After the translation of *Molloy* was completed in December 1954, Beckett proceeded in sequential order to translate *Malone Meurt* to English from 1955 to 1956, and completed his translation of *L'Innommable* by 1958 (Weller xi). According to Beckett, *Act Without Words I* and *II* were written in French around 1956 (Fletcher 110). This was also the year when Beckett tried to translate the third novel of the trilogy from French to English, before "guiltily" (Connor x) abandoning it until 1957 and eventually completing the translation in February 1958. Thus, both plays may be regarded as being conceived in a period of time when Beckett was emerging from translating the trilogy's second novel and frustratingly trying to translate the third novel in sequential order. In this obligation to translate, it is not difficult to see a tension between the dictates of logical sequence and the artist's internal inertia, which could have been transposed to his creative output during this period in the form of his dual conception of time in the mimes.

Shane Weller's observation that Beckett's "approach to his own self-translations" was "a deliberate impoverishment, an attempt to achieve the greatest simplicity, and even a certain stylelessness" (xiv) is supported by the playwriting novelist's explanation that his turn to theater while writing *Watt* in the early years of his career was prompted by "the need to create for a smaller space, one in which [he] had some control of where people stood or moved, above all, of a certain light" (ctd. in Worton 69). Taking into account Beckett's interest in Being as we consider these quotations, his move towards simplicity and stylelessness in his translations reveals a striving towards the effacement of particularities, which could potentially allow him to invoke more accurately in his everyman reader a common intuitive experience of his works. That theater was regarded by him as offering greater authorial control over his characters' positions and movements in physical space compared to textual space, could suggest that he viewed the stage as supplying him with a more direct solution to realizing his dual conception of time in embodied space—one in which the possibility of conceptual distortions through linguistic misinterpretations by audience members is reduced with the abandonment of words in his mimes. Key to this understanding of Beckett's delineations of time in the novels and plays that are examined here is Henri Bergson's opposition to Immanuel Kant's conception of time as a sequential continuum.

Bergsonian philosophy's influence on Beckett's works is receiving increasing attention in Beckett scholarship. S. E. Gontarski helpfully points out that although Bergson's "mystical certainty" ("Recovering Beckett's Bergsonism" 98) had little resonance with Beckett's oeuvre, "it is decidedly opposed to teleology, or what Bergson calls 'mechanism,'" which I agree might have been a position shared by Beckett if we consider the latter's disparagement of habits and routines in his works as ineffectual, yet inescapable. In addition, following Manfred Milz, who identified Bergsonian influence in Beckett's early theoretical writings and fiction from 1929 to 1936 (1), Graley Herren's *Samuel Beckett's Plays on Film and Television* (13) and Colin Gardner's *Beckett, Deleuze and the Televisual Event* (16) are two works that, despite the latter's focus on Deleuze's philosophy, also point to the centrality of Bergson's philosophy in the understanding of Beckett's drama. For instance, Bergson's doubt in the mechanical clock (that has been so instrumental to the scientific understanding of time in relation to human life) contributed to his interrogation of the extent to which reality can be defined by teleological systems. As Gontarski puts it, Bergson saw that "'real time' [. . .] eludes mathematics because it flows" ("Bergson on Movement and Spatialization" 327). Interestingly, Beckett's naming of Georges Pelorson's one-act burlesque of Pierre Corneille's seventeenth-century four-act play *Le Cid* as *Le Kid*, after Charlie Chaplin's film *The Kid* (Knowlson 124), could imply that Beckett saw a parallel between Pelorson's reconfiguration of Corneille's play with an emphasis on the fluidity of Time, and Chaplin's portrayal of how the governing system of the depicted world in *The Kid* is sustained at the expense of the Tramp and the child's desire to stay together. Chaplin's *The Kid* and Pelorson's *Le Kid* seem to articulate a disjunction between constructed systems imposed on lived reality and a subjectively experienced reality.

James Knowlson reports that when Beckett played the part of Don Diègue in *Le Kid*, it was Beckett's idea to "bring an alarm clock on stage with him" (124) to interrupt Don Diègue's famous monologue and wake up the silent figure who controls the hands of a large clock that was set against the backdrop of the stage:

> [H]e knelt down, placed the clock very carefully on the floor and was midway when the alarm went off infuriating him and waking up the man on the ladder. This combined with the speeded-up movements of the hands of the big clock, forced him to go faster and faster until he built up a wild, crazy momentum, producing a torrent of sound that has been aptly compared with the effect of Lucky's extravagant monologue in *Waiting for Godot*. (124)

Although Pelorson might have had a greater part to play in designing this sequence of actions, Beckett's involvement in this particular section of the performance might have influenced his conception of Time as a creatively manipulatable subject in his own works when he began his career as a writer. Further, his equation of *Le Kid* "as a blend of Corneille and Bergson, because of the importance given to time" (ctd. in Knowlson 124), further attests to Beckett's awareness of Bergson's doubt in mechanical time and valorization of an intuitive experience of *la durée*, which the latter asserted was more qualitatively accurate to describe time as it is experienced subjectively. As Gontarski has it, Beckett's "study of Bergson, if only for his preparation for teaching his Trinity students, remained with him as a ghost, an afterimage that informed much of his work for the remainder of his career" ("Recovering Beckett's Bergsonism" 104).

The tension between Bergson's and Kant's concepts of Time is of particular significance to understanding the temporal aspect of the Beckettian project, which I maintain is to activate in his audience and readers an intuitive experience that is normally veiled under the veneer of habitual systems. I posit that the Kantian continuum of sequential time is delineated in the novels through the characters' physical deterioration, and depicted in the two plays, particularly in *Act Without Words II*, as an incarcerating force that traps each of the characters in the performance of an ineffectual sequence of actions that constitute habit. Before demonstrating how the dual conception of time is delineated in the novels and plays, it is necessary to introduce the three modes of Kantian time: Permanence, Succession, and Coexistence, in order to establish how these might relate to Beckett's portrayal of external time as a trap.

None of the three Kantian modes can define time in isolation. They are instead strict rules of one system that govern the relations of phenomenal apparitions. Firstly, Permanence refers to that which is permanent in all phenomena. Kant maintained that "permanence is the object *in itself*, that is, the substance (phenomenon)" (125) that renders the other two modes, Succession and Coexistence, possible. What this means is that any object of experience can only be perceived as successive or coexistent if there is an unchanging foundation of permanence in that object. According to Kant, "it is only by means of the permanent that existence in different parts of the successive series of time receives a *quantity*, which we entitle *duration*." Here, Kant was referring to the idea that it is only because permanence is a foundation of phenomena, that the successive transition from one moment to the next in time, or quantified duration, is perceptible by us.

Secondly, in terms of Succession, Kant posited that "[o]ur apprehension of the manifold of phenomena is always successive" (128). To explain this point,

Kant employed the analogy of a ship floating downstream on a river. The ship's movement from point A to point B, from a higher position to a lower position on the course of the river, cannot be perceived in a reverse order. This "order of apprehension" is "determined" and "regulated" (130). The order is irreversible. Therefore, events in time are similarly perceived in a causally determined order in that each event of change must necessarily be preceded by a prior condition that allows the present state to be possible.

And thirdly, in his definition of Coexistence, Kant stated that "all substances, in so far as they can be perceived in space at the same time, exist in a state of complete reciprocity of action" (138). It is worth noting that he regarded "substances as phenomena" (140) and the two terms are interchangeably employed here. To rephrase his definition of Coexistence, a phenomenon is perceived to exist in terms of its relations with all the other phenomena which it exists with. The "reciprocity of action" refers to how the possibility of perceiving one substance is dependent on the perception of another substance, or how the possibility of perceiving one phenomenon relies on the perception of another phenomenon.

Against the barren landscape of the Beckettian world, the characters' starkly localized and articulated physical and sensory afflictions are in themselves a web of reciprocal relations that is perceived by the characters and also by the audience or reader. More specifically, the "external" time in Beckett's works can also be likened to the Kantian time continuum by virtue of its relations with objects of the physical world of the novels and the plays. With reference to Kant's three modes of time, the following section is an explication of how the characters in the novels, as well as the readers, cannot comprehend the passing of diegetic time without perceiving change in the objects of the portrayed external reality. By "change," I am specifically referring to deterioration and depletion.

The Novels

In *Malone Dies*, Malone describes a man sitting on a "bench" with "his back to the river":

> I have taken a long time to find him again, but I have found him. How did I know it was he, I don't know. And what can have changed him so? Life perhaps, the struggle to love, to eat, to escape the redressers of wrongs. I slip into him, I suppose in the hope of learning something. But it is a stratum, strata, without debris or vestiges. But before I am done I shall find traces of what was. (220)

The passing of a "long time" is discerned through the changes wrought to the man by what Malone assumes to be "Life." He does not know if the man sitting on a bench with his back to the river is the same man he was searching for, but his assumption of a change in this random man that is caused by what he generalizes to be the inevitable struggles of Life implies that the man whom Malone has been searching for could very likely be the everyman. Thus, "Life" or the living body of the everyman is the perceivable phenomenon on which the three modes of time conjugate. The last clause in the quotation draws the reader's attention to the deteriorating life of the figure by suggesting that Life entails "escap[ing] the redressers of wrongs"; that is, the change in the figure can be inferred by the reader as a degeneration from past innocence to irredeemable guilt. As such, the figure of the everyman is presented to the reader as a sinner who can only try to "escape the redressers of wrongs" instead of restoring his state of innocence. Pointedly, this is an indication of the irreversible mode of successive time in which the event of assumed innocence precedes the event of wrongdoing. With reference to the Kantian concept that perceiving one phenomenon relies on the perception of another phenomenon in his definition of Coexistence, Malone is portrayed in the quotation above as a phenomenon with which the phenomenon of the everyman can be compared when Malone "slip[s] into" the everyman in order to learn "something" about the change in him.

However, this "slippage" only yields the result of "stratum, strata, without debris or vestige." The crumbling change from singular to plural, from "stratum" to "strata," suggests a breaking apart of a layer into multiple layers, and may be interpreted by the reader as Malone's slippage into the mind of the man and discovering that it has broken into layers; that is, it has "changed" through fragmentation from a singular simplicity to a plural complexity. Its subsequent disappearance "without debris or vestiges" describes the mind's eventually-pulverizing disintegration. In addition, the reader may interpret the line "before [he is] done [he] shall find traces of what was" as referring to Malone's observation that before he is able to learn anything about this process of disintegration from "stratum, strata [to] without debris and vestiges," all that he shall find are inconsequential traces of all that has come to pass, none of which contributes to his desire to learn the reason and purpose of this perceptible process of debilitating change in the everyman.

Conversely, the Unnamable's desire for observable changes and the absence of such changes further support my postulation that external time could have been specifically conceived by Beckett as only perceptible through the changes that occur in the external reality:

> Some simple thing, a box, a piece of wood, to come to rest before him for an instant, once a year, once every two years, a ball revolving one knows not how about one knows not what, about him, every two years, every three years, frequency unimportant in the early stages, without stopping, it needn't stop, that would be better than nothing, he'd hear it approaching, hear it receding, it would be an event, he might learn to count, the minutes, the hours, to fret, be brave, have patience, lose patience, turn his head, roll his eye, a big stone, and faithful, that would be better than nothing, pending the hearts of flesh. (*The Unnamable* 356-57)

In order to "learn to count, the minutes, the hours, to fret, be brave, have patience, lose patience [. . .]," in other words, to live, perceivable changes in the forms of movements in the external world are necessary. Thus time, tied closely to the state of being in the physical world, is measured in observable changes or movements of objects in the diegetic reality. By movements of objects, I am referring to the "box" that might "come to rest," as well as the ball that might "[revolve]" around the Unnamable. Observing that the Unnamable, as the third and last protagonist of the trilogy, finally presents to the reader a disembodied character, his disconnection from an external reality can be inferred further from his desire to observe the movements of these objects.

In addition, "the hearts of flesh" is a reference to Ezekiel's biblical entry that God will replace the Israelites' "hearts of stone" (KJV, Ezek. 11.19; 36.26) that were pledged to the worshipping of idols with "hearts of flesh." This replacement will enable each of them to now follow His decrees with a restored and undivided faith. In a word, "the hearts of flesh" refer to God's gift of salvation. The phrase in the quotation "pending the hearts of flesh" therefore implies "[im]pending" salvation. Poignantly, as he waits for this, the Unnamable, unlike Malone, has arrived at the brink of an ever-extending impasse of existence because he cannot perceive time and therefore is deprived even of the illusion of being able to estimate when his end might arrive. To reiterate, his existence can be interpreted by the reader as reduced to a state of consciousness that is deprived of physicality and as a consequence, an existence that is devoid of observable time as well as the possibility of intuiting a subjective time. As such, the discerning reader would be able to infer from the novels that the dual conception of time is depicted as inextricably reliant on the perceptibility of the characters' physical reality. Nevertheless, compared to the novels, the mimes, as we shall see in the next section, seem to demand less of the audience in that the spectator does not need to close-read the performance by drawing on their knowledge of, for example, the philosophy of time or the Bible in order to experience Beckett's dual delineation of time.

One difference between Kant's and Bergson's respective concepts of "intuition" is that Kant's is an organized intuition whereas Bergson's is a "simple intuition" (235). In one example, Bergson likened intuition to our ability to "distinguish our right from our left by a natural feeling" (97). An intuition is that "which no formula, no matter how simple, can be simple enough to express" (237). For Bergson, the *durée* is time that is qualitatively apprehended through intuition. As opposed to Kant's formulation of time as an organized intuition which "is in itself a series (and the formal condition of all series)" (388), Bergson's concept of time is a qualitative duration which "consciousness reaches immediately" (127) through simple intuition. As such, Kantian time's inherently organized nature is interpreted in this essay as the characteristic of external time which structures the linear process of physical deterioration in Beckett's works. Crucially, this spatialization of time is likened by Bergson to the limited ticking of the mechanical clock and is consequently deemed as a "spurious concept" (98).

To elaborate upon what he meant by "spurious," Bergson asserted that measurable time is but a construct. The successive units of time evenly divided into hours, minutes, and seconds are contrived by the mind as residing in an imagined homogenous space that allows the setting of two points (i.e. a past moment A and a present moment B) in juxtaposition. Quantifiable time to Bergson is merely a symbolic representation of real duration or *durée*, necessary for the "[adaptation] to the requirements of social life in general and language in particular" (128). As opposed to measurable time, the *durée* is an experience of the process of reality that is unquantifiable. To Bergson, the process of reality can only be genuinely experienced through human intuition, and I posit that this Bergsonian intuition is a concept which Beckett might have sought to convey to his readers through the depiction of his characters' preference for an intuitive experience of time.

In the novels, the characters are painstakingly depicted as spinning stories to invoke the qualitative experience of *durée*, which the reader can only infer from the text itself instead of intuitively experiencing it like an audience member. The spectator's intuitive experience will be elaborated in the next section. It should suffice for now to understand that the characters in the novels are portrayed as seeking to become unconscious of the characteristically slow succession of external time in the Beckettian world. As a result, the *durée* is depicted as a viable shortcut that could plausibly speed up the characters' experience of external time and by implication, speed them towards the end of consciousness. In other words, by turning away from the consciousness of external time, the characters are delineated as hoping to invoke the intuitively perceptible internal time or *durée*. The desired outcome of invoking the *durée* is that it will allow the characters to unconsciously pass enough external time so as to experience a quicker arrival at their ultimate point of demise. Since the slow passage of external time appears to withhold an end of consciousness from the characters, one possible way out of this rut is to turn away from the consciousness of it. Further, the characters' storytelling and inventory recording entail the commingling of both past and imagined memories. As a character's conscious mind turns from the unitary succession of time to these anachronical distractions, the character is portrayed as attempting to "leap" through external time in these moments of displaced consciousness.

The end of consciousness as a desired outcome is evident in Malone's yearning for death: "I shall be quite dead at last" (173). The words "at last" suggest that death would bring relief from the perceptibly slow succession of external time and this slowness can be inferred from the following: "But let us leave these morbid matters and get on with that of my demise, in two or three days if I remember rightly" (229). One of the "morbid matters" that Malone is referring to is the possibility that one day he might find that "there is nothing more to be said" (229). He may no longer be capable of composing stories to distract himself from the passage of time and as a consequence, have no relief from the conscious experience of external time as his "demise" will appear starkly to him as delayed indefinitely.

Malone's confinement to a "bed" (177) in an "ordinary room" since his "body is what is called, unadvisedly perhaps, impotent" (180) implies that the character's body is no longer capable of movement and so his only distraction is telling stories. Again, the reader's attention is directed to the deteriorating body of the protagonist as a seemingly interminable entrapment, and the notion that respite can only be found by turning its attention away from the body is implicit in Malone's story of Saposcat:

> Here truly is the air I needed, a lively tenuous air, far from the nourishing murk that is killing me. I shall never go back into this carcass except to find out its time. I want to be there a little before

> the plunge, close for the last time the old hatch on top of me, say goodbye to the holds where I have lived, go down with my refuge. (187)

"Here" refers to his conscious retreat into the internal world of stories. The retreat into his mind provides the "air" that he needs to get on with his life while the air in external reality is described as "nourishing murk that is killing [him]." The "air" invented through the imagination effectively contrasts with the "murk[y]" air in external reality to create the impression of a more desirable condition while his consciousness is turned to the imaginative state. The "murk" combined with his obviously ailing body constitute the "carcass" that he has no wish to be conscious of except to "find out" if it is nearing its end. Alternating between his imagination and the external reality, it is the ultimate end that Malone strives to arrive at by intuition. However, the repetitive alternations between these two points throughout the novel indicate his inability to while away enough of his time through storytelling in order to intuitively land on his desired absolute end. As he emerges from the invention of stories, he finds that his invocation of the *durée* persistently falls short of his goal because the end has not arrived. But he continues to invent stories anyway for temporary relief from the tedium of his inestimable wait for the end of consciousness.

Compared to the peopled worlds in *Malone Dies*, the extraneous world of *The Unnamable* is largely silent and inhabited by "nothing" (383). The protagonist is utterly "alone" (286) and completely incapable of physical movement:

> Can it be one day, off it goes on, that one day I simply stayed in, in where, instead of going out, in the old way, out to spend day and night as far away as possible, it wasn't far. Perhaps that is how it began. You think you are simply resting, the better to act when the time comes, or for no reason, and you soon find yourself powerless ever to do anything again. (286)

By "staying in," the titular character may be referring to his inability to sway his consciousness back to the external world from his internal mind. He is utterly unable to "do anything again" physically because his body has deteriorated to the point of paralysis. He cannot count on his corporeality because it is no longer receptive to external stimuli. The opening questions in the novel are "Where now? Who now? When now?" (285) and these questions indicate that place, identity, and time are no longer observable "now," but it is important to note that this perceived absence of an external world is not total. Since the external time continuum is pegged to living consciousness, insofar as the conscious mind continues to exist, the linear external time continuum continues to be valid in spite of the character's seeming disengagement from his external body. Nonetheless, the trouble with not being able to turn his consciousness back to the external world is his inability to intuitively experience the "leap" to a future point in external time when his stories end. As external time continues to "[pass]" (383) and "[pile]" ceaselessly upon the Unnamable, the only indication of some form of advancement would be the absolute cessation of this accumulation. Further, in contrast to Malone, the Unnamable has taken to "[weaving]" (333) identities for himself with words instead of inventing stories in order to "pass the time":

> Perhaps it's by trying to be Worm that I'll finally succeed in being Mahood, I hadn't thought of that. Then all I'll have to do is to be Worm. Which no doubt I shall achieve by trying to be Jones. Then all I'll have to do is to be Jones. Stop, perhaps he'll spare me that, have compassion and let me stop. The dawn will not be always rosy. (333)

"The dawn will not be always rosy" confesses a lack of desire to see another day and supports the idea that the Unnamable's ultimate goal is to stop "being." On top of claiming to be the creator of the first two novels of the trilogy, the narrator also indicates to the reader that he could be Molloy and Malone. The title, *The Unnamable*, poignantly points to an indeterminable identity as the subject of the text. As the narrator continues to invent identities, the reader would notice that storytelling as a distraction in the previous novels has effectively been reduced to plotless identity invention by this last instalment of the trilogy. Therefore, when regarded in sequential order, the final novel seems to allude to an exhaustion of creative efforts. The narrator in the final novel is portrayed as being so exhausted that he is unable to completely extricate himself from his invented identities; so much so that he is perpetually conflated with his invented characters by himself as well as by the readers. For example, having seemingly managed to cease to be Mahood, he wonders if he can finally be "left in peace" (339) and stop "being." This is the moment in which his consciousness would turn to the external time and he would find himself at the gates of his expiration. But "[i]t doesn't look like it, [he seems] to be going on talking" and he is aware that he "shall no doubt be launched again, grit with better arms, against the fortress of mortality." In other words, time seems to persist unceasingly, death remains out of reach, and the tedium of invention must go on, no matter how little the Unnamable has left to say. More crucially, deprived of an observable external time, the *durée* cannot be invoked as there is no external continuum from which he may emerge from his invention of identity.

Conceptually, an exhaustion of a character's creative efforts would return him to the consciousness of successive time and this return should seem to the character as if he had taken a "leap" to a future point in time. More specifically, the sense of having advanced un-consciously through external time marks the intuitive experience of the *durée*. Nonetheless, shaping his characters through elliptical utterances, Beckett's characters in the novels are set on a quest for expiration that is destined to fail as long as they remain conscious. As Beckett has it in *Proust*, "[d]eath has not required us to keep a day free" (514); the characters are directed towards a definite demise yet prevented from knowing the "when" and the "how." As much as death is an inevitable end to all that is knowable, the novels emphasize this "unknown" as the ceiling of all that is knowable. As a relentless gap in an unceasing consciousness that is governed by the external time continuum, it is precisely the irresolvable awareness of unknowability that the characters seek to end. But as usual with Beckett, the paradox of his characters' search for an end of consciousness is that it must entail an awareness of this end once it arrives. Indeed, because one cannot be conscious when consciousness ends, Beckett's characters' desired experience of this end through the invocation of the intuitive *durée* in the novels is destined to be an absurdly futile one. Having demonstrated in this section how a reader might discursively understand Beckett's delineations of external time and internal *durée* in the novels, the following section establishes how an audience member might more intuitively experience Beckett's portrayal of time as dual in the mimes.

The Mimes

Knowlson's suggestion that *Act Without Words I* "reflects Beckett's readings in behavioural psychology as a young man in the 1930s, when he looked at Wolfgang Kohler's book, *The Mentality of Apes*" (419) is supported by the experimental setting of the mime, in which the *mise-en-scène* delineates a controlled environment that is being manipulated by an invisible entity. Nevertheless, more than just another depiction of the futility of the everyman's condition of being in the world, the play can also be regarded as the playwriting novelist's experiment with isolating embodied space from extraneous space, and as a result more concretely presenting to the audience member, the everyman's body as an observable phenomenon. As Ruby Cohn put it, Beckett's wordless dramas "show us man from the outside, without penitential self-examination" (5) and "imply Beckett's mistrust of language" (6), which is more susceptible to distortion or misinterpretation compared to gestures. Asserting that "[g]esture is apparently keener and cleaner than phrase," Cohn went on to observe that in *Act Without Words I* space is exploited "up and down, in and out, back and forth; a human being sits, falls, stands, lies, and moves about" (21). Nonetheless, this mime is more than an exploitation of space. It is likened in this essay to an experiment to isolate extraneous space from embodied space because Beckett's depiction of a controlled space in which the original condition of space is restored by the end of the play implies that the only observable change in the play by the audience is the protagonist's eventual resignation to the ineffectualness of his actions; that is, like the novels examined in the previous section, the focus—of delineating the protagonist's futile coexistence with the unattainable objects of his reality—remains on the accentuation of the everyman protagonist's exhausted body as an observable phenomenon.

Moreover, while the manipulation of space is stark in *Act Without Words I*, time features prominently in *Act Without Words II* alongside the depiction of space, which indicates that a compelling formal development from the first to the second *Act Without Words* has occurred. As such, if *Act Without Words I* is regarded as the demonstrations of the everyman's body as phenomenon, *Act Without Words II* develops this further to suggest that the everyman's body is a phenomenon from which external spatial time and internal *durée* are perceived and intuited, respectively. In turn, a dual conception of time is conveyed to the audience member as her intuition is invoked when she views *Act Without Words II*. As opposed to the novels examined in the previous section, in which intuitive time may be inferred by the reader as a qualitative experience that the characters attempt to invoke through storytelling, the mime directly implicates the audience member by invoking her intuitive experience of time.

Beckett's portrayal of external time as a closed system of interminable successive time can be observed by the audience through the actors' performance of the characters' habitual routines. Even while Beckett's stage directions in *Act Without Words II* indicate that "A is slow, awkward (gags dressing and undressing), absent" (209) whereas B is "brisk, rapid, precise," Beckett also emphasizes that both sequences "should have approximately the same duration" as the two actors execute their respective routine in sequential order. The mime is intended to be performed "on a low and narrow platform at the back of the stage" that is "violently lit in its entire length" to present a "[f]rieze effect" (209). As such, A and B will each take an approximately similar duration to perform along this single strip of lit path. Since each routine should be timed to achieve an approximately similar duration, A's performance would, according to Beckett's diagram, traverse the first half of the strip and B's routine would complete at the end of the strip. Of course, in a characteristically Beckettian move, before the curtain falls, the goad would enter again to suggest to the audience that A's and B's routines will continue interminably. Whereas in the novels the interminability of external time is textually presented to the reader through an intricate crafting of the characters' turn to storytelling to distract them from the seemingly never-ending continuum, this interminability is indicated succinctly to the audience member upon the goad's third entrance in the mime.

Effectively, while the narrow strip of light—and the actors' timed, linear, and successive movements through it—represents the quantifiable duration of external time, the closing suggestion that the mime will continue indefinitely points to time as a continuum. More importantly, even though both routines would take an approximately similar amount of quantifiable time to complete, the audience, without the aid of a mechanical watch, would qualitatively experience the timings as dissimilar; that is, the subjective *durée* may be experienced by an audience member when she watches A's "slow" and "awkward" performance and intuits it to be longer and more tedious than B's "brisk, rapid, precise" performance.

Further, it is worth noting that the sluggish character A begins his routine with a prayer whereas the energetic character B begins each action of his routine by consulting his watch. Here, two structuring orders of life are presented to the audience: religion and science. By portraying both routines as taking an approximately similar amount of time to be completed, Beckett could be implying a common contrivance between the two systematic structures. This effectively brings us back to the interpretation early in the essay that the title of *Le Kid* could indicate Beckett's interest in the disjunction between a subjectively experienced reality and its rigid governance by constructed systems. In essence, the audience's subjective experience of the durations of the two routines as dissimilar poignantly indicates that the play invokes in it a non-successive form of time that eludes clearly defined sequencing and timing.

Indeed, even before *Act Without Words II*, in *Waiting for Godot*, Didi and Gogo's exchange after Pozzo and Lucky leave them in the first act, already gestures towards Beckett's acute awareness of the difference between a quantitative and qualitative experience of time:

> [*Long silence.*]
> VLADIMIR. That passed the time.
> ESTRAGON. It would have passed anyway.
> VLADIMIR. Yes, but not so rapidly.
> [*Pause.*] (46)

In these three short lines, the dual conception of time emerges. Poignantly, Pozzo and Lucky's antics had offered Didi and Gogo a distraction from their external time and the result is Didi's perception that time passed "rapidly" when his attention was turned away from it. Gogo's response that time "would have passed anyway" refers directly to the irreversibly successive and sequential external time continuum whereas Didi's response to Gogo's observation is a reference to time that is experienced subjectively, in other words, a *durée* that is experienced internally.

Therefore, time can be regarded from the outset as quantitatively and qualitatively conceived and presented by Beckett to the audience. The two concepts of time crucially depend on the audience's expectation that time is a quantifiable and successive continuum, so that this expectation can be disrupted by the characters' incongruent enactments and descriptions of time despite residing in the same diegetic space. Although the audience may not necessarily find the words to articulate their intuition of Beckett's dual delineation of time, their direct experience of temporal uncertainty is testament to the disruption of this specific expectation as they view the plays.

After the mimes, Beckett's stage plays seem to draw upon the novels' delineations of time by marrying the performance of temporal uncertainty with storytelling in order to offer the audience member an opportunity to intuitively experience the two modes of time through the stage characters' alternation between storytelling and an awareness of their diegetic reality. However, I have limited the scope of this essay to the mimes due to the constraints of space.

To conclude, the mimes seem to offer the playwriting novelist a more effective way to direct the audience member towards experiencing time as an external time continuum and an internal *durée*. Unlike the reader of the novels who can only interpret these two modes of time through meticulous textual inferences, the spectator of the plays, specifically of *Act Without Words II*, is directed towards an intuitive experience of Beckett's dual depiction of time.

WORKS CITED

Beckett, Samuel. *Act Without Words I. The Complete Dramatic Works*. London: Faber and Faber, 2006. 201-206. Print.

—. *Act Without Words II. The Complete Dramatic Works*. London: Faber and Faber, 2006. 207-211. Print.

—. *Malone Dies. Samuel Beckett: The Grove Centenary Edition*. Ed. Paul Auster. Vol. 2. New York: Grove Press, 2006. 171–282. Print.

—. *Molloy. Samuel Beckett: The Grove Centenary Edition*. Ed. Paul Auster. Vol. 2. New York: Grove Press, 2006. 1–170. Print.

—. *The Unnamable. Samuel Beckett: The Grove Centenary Edition*. Ed. Paul Auster. Vol. 2. New York: Grove Press, 2006. 283–408. Print.

—. *Waiting for Godot. The Complete Dramatic Works*. London: Faber and Faber, 2006. 7-88. Print.

Bergson, Henri. *Time and Freewill: An Essay on the Immediate Data of Consciousness*. Trans. F. L. Pogson. 3rd ed. London: G. Allen, 1913. Print.

Cohn, Ruby. *Just Play*. Surrey: Princeton UP, 1980. Print.

Connor, Steven. Preface. *The Unnamable. By Samuel Beckett*. London: Faber and Faber Ltd., 2010. vii-xxv. Print.

Fletcher, Beryl S., et al. *A student's guide to the plays of Samuel Beckett*. London: Faber and Faber Ltd., 1978.

Gardner, Colin. *Beckett, Deleuze and the Televisual Event: Peephole Art*. New York: Palgrave Macmillan, 2012. Print.

Gibson, Andrew. *Beckett and Badiou: The Pathos of Intermittency*. Oxford and New York: Oxford UP, 2006. Print.

Gontarski, S. E. "Bergson on Movement and Spatialization." *Understanding Bergson*,

Understanding Modernism. Eds. Paul Ardoin, S. E. Gontarski, and Lacci Mattison. London and New York: Bloomsbury Academic, 2014. 327-9. Print.

—. "Recovering Beckett's Bergsonism." *Beckett at 100: Revolving it all*. Eds. Linda Ben-Zvi and Angela Moorjani. Oxford: Oxford University Press, 2008. 93-106. Print.

Herren, Graley. *Samuel Beckett's Plays on Film and Television*. New York: Palgrave Macmillan, 2007. Print.

Kant, Immanuel. *Critique of Pure Reason*. Trans. J. M. D. Meiklejohn. New York: Prometheus Books, 1990. Print.

Kelly, Michael R. "Bergson's Phenomenological Reception: the Spirit of a Dialogue of Self-Resistance." *Bergson and Phenomenology*. Ed. Michael R. Kelly. Hampshire: Palgrave Macmillan, 2010. Print.

Knowlson, James. *Damned to Fame: The Life of Samuel Beckett*. London: Bloomsbury Publishing, 1996. Print.

Levy, Eric P. "The Beckettian Mimesis of Time." *University of Toronto Quarterly* 80.1 (2011): 89-107. Project Muse. Web. 28 Apr. 2014.

Milz, Manfred. "Echoes of Bergsonian Vitalism in Beckett's Early Works." *Borderless Beckett / Beckett sans frontières*. Ed. Minako Okamuro. *Samuel Beckett Today/ Aujourd'hui* 19. Tokyo: Rodopi, 2006. 143-54. Print.

The Holy Bible, King James Version. Cambridge Edition, 1769. *King James Bible Online*. Web. 23 Aug. 2014. <http://www.kingjamesbibleonline.org/>.

Weller, Shane. Preface. *Molloy. By Samuel Beckett*. London: Faber and Faber Ltd., 2009. vii-xx. Print.

Worton, Michael. "Waiting for Godot and Endgame: Theatre as Text." *The Cambridge Companion to Beckett*. Ed. John Pilling. Cambridge: Cambridge UP, 1996. 67-87. Print.

BARTOSZ LUTOSTAŃSKI

THEATRICAL NARRATIVE—SAMUEL BECKETT'S *MOLLOY*

"I am in my mother's room. It's I who live there now. I don't know how I got there. Perhaps in an ambulance, certainly a vehicle of some kind. I was helped. I'd never have got there alone" (3).[1] Thus begins *Molloy*, the first novel from Samuel Beckett's trilogy that also includes *Malone Dies* and *The Unnamable*. The beginning of a literary work is believed to signal the most important properties of its entirety.[2] Indeed, the initial sections of *Molloy* present a number of features that transpire as fundamental to its structure and composition. Molloy's part opens with "I." The frequency of the first-person pronoun (six times in the six-sentence excerpt above) suggests the significance of the narrative subject. Molloy is not only overt and explicitly self-conscious but also hypersensitive about his spatiotemporal location: the "here" and the "now." These two parameters constitute his narrative situation,[3] and are associated with the zero point of time orientation.[4] Therefore, the narrative action is performed in the room and firmly lodged in the present moment although the past tense introduced in the third sentence implies the existence of another spatiotemporal dimension embedded in the "here-and-now." The dimension is fully established in the second paragraph: "So I saw A and C . . ." (4).

The analysis of *Molloy*'s opening demonstrates that three devices seem to be most important not only in the initial paragraphs of the novel but also

1 All of the following quotations from Molloy come from *Samuel Beckett, Molloy. Malone Dies. The Unnamable. How It Is. Novels. Volume II. The Grove Centenary Edition.* Introduction by Salman Rushdie. New York: Grove Press 2006. Hereafter each quotation from this source is followed by page number.

2 See, for example, *Narrative Beginnings* edited by Brian Richardson for a useful conceptualisation and insightful discussion of introductions in prose literature.

3 I define "narrative situation" as a "sphere of storyteller's activity" and "construction external to plot" which is the "sphere of characters' activity" (Głowiński, Okopień-Sławińska, Sławiński 320). It is important to note that narrative situation constitutes the "*mediating* process through which the narrated is presented," as Gerald Prince asserts, following Stanzel and Genette (64; italics mine). It should be associated with orientation centre, defined by Franz Stanzel as "spatiotemporal orientation in the represented reality; 'here and now' of a narrator" (226).

4 "[T]he moment in which the narrator is telling the text" (Wysłouch 106).

in its entirety. These devices are concurrency, monologue and scene.[5] In this essay, I examine these devices in three respective sections and argue that their particular employment profoundly affects the semantics of the novel. In the final section, these semantics are regarded as "theatrical" and I look into their effects on reading. That is to say, the "theatrical" semantics necessitate an alternative reading approach by challenging conventional novelistic reception strategies. This approach is referred to as "performative" to differentiate it from a global and general semantic mechanism in Beckett's work.

1. Concurrency

The account of Molloy's stay at Lousse's spans about three pages (32-35). It teems with sentences and phrases that attract attention to the narrative agency and the process of narrating. "What a story!" or "It might be worth looking into," for instance, are indicative of Molloy's self-consciousness. This category can be subdivided into control, intrusiveness and digressiveness.

Firstly, "I recount these moments with a certain minuteness" and "she kept up a chatter of which I did not understand the hundredth part" demonstrate Molloy's control over the narrative selection and distribution process as he decides what and how to recount. The control is licensed by his posterior narrative position (in the "here-and-now") that endows him with authority over the representation of past events. Furthermore, control comments disrupt the narrative object as they divert readers from it and in turn accentuate Molloy and his mediating position.

Secondly, the account of the burial is frequently punctured with inserted comments that break its linear progression.[6] Consider the underlined phrases

5 In my PhD dissertation, *Gombrowicz-Beckett. Beckett-Gombrowicz. A Comparative Study*, I discuss concurrency, monologue and scene as three general narrative devices impacting the semantics of the successive two parts of Beckett's first "trilogy" as well. The following analysis of the devices might be considered as an exemplification and illustration of a complex meaning mechanism generated by the devices.

6 Auto-reflexive intrusions have a prominent place in Molloy's narrative arsenal. He frequently breaks his narration with a comment on a correct word for an object, "that's the word" (56); on his story: "I didn't feel I missed my bicycle, no, not really, I didn't mind going on my way the way I said, swinging low in the dark over the earth, along the little empty country roads" (61) or on the nature of writing in general: "But in order to blacken a few more pages may I say I spent some time at the seaside, without

in the following, "He smelt bad, if you like, but bad like an old dog, not like a dead dog. He too had dug holes, perhaps at this very spot. We buried him as he was, no box or wrapping of any kind, like a Carthusian monk, but with his collar and lead" (32). This puncturing profoundly influences the syntactic construction of Molloy's part. It is not only of an incremental structure but also of an arborescent one. Branching out in various directions, sentences and individual phrases generate additional meanings. This unusual phenomenon is even more pronounced in the case of digressions.[7] The account of Teddy's burial alone presents digressions to a larch, a vet, a parrot, and a beard.[8] Like intrusions, they heavily influence the reading process although in a functionally different way. For while intrusions disrupt the linear sequencing of a sentence (syntactic disruptions), digressions disrupt the linearity of larger semantic units, summary, or scene, by means of pause (formal disruptions). Both affect the progression of the story and the development of alternative narratives, established by persistent shifts between the "primary" and the "subsidiary" contents. The shifts result in a complex compound sentence structure and the information load of single sentences significantly increases with new clauses unboundedly added. Extensive blocks of text are constructed with parataxic sequencing while the narration incessantly intercuts as short, separate sentences and clauses are divided and dismembered by commas, comma splices and full stops.[9]

Due to an accumulation of seemingly auxiliary and superfluous elements, Molloy's story seems spontaneous, provisional and ad-hoc. Other textual phenomena such as (rhetorical) questions, exclamations, unfinished sen-

seaside" (63). At another moment he tries to elucidate, "Let us try and get this dilemma clear. Follow me carefully" (71). Another vital type of intrusion is the metaleptic intrusion (violating the diegetic construction of the story): "Tears and laughter," "Pets often change," "It may seem strange," "My sleep as a rule," "My beard grows properly."

7 I define digressions as an "illicit straying from the straight and narrow path of narration into a terrain that does not properly belong to it" (Cohn *Minds* 187-188; see Prince 46).

8 The most prominent digressions are auto-reflexive, for example, "And though it is no part of my tottering intentions to treat here in full, as they deserve, these brief moments of the immemorial expiation, I shall nevertheless deal with them briefly, out of the goodness of my heart, so that my story, so clear till now, may not end in darkness" (73).

9 Syntactic and formal disruptions affecting the narrative structure can be observed in *The Unnamable*.

tences, ontological hesitations, anacoluthons, or informal expressions contribute further to that impression. These "speech conventions" comply with syntactic and formal disruptions, and indicate that the story is narrated, to borrow Molloy's expression, "in the heat of composition." Whilst narrating, Molloy corrects his mistakes, clarifies and complements his narration, goes off on tangents to talk about, for example, larches or sea-pebbles, invariably meandering to and fro the main story line. Consequently, as H. Porter Abbott (109), James H. Reid (81) and Wojciech Kalaga (56-67) argue, Molloy hardly devotes himself to recounting his past experiences (the "happenedness") but instead focuses on the creative act (the "inventedness"). As a consequence, the process of retrieving the past is exposed as ambivalent and heterogeneous since the domain of the "happenedness" is not only influenced but also frequently replaced by the "inventedness." In terms of narration, the point of gravity of the story shifts from the represented reality to the act and process of representing. Plot, characters, setting, and time are less important than the narrator's ongoing representation of them. Hence the narrative action moves from long blocks of text to individual sentences and phrases, or, in short, from large to small semantic units.

Molloy's story can be thought of, to borrow Uri Margolin's words, as "an unfolding sequence of concurrent temporal stages or intervals which put together make up the course of events being reported." In this sense, it can be argued that simultaneity is employed. In an online article "Simultaneity in Narrative" Margolin defines this device as "the property of two or more events, actions or processes which satisfy the following formula for temporal location: x is simultaneous with y if and only if for every time point or interval in which x is (or was or will be) present, y is (or was or will be) present." With regard to Molloy's story, x is a past event (the narrated) and y is the present moment of its narrating. A type of simultaneous narration obtained at the nexus of the narrated and the narrating is called concurrent narration. It significantly alters the temporal status of Molloy's memories. Usually presented in the past tense, past events are now embedded in the present moment of narrating, i.e., Molloy is recollecting *now* what happened *then*. "[T]he narrated domain takes shape as it is being narrated and is not a bounded whole," writes Margolin. Because Molloy is (re)constructing the content of his memory *when* writing at a specific time, his story is being conceived "in front of our eyes," as it were, and it therefore breeds all the instances of disrupted and de-chronologized rendering of the events in question (see Cohn *Minds* 182).

2. Monologue

In the Molloy part the narrating self and the narrated self are homologous. With one entity simultaneously playing two roles and the temporal status of the main narrative material (past), it is a textbook example of fictional autobiography (Keen 36; Martin 75; Genette 245). Indeed, it is frequently used as the genre paradigm for *Molloy* (Pavel 196; Cohn *Minds* 154). With nobody else speaking in the text, Molloy's story can also be considered a monologue.[10]

Crucially, it is impossible to indisputably categorise the monologue as oral, written or interior. A good case in point is the oral type. On the one hand, Molloy's monologue acquires a manifestly oral status because of the multiplication of various orality devices as well as the emphasis on a close relation between narrator and language (Banfield 536; Ejchenbaum 487-490; Głowiński *Gry* 126-127). On the other hand, it lacks essential features of the form such as those theorized by Wolf Schmid ("double-voicedness," "restrictedness of intellectual horizons" and "dialogicity"). Therefore, rather than arguing for one particular mode, it seems more fruitful to treat Molloy's story generally as a monologue and syncretically highlight points of convergence between its diverse types.

One major point of convergence is a strong emphasis on the narrator. As Sabine Buchholz and Manfred Jahn argue, monologue invariably "throws a focal spotlight on the speaking character" (124). Molloy plays the leading role in his narrative: he is self-conscious, controlling, intrusive and digressive. Also, the auto-reflexive utterances (see footnotes 6 and 8) form an integral

10 The category of monologue, used for the first time by Nadeau in his review of *Molloy* (34), reappears in a plethora of critical works on Beckett. It is used, for example, by Gontarski 2004; Kennedy; Pavel. Surprisingly, there is no serious study of the function and implication of this theatre-derived device in Beckett's prose fiction.

part of his repertoire as he tells the story as well as scrutinizes and evaluates it. Another similarity is time treatment. When discussing his works, Samuel Richardson used the phrase "instantaneous description" to suggest a momentary rendering of action in his epistolary novels (ctd. in Głowiński *Gry* 98-101). In other words, the narrative subject is presented in the moment of writing, and the writing becomes "an active element of his narrative situation" (see Głowiński *Powieść* 238-239). Time is reduced to a moment—to the narrator's present—or, in narratological terms, to the "discourse time" (Genette 219). It is realized chiefly in the narrating: the narrated time becomes the evoked time and thus loses its autonomy, being only actualized when reappearing in Molloy's consciousness. The present dominates his section: timeless and unrolling with the telling; direct and non-mediated; spontaneous and synchronized. Głowiński's concept of "temporal dialectics" can be employed here, in which the present speaks about and influences the past (*Gry* 132-133), or even absorbs it.

3. Scene

Molloy's part is a concurrent monological narration. Concurrency is characterised "by necessity" as "durative, *scenic* and coterminous with the events being reported" (Margolin; my italics). Margolin thus marries the concept of concurrency with scene, generally defined as "a canonical narrative tempo" distinguished by "some sort of equivalence between a narrative segment and the narrated it represents" (Prince 85). A fundamental correlation between concurrency and scene is therefore an identical formula operative for both: discourse time = story time. The present-tense, concurrent "I am in my mother's room" (3) establishes a scene. In Molloy's case, however, the scenic structure might be seen as unconventional because of its complexity.

The here-and-now embeds a story about specific past events (Molloy's journey home). The story-within-a-story construction goes roughly along the logical and chronological axis of past events. Both levels—since they entail separate spatiotemporal and deictic domains—are usually considered autonomous. However, they are not autonomous in Molloy's story due to two formal phenomena. The first is metalepsis, which accounts for violations of diegetic separateness (see footnote 6), and another is interdiegesis, which conceptualizes a conditional abolition, indeterminacy or suspension of actual boundaries between intradiegesis (the past) and extradiegesis (the present).[11] Metalepsis and interdiegesis confirm that the narrator's principal narrative situation is the "here-and-now" because this very position enables and legitimises unrestricted movements from one diegetic level to another and back. Furthermore, the temporal distance between the narrated and the narrating is considerably reduced or, one might say, annulled. In that case we may speak about temporal selfsameness, understood as conflation of the narrating and the narrated, which thematically and symbolically correlates with the spatial selfsameness: the room that the narrator never leaves for the duration of the narrative. The "here" and the "now" function as the vantage point or gauging device for varying spatiotemporal locations and fluctuating temporal horizon.[12] Through syntactic, textual, and formal operations, Molloy attains a considerable degree of a "seamless continuity" between "outer and inner reality, report and reflection" and there is no problem with "mediating memory" (Cohn *Distinction* 107).

All things considered, the diegetic "then" is produced, included and embedded in the "now" and the relation between these two domains resembles a quotation. The scenic, present narrative situation subjugates the quoted past domain as intradiegetic, second-degree scenic narrative. Functionally, the macro-scene of Molloy's first-degree story comprises second-degree summaries and ellipses, (intrusive and digressive) pauses and slowdowns, scenes and scenelets. This complexity on no account undermines the semantics generated by the scenes. On the contrary, together with monologue, the scene foregrounds the subject's homology, and with concurrency it emphasises temporal homology insofar as scene corresponds to "moment-by-moment action,

11 For a more detailed analysis of interdiegesis see Lutostański. I am currently working to theorize the phenomenon.

12 Kazimierz Bartoszyński defines the narrow temporal horizon as an utterance with a narration from a mobile point of view, accompanying the narrated events, situated in their temporal location but actualized in the discourse time. There is a close and strict relation between the narrator and the narrated world inasmuch as the process of its narrating remains in the discourse framework (253).

careful detailing of specific events" (Prince 85-6), "abruptness and speed" of experiencing (Chatman 72-8) or "the strong periods of the action coinciding with the most intense moments of the narrative" (Genette 109).

4. Narrative as Theatre

It is frequently emphasised that monologue, concurrency and scene are non-narrative because of their limiting of the Genettean narrative function and low degree of mediation.

According to Gérard Genette, the narrator's quintessential function is to narrate: "no narrator can turn away from [it] without at the same time losing his status as narrator" (255). The reduction of the function results in the reduction of narrative quality in a text. In the Molloy part it is considerably restricted by three other functions: the directing (stemming from the considerable extent of auto-reflexive devices), testimonial (having to do with a narrator's indicating "the source of his information, or the degree of precision of his own memories, or the feelings which one or another episode awakens in him") and communication (stressing the communication between the narrator and the narratee) (Genette 255-259). Since they concertedly correspond to the narrative subject, I will employ the Jakobsonian expressive function as an umbrella term for the three functions.

Secondly, Alber and Fludernik assert that the lower the degree of mediation, the lower the degree of narrativity. Monologue, concurrency, and scene are non-narrative because they substantially reduce mediation. Monologue for Franz Stanzel is an expression of "a self that already exhibits the characteristic features of a reflector-character: *it does not narrate or address* a listener or reader, but reflects in its consciousness its own momentary situation" (ctd. in Cohn *Distinction* 100; Cohn's italics). Therefore, "the event [of narration] is none other than the unrolling of the monologue itself, independently of the reported 'facts,' which become immaterial" (Cohn *Minds* 189). In addition, concurrency, Genette contends, also circumvents narratorial mediation (174, 216-217). "Since the action is inevitably represented as a series of successive events as they occur, the reporting is endowed with scenic *immediacy* . . ."

(Margolin; my italics). On the whole, the first part of *Molloy* can be considered as a text in which global semantics are generated by non-narrative devices that aim for a non-mediated and direct representation. They reduce the importance of contents and foreground the agent and act of narration.

According to a number of critics, Beckett belongs "to a lineage of antinovelists that includes Cervantes, Furetiére, Swift, Sterne, and Diderot" (Pavel 180). The first critic to call him an "anti-novelist" was Christine Brooke-Rose in her article "Samuel Beckett and the Anti-Novel" in *London Magazine*, December 1958, but Nadeau attributed the term "non-work" to *Molloy* as early as 1952 (35). Moreover, Gerald Prince in his *Dictionary of Narratology* quite tellingly describes *Molloy* as an "antinarrative" because it adopts the "trappings of narrative" but "systematically" calls "narrative logic and narrative conventions into question" (6). Similarly, we might associate Beckett's "trilogy" with terms such as Chatman's "antinarrative" (a narrative contravening "narrative logic") or "antistory" (any narrative that "may be defined as an attack" on narrative conventions) (56-59), or Cohn's "non-narrative" (texts that reduce their mediating apparatus) (*Distinction* 97-100). Elsewhere we also encounter "anti-literature" or "antinarrativity" (see Alber). However, all the negative terms have been applied to account for violations of traditional story parameters in Beckett's prose fiction so often as to render them obsolete in describing the meaning-making mechanism in *Molloy*'s first part. Therefore, I would like to offer here an alternative take on its semantics.

The theoretical discussions on monologicity, concurrency, scene as well as orality and auto-reflexivity suggest that the chief organisational principle of Beckett's novel relies on two elements: language and narrator. As Głowiński asserts, "[T]he more restricted the story, the more linguistic factors appear organizational, [and] the more the discourse comes to the foreground," (*Powieść* 181).[13] Julia Kristeva posits that in non-narrative novels literary signification moves toward "the exploration of grammaticality and/or toward enunciation" (57). Molloy transcends the "grammar of prose fiction" because he resigns from macro-narrative structures in favour of micro-narrative phe-

13 Translation mine – BL.

nomena. In other words, the narrative action transposes from the high orders of narrative organisation (time, space, plot or character) to the low orders (syntax, sentence, words and word segments), and from the representation of events to the representation of representation (see Rabinovitz 137-139). The five properties are thus employed to challenge the conventions of the novel, dynamise its elements, relax its deep-rooted rules, and, ultimately, demonstrate the innovativeness of Beckett's literary enterprise.

The novel's second foundational element is narrator. Molloy functions as a subjective modal frame since his monologue provides a matrix for the story's coherence. He controls, structures and codifies his stories. He self-consciously narrates the substance of his consciousness. His narrative is expressive and auto-reflexive, marked with strong oral qualities. As well as this textual evidence, there are also formal suggestions of the narrator's dominating role such as metalepses, interdiegesis and monologicity. All of the elements come together to foreground the immediate, direct and intimate act and process of narration.

All in all, the need for a new interpretive paradigm in terms of Beckett's *Molloy* (or at least its first part) is stressed by: a language and narrator being two organisational principles; a monologicity, concurrency and scenicness corresponding to drama-like immediacy and spatiotemporal selfsameness (Chatman 72; Rimmon-Kenan 108; Genette 109-112; Prince 86); and an orality and auto-reflexivity indicative of performance (Fludernik "Speech" 539). In this essay I will not refer to that paradigm as non- or anti-narrative but "theatrical." Following this trajectory, *Molloy* becomes a "theatrical" novel.[14]

Theatricality, Erika Fischer-Lichte explains, is the "sum total of materials or sign systems used in a theatrical performance beyond the literary text of the drama which define the theatrical performance such as movements, voice, sounds, music, light, colour, and so on" (Fischer-Lichte *Semiotics* 86; Elam 2). In this essay I understand theatricality as "a particular mode of using

14 My term is a reversal of S. E. Gontarski's concept of "narrative theater," which is used to account for the "narrative mode" (199) in Beckett's late drama. According to Gontarski, narrative dominates Beckett's late prose and theatre texts. This semantic proximity, Gontarski claims, might have prompted "so many theatrical directors to stage, to perform the prose fictions" (199).

signs or as a particular kind of semiotic process in which particular signs . . . are employed as signs of signs—by their producers, or their recipients" (Fischer-Lichte *Semiotics* 88). Beckett's novel is "theatrical" in the sense of its intense accumulation of non-narrative devices, which through their specific configuration, become "theatrical" signs and generate a "theatrical" semantics in a prose fictional medium.

The "theatrical" semantics of *Molloy* explores the mimetic dimension of literature. The word "theatre" comes from Greek word "thea" ("to show") or "theasthai" ("to look on") (Fischer-Lichte *Introduction* 7) and the binary opposition of diegetic (or telling) and mimetic (showing) traditionally corresponds to literature and theatre respectively (Rimmon-Kenan 108; Genette 162-170; Nünning and Sommer 337). In Keir Elam's words, dramatic representation[15] is generally "mimetic rather than strictly diegetic—acted rather than narrated" (73). An intense discussion of the diegetic and the mimetic reopened at the dawn of the twentieth century when a number of American and English writers advocated a more pronounced use of the mimetic in prose fiction. Henry James, for example, famously exhorted, "Dramatise it! Dramatise it!" in the preface to "The Altar of the Dead" (251). In fact, in his oeuvre he "gives explicit priority to modes of [mimetic] immediacy such as rendering the characters in their own voices or portraying the events through their eyes and minds in order to achieve empathy and a 'scenic' impression of life" (Berns). Likewise, Joseph Conrad in the "Preface" to *The Nigger of the Narcissus* writes that his main ambition is to make the reader *see* (1955).

Subsequently, in the twentieth century many theoreticians rendered diegesis and mimesis key terms in their theories. They concur that "[t]he verbal fictional narrative is inherently diegetic, it is always told by virtue of being a verbal representation" and that the showing mode presupposes "the character being presented through actions, speech, through nonevaluating description etc." (Johansson 148-149; see Alber and Fludernik). Yet instead of perceiving

15 In the following analysis I use the terms theatrical/theatre and dramatic/drama interchangeably for the sake of simplicity. It might seem a controversial move yet in this study I solely focus on the mimetic dimension of the mode and hence the theoretical and practical differences between the theatrical and the dramatic can conditionally be abolished.

the diegetic and the mimetic in prose, poetry, and drama as binary oppositions, some narratologists locate these concepts within a continuum. Brian McHale classifies particular narrative devices as a typology ranging from "purely" diegetic figures (such as summary) to "purely" mimetic (free indirect discourse) (195-196). Likewise, for Chatman, reports and summaries are diegetic, and dialogues and internal monologues are mimetic (Chatman 146-147). McHale's and Chatman's conclusions concur with my own observations: as a monologue and free indirect discourse, *Molloy* needs to be considered as excessively mimetic.

Further, in accordance within a paradigm of dramatic plays that "represent 'acts of narration,' with characters serving as intradiegetic storytellers" (Nünning and Sommer 337), the novel can be understood as an (self-conscious and auto-reflexive) act (or "staging"[16]) of narration. Considerably accumulating mimetic principles penetrate and permeate each and every aspect of the novel leading to the generation of "theatrical" semantic, which, to some degree, approximates theatre.

The first evidence for that approximation is a modal proximity between monologues in prose fiction and drama. Głowiński pointed out that "there are no essential differences between monodrama and oral monologue (*Gry* 146) while Dorrit Cohn contends that "Virtually any monologue is potentially theatrical work" (*Minds* 255). Beckett's oeuvre provides plenty of examples of such works. Gontarski observes that *A Piece of Monologue* and *From an Abandoned Work* are "almost indistinguishable from late prose fiction" (198-199).[17] *The Unnamable* has been adapted as a radio play and *Company* has been staged by "some six major theatre companies" (Gontarski 199). Both prose works feature monologicity, concurrency and scene, and one might argue that *Molloy* could become adapted as a theatrical performance through similar adaptive mechanisms.

Additional evidence for the approximation of the non-narrative seman-

16 The concepts of "staging," and "performance" too, are frequently employed to capture the non-narrative properties of the "trilogy" (see Bolin 154 and 173).

17 *From an Abandoned Work* was initially collected with other theatrical works in *Breath and Other Shorts* (1971) but it is now anthologized as short fiction.

tics to theatre is the issue of immediacy. Typically, in Manfred Pfister's words, "the receiver of a dramatic text feels directly confronted with the characters represented" (3). Dujardin, the first prominent theoretician and practitioner of monologue in fiction, was aware of the fact and employed monologue in the quest for eliminating authorial interventions (Cohn *Minds* 256). In *Molloy* the use of monologue, concurrency, and scene is also expected to minimize the mediacy and maximize directness in communication between narrator and reader.

Molloy is also "theatrical" in terms of how it recalibrates reception. Because of its immediacy, directness, concurrency, autodiegesis, scenicness, spontaneity, and orality, Beckett's novel should be read not as "text" but "script." Enoch Brater defines the former as "ominously monumental, even *finished*" whilst the latter is "imminent, performable, something always on the verge of *becoming*" (ix). Consequently, a third reason for a semantic proximity between *Molloy* and theatre is the reception approach in which typical prose fictional reception and interpretation no longer suffice and need to be enriched with techniques derived from theatre. I term this approach "performative".[18]

Traditionally, performance is defined as "any event in which all the participants find themselves in the same place at the same time, partaking in a circumscribed set of activities . . . The performance is created out of the interactions of participants" (Fischer-Lichte *Introduction* 18). There are, however, alternative understandings of performance, more fitting for phenomena discussed in Beckett's novel. According to Ute Berns, performativity divides into two senses with "performativity II" referring to "the imitation or illusion of a performance." It is a "non-corporeal presentation of actions not mediated by a narrator" corresponding to or being modelled on "scenic performances" of the act of narration.

The Molloy part requires a "performative" reading for three reasons. Firstly and obviously, it necessitates participants (the narrator and the narratee) in the same place at the same time to take part in a circumscribed set of activi-

18 See "The Performance Issue" of *Journal of Beckett Studies* (23.2 (2014)) for more theoretical and practical examinations of the interface of prose, theatre and performance. (My thanks to Hui Ling Michelle Chiang for referring me to the issue.)

ties (the narrating and the reading). Secondly, in terms of structure, the focus of "performative" reading is not on the high orders of narrative organisation such as plot, time and space but on the low orders: sentences, word blocks and words. Consequently, in *Molloy*, as in any performance, the experience of reading is, to borrow Fischer-Lichte's terms, "an art event" rather than "a work of art" insofar as the interest is in how the novel is perceived and experienced, how it affects the readers, and what kind of impact it has on them ("Sense" 70-7). This aspect of "performative" reading comes to account for the readers' subjective experiences of and individual reactions to the novel, occurring in a specific place and time, varying from one reading to another as well as from one reader to another.

Thirdly, with immediacy, intimacy and indirectness, the "performative" reading inherently pertains to the event of reading. To "perform" the reading is not just to read Beckett's novel but also to experience the contact with the narrator and to interact with him, to pay intense attention to his being and narrating, and to "privilege involvement over content" (Kacandes 155). The interaction in prose fiction, Irene Kacandes asserts in *Talk Fiction*, is usually contrived in such a way as to demand readers' immersion into the fictional world (see Rabinovitz 16) and their "attention to the matter raised by the speaker" (Kacandes 155). The readers can imagine themselves, as Margolin put it, "being *on the scene then and there, viewing* the events as they unfold, *experiencing* them with narrator and characters" (my italics).

The "performativity" of Molloy's part is directly generated by the "theatrical" semantics. The former functions as a consequence or effect of the latter, and must be regarded as one of many interpretive strategies a reader can apply to the novel. "Theatricality" is a more general term that describes a specific narrative structure and meaning-making mechanism. As opposed to "performative" reading, which is inherently linked to the moment or event of reading and subjective reactions, "theatricality" is a universal and objective semantic concept that is changeless over time and immune to individual readings. This essay examines the semantics of the Molloy part and not its particular reception, hence its title.

In order to illustrate how the "theatrical" devices require "performative" reading it is important to look into each principal narrative device in the Molloy part and present its potential reading approaches. To begin, concurrency requires a specifically intensive reader's activity since "on the level of the narration the text's coherence is disrupted and the reader [. . .] needs to [. . .] integrate particular fragments together" (Wysłouch 34-35; see Margolin).[19] Orality, as Tynjanov, Schmid and Fludernik argue, forces the reader to "introduce" him/herself into the work. It highlights the narrator's non-mediated communication of the contents in his consciousness, which simultaneously functions as self-reference and the dynamic act and process of narrating. The narrating becomes an event that we "performatively" attend whenever we start reading (see Fludernik "Speech" 539). Monologicity signals direct and non-mediated communication, and the narrative "you" address (especially its phatic and conative functions) orient the text towards the reader (see Fludernik "Speech" 539; see Głowiński *Gry* 61).

Molloy contributes to the burial of Teddy solely with his presence. Writing, to use Molloy's expression, "contributes presence" in an analogously passive, crippled and superficial way. It therefore needs to be set in motion by various "theatrical" devices. Underlying this need is the contention that written language is no longer sufficient in literary communication, and must be improved. Language distances the subject from the object of narration and from audience. In order to bring them as close as possible, Molloy employs the techniques of *showing*. The "theatrical" semantics in Beckett's "trilogy" with its requirements for their "performative" reading seems to revolve, in my view, around one issue: the narrator. Molloy endeavours to render his voice direct, close, and almost audible to the readers, in the event of its being read. By foregrounding Molloy's voice, Beckett pushes the "concrete world of objects, acts, time" (Schulz 94) to the background by abolishing ontological boundaries of the stories and annulling the spatiotemporal divisions (the unity of time and space). Molloy is depicted as crying out for attention, and for direct and immersive communication. What is at stake is the desire to speak and to be heard "here and now."

19 Translation mine – BL.

WORKS CITED

Abbott, H. Porter. *The Fiction of Samuel Beckett*. Berkeley, Los Angeles, London: University of California Press, 1973. Print.

Ackerley, C. J. and S. E. Gontarski. *The Grove Companion to Samuel Beckett*. New York: Grove Press, 2004. Print.

Alber, Jan. "The 'Moreness' of 'Lessness' of 'natural' narratology: Samuel Beckett's 'Lessness' Reconsidered." *The Free Library*. Northern Illinois University, 22 Mar. 2002. Web. 6 Jan. 2013.

Alber, Jan and Fludernik, Monika. "Mediacy and Narrative Mediation." Eds. Peter Hühn et al.: *the living handbook of narratology*. Hamburg: Hamburg University Press, 8 Jun. 2011. Web. 23 Dec. 2013.

Banfield, Ann. "Skaz." *The Routledge Encyclopedia of Narrative Theory*. Eds. D. Herman, M. Jahn and M.-L. Ryan. London and New York: Routledge, 2005. 535-536. Print.

Bartoszyński, Kazimierz, "Problem konstrukcji czasu w utworach epickich." *Problemy teorii literatury*. Ed. H. Markiewicz. Vol. 2. Wrocław: Ossolineum, 1987. 211-265. Print.

Beckett, Samuel. *The Grove Centenary Edition. Volume II: Novels*. New York: Grove Press, 2006. Print.

Berns, Ute. "Performativity." Eds. Peter Hühn et al.: *the living handbook of narratology*. Hamburg: Hamburg University, 19 Dec. 2012. Web. 7 Jan. 2014.

Bolin, John. *Beckett and the Modern Novel*. Cambridge: Cambridge UP, 2012. Print.

Brater, Enoch. *The Drama in the Text*. New York and Oxford: Oxford UP, 1994. Print.

Buchholz, Sabine, Manfred Jahn. "Dramatic Monologue." *The Routledge Encyclopedia of Narrative Theory*. Eds. D. Herman, M. Jahn and M.-L. Ryan. London and New York: Routledge, 2005. 124-125. Print.

Cohn, Dorrit. *Transparent Minds. Narrative Modes for Presenting Consciousness in Fiction*. New Jersey: Princeton UP, 1978. Print.

—. *The Distinction of Fiction*. Baltimore and London: The Johns Hopkins UP, 1999. Print.

Connor, Steven. *Samuel Beckett. Repetition, Theory and Text*. Colorado: The Davis Group Publishers, 2007. Print.

Conrad, Joseph. "Preface to The Nigger of the 'Narcissus.'" *The Norton Anthology of English Literature.* Vol. 2. 7th ed. Eds. M. H. Abrams et al. New York and London: W.W. Norton & Company, 2000. 1954-1956. Print.

Chatman, Seymour. *Story and Discourse.* Ithaca and London: Cornell UP, 1980. Print.

Ejchenbaum, B. M. "Iluzja narracji mówionej." *Rosyjska szkoła stylistyki.* Eds. M. R. Mayenowa and Z. Saloni. Warszawa: PIW, 1970. Print.

Elam, Keir. *The Semiotics of Theatre and Drama.* London and New York: Routledge, 1980. Print.

Fischer-Lichte, Erika. *The Routledge Introduction to Theatre and Performance Studies.* Trans. Minou Arjomand. London and New York: Routledge, 2014. Print.

—. "Sense and Sensation: Exploring the Interplay Between the Semiotic and Performative Dimensions of Theatre." *Journal of Dramatic Theory and Criticism.* 22.2 (2008): 69-81. Print.

—. *The Semiotics of Theater.* Trans. J. Gaines and D. L. Jones. Bloomington and Indianapolis: Indiana UP, 1992. Print.

Fludernik, Monika. *Towards a "Natural" Narratology.* London and New York: Routledge, 1996. Print.

—. "Narrative and Drama." *Theorizing Narrativity.* Eds. J. Pier and J. A. G. Landa. Berlin and New York: Walter de Gruyter, 2008. 355-385. Print.

—. "Mediacy, Mediation, and Focalization. The Squaring of Terminological Circles." *Postclassical Narratology: Approaches and Analyses.* Eds. J. Alber and M. Fludernik. Columbus: The Ohio State UP, 2010. 105-137. Print.

—. "Speech Representation." *The Routledge Encyclopedia of Narrative Theory.* Eds. D. Herman, M. Jahn and M.-L. Ryan. London and New York: Routledge, 2005. 558-563. Print.

Genette, Gérard. *Narrative Discourse.* Trans. Jane Lewin. Ithaca and London: Cornell UP, 1980. Print.

Głowiński, Michał. *Gry powieściowe.* Warszawa: PWN, 1973. Print.

—. *Powieść młodopolska: Studium z poetyki historycznej.* Kraków: Universitas, 1997. Print.

—. *Porządek, chaos, znaczenie.* Warszawa: PIW, 1968. Print.

—. *Aleksandra Okopień-Sławińska, Janusz Sławiński. Zarys teorii literatury.* Warszawa: Wydawnictwa Szkolne i Pedagogiczne, 1975. Print.

Gontarski, S. E. "Beckett and Performance." *Palgrave Advances in Samuel Beckett Studies.* Ed. Lois Oppenheim. Hampshire and New York: Palgrave Macmillan, 2004. 194-209. Print.

James, Henry. "Preface to 'The Altar of the Dead.'" *The Art of the Novel.* Chicago and London: University of Chicago Press, 2011. 241-266. Print.

Johansson, Christer. "Telling and Showing: A Semiotic Perspective." *Disputable Core Concepts of Narrative Theory.* Eds. G. Rossholm and C. Johansson. Bern et al. Berlin: Peter Lang, 2012. 147-183. Print.

Kacandes, Irene. *Talk Fiction: Literature and the Talk Explosion.* Lincoln and London: University of Nebraska Press, 2001. Print.

Kalaga, Wojciech. *Mental Landscape: The Development of the Novel of Samuel Beckett.* Katowice: Uniwersytet Śląski, 1982. Print.

Keen, Suzanne. *Narrative Form.* New York: Palgrave Macmillan, 2003. Print.

Kennedy, Andrew. *Samuel Beckett.* Cambridge: Cambridge UP, 1989. Print.

Kędzierski, Marek. *Samuel Beckett.* Warszawa: Wiedza Powszechna, 1990. Print.

Kristeva, Julia. *Revolution in Poetic Language.* Trans. Margaret Waller. New York: Columbia UP, 1984. Print.

Lutostański, Bartosz. "Nienaturalna narratologia." *Tekstualia* 1.36 (2014): 181-194. Print.

Margolin, Uri. "Simultaneity in Narrative." Eds. Peter Hühn et al.: *the living handbook of narratology.* Hamburg: Hamburg University, 6 May 2012. Web. 15 Jan. 2014.

Martin, Wallace. *Recent Theories of Narrative.* Ithaca and London: Cornell UP, 1987. Print.

McHale, Brian. "Free Indirect Discourse: A Survey of Recent Accounts." *Narrative Theory: Critical Concepts in Literary and Cultural Studies.* Ed. Mieke Bal. Vol. 1. London and New York: Routledge, 2004. 187-222. Print.

Nadeau, Maurice. "Samuel Beckett: Humour and the Void." *Samuel Beckett: A Collection of Critical Essays.* Ed. Martin Esslin. New Jersey: Prentice-Hall Inc., 1965. 33-36. Print.

Nünning, Ansgar, Roy Sommer. "Diegetic and Mimetic Narrativity: Some further Steps towards a Narratology of Drama." *Theorizing Narrativity.* Eds. J. Pier and J. A. G. Landa. Berlin and New York: Walter de Gruyter, 2008. Print.

Pavel, Thomas G.. "Naturalizing Molloy." *Understanding Narrative.* Eds. J. Phelan and P. J. Rabinowitz. Columbus: Ohio State UP, 1994. 178-199. Print.

Pfister, Manfred. *The Theory and Analysis of Drama.* Cambridge: Cambridge UP, 1988. Print.

Prince, Gerald. *A Dictionary of Narratology.* Rev. ed. Lincoln and London: University of Nebraska Press, 2003. Print.

Rabinovitz, Rubin. *Innovation in Samuel Beckett's Fiction.* Urbana and Chicago: University of Illinois Press, 1992. Print.

Richardson, Brian, ed. *Narrative Beginnings: Theories and Practices.* Lincoln and London: University of Nebraska Press, 2008. Print.

Rimmon-Kenan, Shlomith. *Narrative Fiction.* 2nd ed. London and New York: Routledge, 2002. Print.

Schmid, Wolf. "Skaz." Eds. Peter Hühn et al.: *the living handbook of narratology.* Hamburg: Hamburg University, 22 Jan. 2013. Web. 6 Jan. 2014.

—. "Narratee." Eds. Peter Hühn et al.: *the living handbook of narratology.* Hamburg: Hamburg University, 22 Jan. 2013. Web. 6 Jan. 2014.

Schulz, Hans-Joachim. *This Hell of Stories: A Hegelian Approach to the Novels of Samuel Beckett.* The Hague: Mouton, 1973. Print.

Wysłouch, Seweryna. *Problematyka symultanizmu w prozie.* Poznań: Wyd. Nauk. Uniwersytetu im. A. Mickiewicza, 1981. Print.

CONTRIBUTORS

WILLIAM C. BOLES, Professor of English at Rollins College, authored *Understanding David Henry Hwang* (University of South Carolina) and *The Argumentative Theatre of Joe Penhall* (McFarland). He is a board member of the Comparative Drama Conference.

H. L. MICHELLE CHIANG received her PhD from the University of Leeds in 2015. Her research interests lie in the intersections between literature, the Philosophy of Time and Abnormal Psychology.

JANE WONG YEANG CHUI is Assistant Professor at Nanyang Technological University (NTU), School of Humanities and Social Sciences. She teaches Asian Literature and Renaissance Literature at NTU. Her research interests range from early modern historiography and literature, modern Asian fiction in English to modern drama. She has published articles and essays on Harold Pinter's works, including a recent book entitled *Affirming the Absurd in Harold Pinter* (Palgrave, 2013).

GRALEY HERREN is Professor and Chair of English at Xavier University in Cincinnati. He is the author of numerous articles on twentieth-century drama and fiction, as well as the book *Samuel Beckett's Plays on Film and Television*. He edits the annual book series *Text & Presentation* for McFarland.

DANIEL K. JERNIGAN is Associate Professor of English Literature at Nanyang Technological University (NTU), Singapore. He has written extensively on Tom Stoppard, including his recent monograph, *Tom Stoppard: Bucking the Postmodern* (2013). He also edited *Flann O'Brien: Plays and Teleplays* (2013), and Aidan Higgins collection of radio plays, *Darkling Plain: Texts for the Air* (2010).

BARTOSZ LUTOSTAŃSKI is a PhD candidate at the University of Gdańsk. He has actively participated in organising five literary conferences in Poland "Between.Pomiędzy." The list of his publications includes studies of narratology, contemporary Polish and British literature, poetry and radio drama. He is also a translator and musician.

NEIL MURPHY teaches contemporary literature at Nanyang Technological University (NTU), Singapore. He is the author of *Irish Fiction and Postmodern Doubt* (2004) and editor of *Aidan Higgins: The Fragility of Form* (2010) and of the revised edition of Higgins's *Balcony of Europe* (2010). He co-edited (with Keith Hopper) a special Flann O'Brien centenary issue of the *Review of Contemporary Fiction* (2011), *The Short Fiction of Flann O'Brien* (2013) and the forthcoming four-volume series of books related to Dermot Healy's work (2015-16).

JOSEPH H. O'MEALY is Emeritus Professor of English and former Dean of the College of Languages, Linguistics, and Literature at the University of Hawaii, Manoa. He is the author of *Alan Bennett: A Critical Introduction* (Routledge, 2001), several essays on Bennett, most recently in *Modern British Drama on Screen* (Cambridge, 2013), as well as essays on Dickens, Conrad, and Margaret Oliphant.

KEVIN RIORDAN is an Assistant Professor of English at Nanyang Technological University (NTU), Singapore. His research focuses on the ways performance travels, and his writing has appeared or is forthcoming in *Modern Drama*, *Theatre Annual*, *Modernism/modernity*, *Theatre Topics*, *Performance Research*, and *Intertexts*. He now is at work on a book project, a performance history of the around-the-world tour.

JEFFREY SEVERS is assistant professor of English at the University of British Columbia. He co-edited (with Christopher Leise) *Pynchon's* Against the Day: *A Corrupted Pilgrim's Guide* (Delaware, 2011), and his articles on Pynchon, Philip Roth, and David Foster Wallace have been published or are forthcoming in *Twentieth-Century Literature*, *Studies in American Fiction*, and *Critique*. He is completing a book project titled "David Foster Wallace's Balancing Books: Fictions of Value."

W. MICHELLE WANG recently completed her PhD at The Ohio State University; her dissertation focuses on post-1945 British and American fiction. She specializes in areas of narrative theory and aesthetic theory, and has published articles in the *Journal of Narrative Theory* and *The Review of Contemporary Fiction*. Her scholarly interests also extend to East Asian popular culture and televisual narratives.

MIKE WITCOMBE recently completed a PhD at the University of Southampton, during which he researched depictions of sex and sexuality in Philip Roth's 'Kepesh' novels. He has additional research interests in gender theory, psychoanalysis and baseball fiction.

BOOK REVIEWS

Valeria Luiselli. ***Faces in the Crowd.*** Trans. Christina MacSweeney. Coffee House Press, 2014. Paper: $15.95.

Valeria Luiselli. ***Sidewalks.*** Trans. Christina MacSweeney. Intro. Cees Nooteboom. Coffee House Press, 2014. Paper: $15.95.

The title of Luiselli's first novel derives from Ezra Pound's poem "In a Station of the Metro," which reads in its entirety: "The apparition of these faces in the crowd; / Petals on a wet, black bough." As we learn from the novel, Pound wrote the poem after seeing a flash of his friend Henri Gaudier-Brzeska in the subway—he'd died in the trenches some months before. Later, Pound reduced some three hundred lines to two, so that it would be "exactly as brief as his friend's appearance, exactly as startling." Luiselli aims for, and often achieves, the same level of startling compression in this deft short novel, which is remarkable for its fluid treatment of time and the boundaries between the living and the dead. An unnamed young mother in Mexico City starts a novel about her time in New York, where she worked at a small publishing house specializing in translation, and became obsessed with the early twentieth-century Mexican poet Gilberto Owen. Her campaign to publish Owen's works ultimately becomes something much deeper and stranger, a kind of ontological overlapping. Luiselli structures her work in short prose bursts that allow for childish interruption—the sentences "dense, porous . . . like a baby's heart" (US readers may be reminded of another brilliant recent novel about motherhood, Jenny Offill's *Dept. of Speculation*). Later, Luiselli utilizes this form to break down distinctions of geography and linearity: Mexico City and New York begin to feel continuous, while Owen's voice creeps into the narrative. Between meetings with Zukofsky, García Lorca, and others, he begins to see a woman in a red coat on the subway, a flash of our original narrator. *Faces in the Crowd* becomes a meditation on the ways in which reading and writing engage us in a double ghost story, each of us communicating with an absent other. While Owen's highly stylized voice is less compelling than the young mother's, the audacity and style of Luiselli's narrative footwork demands admiration. Her idiom is entirely her own but nourished by an unusually rich topsoil of literary history.

Coffee House Press will simultaneously release *Sidewalks,* a collection of Luiselli's essays. These erudite yet limber pieces chronicle a visit to Joseph Brodsky's grave in Venice, the lost rivers of Mexico City, and *relingos*, empty spaces of play and possibility in the city. Luiselli can be both lyrical and sharply epigrammatic, as when she writes: "The outcome of a long-awaited first meeting is often disappointing. The same is true of an encounter with a dead person, except that there's no need to hide the disappointment: in that sense, a dead person is always more agreeable than a living one." Luiselli is a major Latin American writer whose distinctly belated talent seems to grasp the ghostliness of our century. She speaks to us with almost posthumous confidence: as she puts it in *Faces*, "the difference between being alive and being dead is just a matter of viewpoint: the living look from the center outwards, the dead from the periphery to some sort of center." [ERIC LUNDGREN]

Ahmad Faris al-Shidyaq. *Leg over Leg: Volume I.* Trans. Humphrey Davies. Foreword by Rebecca C. Johnson. NYU Press, 2013. 416 pp. Cloth: $40.00.

One cannot accuse Ahmad Faris al-Shidyaq of pulling any punches. *Leg over Leg*, a four-volume nineteenth-century Arabic novel, begins with a note of cheerful forewarning: "Another of the book's excellent qualities is that, when it mentions something, it says everything there is to say about it, while also taking into consideration every aspect of any similar works." And al-Shidyaq lives up to this promise: Loosely draped around the picaresque story of the young Fariyaq, the novel uses each stage of his journey as an occasion to halt, digress, challenge, and muddle the narrative. In just the first volume, a depiction of earthly beauty gives way to a four-page list of sexual perversions; a discussion of the turban digresses into intimations of cuckoldry; a nested story about a priest ends with a list defining the "rare words mentioned above."

Indeed, *Leg over Leg* is concerned less with plot and character than it is with its own form and how to fill it: "Words are but the Matter pertaining to the Form in which various meaning may be *expressed*, and this Matter alone is of no use if the Form . . . has not been *impressed*." The content that ends up filling this form runs the gamut of creative miscellanies: lists, catalogues, lexicography, jokes, errata, and so forth. While often funny, al-Shidyaq does let in one tragedy too real for fiction. A late chapter, aptly titled "Emotion and Motion," finds the author reminiscing on his brother's real-life conversion to Protestantism and the subsequent arrest and brutal imprisonment that led to his death. The rage and sadness lifts right off the page: "Did you feel no compassion, you bull-necked thugs, for his youth and beauty? Were your hard hearts not affected by the pallor of his face when you kept him from the light and air . . . ?" In its lengthy digressions, playfulness with form, and willingness to turn a phrase directly at its audience, *Leg over Leg* is something of a Middle Eastern *Tristram Shandy*, rich and generous in its narrative abundance. Al-Shidyaq's nineteenth-century prescience encompasses not only the aesthetics of our contemporary fictions, but perhaps sees farther still, into their future. It seems we have a lot of catching up to do. [HAL HLAVINKA]

Karl Ove Knausgaard. *My Struggle: Book Three: Boyhood.* Trans. Don Bartlett. Archipelago Books, 2014. 427 pp. Cloth: $27.00.

Far removed from childhood while writing in 2008 this installment of the six-volume account of his life, Karl Ove Knausgaard presents experiences dating back to when he was ages six to thirteen, with the adult awareness that his earliest years are more holes than cloth and that what he recalls is the product of "sly and artful" memory. Initially readers may be surprised, and perhaps disappointed, that the heightened philosophizing of the first two volumes is missing, yet the lack of verbal and metaphysical fireworks is part of an effective and, as far as this word can legitimately go, truthful method that strives to express plainly, with only occasional chronological jumps and metafictional flourishes, what boyhood meant to Knausgaard. His parents and brother

Yngve, as well as many friends, come to full life—especially his mother, who till now has been somewhat shadowy—and what we learned in the first two books about the narrator's approach to the world gains in resonance due to this volume's low-keyed approach. In the vein of self-laceration that's familiar from the first two books, Knausgaard depicts the often hapless navigation of the political worlds of classrooms and boy-girl relationships of a boastful child, proud of his book intelligence but frequently insensitive to others, who is consumed by anxieties common to many at that age, prone to tears at the slightest blows to his self-esteem, and fearful of his father who, alive or dead, is always around, even in 2008: "Sitting here now, hearing [his voice] in my inner ear, I almost start crying." We read with unease, aware that at any moment a harrowing scene might occur, its cruelty amplified by the inexplicable behavior of Knausgaard's mother. This volume deepens and enriches the picture we have from the first two volumes, and is an essential work in this brilliant memoir sequence. [JEFF BURSEY]

Miklós Szentkuthy. *Toward the One and Only Metaphor.* Trans. Tim Wilkinson. Contra Mundum Press, 2013. 408 pp. Paper: $22.00.

In this remarkable work, resplendent with metaphor, itself an extended metaphor, Szentkuthy gives free rein to invention, evoking streams of images and associations with which to suggest the panoply of conjunctions and intimacies central to his life and thought. To begin, he invokes a succession of convenient dualities—demotic and natural, form and order, objective and lyric, garden and flower—with which to examine and classify several characteristic obsessions: encounters real and imagined with alluring women, philosophical puzzles, fascination with mathematics, religious asceticism. Some reflections ripen into extended scenes depicting historical figures—Charles II of England, the painter Richard Parkes Bonington—encountering women in compromising circumstances, leading to mordant inquiries on the nature of love in its physical, moral, and spiritual manifestations. But in the midst of such ruminations, the siren song of Flora in her garden arrests his attention.

How is one to bear so much intellectual strain when the soothing, dispassionate delights of nature beckon? Yet the writer cannot leave any such hint of momentary refreshment alone, for soon he is caught up in analyzing, categorizing, finding analogies and correspondences, providing anecdotes to extend and modify his ever-shifting perspective. Moving back and forth among grandiose conceptions and trivial ephemera as his overwrought fancy leads him, Szentkuthy traverses a multitude of fields of inquiry suggested by free associations on God, disease, boredom, consciousness . . . the list only pauses when he puts down his pen. His companions in art—Goethe, Freud, Aquinas, Sir Thomas Browne, among others—quicken his consciousness into reawakening each time his enthusiasm threatens to flag. Learned references and allusions abound, as well as self-conscious scrutiny of the literary art he practices and sends up in his teeming catalogue of mental furniture. There is abundant entertainment in this brilliant assembly, a treasure trove literally without peer. [MICHAEL PINKER]

Mieko Kanai. ***Oh, Tama!*** Trans. Tomoko Aoyama and Paul McCarthy.
Kurodahan Press, 2014. 190 pp. Paper: $13.00.

Takashi Hiraide. ***The Guest Cat.*** Trans. Eric Selland.
New Directions, 2014. 140 pp. Paper: $14.95.

Both Mieko Kanai's *Oh, Tama!* and Takashi Hiraide's *The Guest Cat* are "cat novels," so to speak, but their ambitions range far from the feline. Given that Kanai and Hiraide are recognized as being among the most innovative Japanese writers working today—Kanai mostly for her prose, though she's also a prize-winning poet; Hiraide mostly for his poetry, though he's also won prizes for his prose—this is hardly a surprise. Kanai's novel is part of her "Mejiro" (a Tokyo neighborhood) series, books known for the lightness and humor with which they survey the human comedy. Kanai has written that "in [her] 'Mejiro tetralogy,' the relationships among the characters are ruled by 'coincidence' . . ." This applies not only to the human characters, but also to the feline, in this case the pregnant Tama, who enters the protagonist's life unlooked for. Unable, it is assumed, to identify the father of her kittens, her condition mirrors that of the human characters who, in a novel that has much to do with maternity and paternity, have tenuous links to their own biological kin. We see, as the novel unfolds, how several of these unmoored characters form a family of sorts for themselves, a family no better or worse than a typical biological family. This may sound trite—aren't several TV sitcoms built on the same premise?—but Kanai's art makes it otherwise. The odd bits of life that Kanai captures in the interactions of her characters draw us in even as they are never exactly the important events that would drive another kind of novel, even as what would be tragedy in those novels approaches comedy in *Oh, Tama!*

The Guest Cat shares with *Oh, Tama!* a focus on the mundane and a concern with family. The family in Hiraide's novel is a childless couple, freelance writers whose lives are enriched when the neighbors' pet begins visiting their small home and turns into a regular guest. The couple becomes increasingly involved with the cat, and as they do so, the warmth between them seems to grow, as does their engagement with the world away from their desks. A lesser writer would have made this into a simple story about how the love of an animal awakens in its people a love for each other and for life. Cats, however, don't live forever, and guesthouses in leafy Tokyo neighborhoods with rents that freelancers can afford are just as transitory. The story, deceptively simple, grows complicated, and so does the form the novel takes: It is, we learn, the story of its own genesis, a birth that, without the guest cat, may not have happened. [DAVID COZY]

Saadat Hasan Manto. ***Bombay Stories.*** Trans. Matt Reeck & Aftab Ahmad. Vintage, 2014. 246 pp. Paper: $16.00.

Saadat Hasan Manto, known as an important Urdu writer of Partition, has nonetheless been largely overlooked as a major modernist more broadly. His frequently anthologized stories, such as "Toba Tek Singh," detail the brutality of mid-century South Asian politics, but they also express the alienation, disembodiment, absurdity, banality, and irony endemic in the writing of his generation (e.g., Camus, Beckett, Nabokov, Ellison). *Bombay Stories*, a much-needed new collection of Manto's writing, separates itself from conventional approaches to Manto by focusing on Bombay, the city he adored. Manto lived in Bombay between 1936–1941 and 1942–48; he didn't leave immediately after Partition but stayed until his dismissal from the Bombay film industry, when he moved to Pakistan, felt adrift, and died of alcoholism in 1955 at the age of forty-three. Manto wrote after arriving in Lahore in 1948, "I am a walking, talking Bombay. Wherever I happen to be, that is where I will make a world of my own . . . I loved the city then as I love it today." Manto explores this personal relationship to Bombay throughout *Bombay Stories*, particularly with stories such as "Barren" and "Rude," which feature a Manto-as-character managing his life as a writer, husband, and communist. He does so with sketches of the so-called immoral or dispossessed—characters who are uncertain, lost, or confused—moving ordinary and overlooked lives to the fore. Until recently, Khalid Hasan was responsible for translating the bulk of Manto's work into English, but this edition by Matt Reeck & Aftab Ahmad crucially calls attention to Manto's continued relevance and his significance as one of the great late modernists. [STEFANIE SOBELLE]

Jim Crace. *Harvest.*

Vintage, 2013. 243 pp. Paper: $15.00.

It has become a hallmark of Jim Crace's novels for their action to be tightly localized and *Harvest* is no exception. Set in a manor on the eve of enclosures in the late sixteenth century, the novel describes the disturbing effect of seemingly random acts of violence starting with the burning of the squire's stables and the killing of a horse. These acts coincide with, but aren't necessarily caused by rumors of imminent change in the estate. The initial sign of change is the arrival of a man who proceeds to measure out the land and produce a map of the area, but this surveying is then taken over by the squire's well-named assistant, Mr. Quill, who takes the narrator with him on an extended tour of the estate. The composition of Quill's illuminated map takes place in parallel to the increasingly violent sequence of events and clearly functions as a metaphor for the novel's narrative assembly. Publicity flyers for *Harvest* notwithstanding, the novel does not show local life to be a pastoral idyll, but instead stresses the hard manual labor of the field hands and their frequent injuries. Because Crace situates us so closely within the village community, key events involve the arrivals of outsiders, itinerant workers of dubious morality and figures acting on the instructions of a rival claimant to the estate. The latter prefigure a near future of fences, dykes, and walls as the land will be separated into different commodities; where common land will become a thing of the past and livestock will replace crop farming. Two aspects of Crace's narrative stand out as particularly impressive. The farming community is virtually nonliterate and functions on tradition; indeed, the novel dramatizes the violent punitive reactions of the locals to inexplicable events. But more generally, Crace skillfully avoids historical markers in his language and throughout engages the reader through his evocation of the physical immediacy of rural life. [DAVID SEED]

Bohumil Hrabal. *Harlequin's Millions.* Trans. Stacey Knecht.
Archipelago Books, 2014. 260 pp. Paper: $18.00.

To an unnamed pensioner, "Harlequin's Millions" is the background music for the reckoning of her life, perpetually rewound in a retirement home housed in the one-time castle of Count Špork in the Czechoslovak countryside. One day she walks to a park on the castle grounds lined with statues of lissome figures who portray, in red sandstone, the months and seasons. Their careless grace summons a feeling of loss for her vanished youth. On her desultory rambles she meets three "witnesses to old times," who proudly regale her with precious anecdotes of The Town Where Time Stands Still, her birthplace, where the brewery her husband managed still stands. (According to Hrabal's endnote, the actual recorded memories of ordinary citizens, families with colorful nicknames and reputations, tradesmen of all stamps a hundred years and more before, inspired this book.) She relives her two months as a shopkeeper in Prague, the happiest days of her life, which to her shame came to naught, a touching calamity of hopeful ambition. Glimpses of her fellow pensioners, recollections of her fashionable past, melancholy paeans of wistful regret accompanying the relentless passage of time, reveal her fervent desire to leave a lasting impression: "Here in this castle I lived every day in the mystery, in the strata of human destinies of people who had long since been buried, but I brought them back to life." At length our heroine seems to retract some of her narrative, the witnesses themselves appearing to dissolve into figments, narrative truth losing its moorings as powerful winds devastate the villa where she and her husband had intended to spend their days after collectivization threw out the old regime following World War II. Hrabal's novel is a loving testament to the mixed feelings attendant upon old age, swept away in an instant. [MICHAEL PINKER]

Joanna Ruocco. *Dan.*

Dorothy, A Publishing Project, 2014. 152 pp. Paper: $16.00.

Much like her previous works, Joanna Ruocco's fifth book *Dan* is a departure from the expected. It is a departure from logic and order. It is a world of fabricated ponderances: the protagonist Melba Zuzzo worries about the substance of time—jelly or miasma?—she concerns herself that perhaps she is not Melba Zuzzo at all but a reincarnation of the very dead Bev Hat, and so on. When considering why her principal liked her, she reaches epiphany: "Perhaps [Principal Benjamin] had been drawn to Melba precisely because he had sensed in her an utter lack of distinction, a pinched, lackluster quality that would only intensify with the years, eventually yielding a person so small and blanched he could put her in the pocket of his mustard-colored frock coat, marking her absently from time to time with his thumbnail as he might mark a nutmeat." Dan is a place without space, or a space without space: a town filtered of rationality, a novel part noir, full on fairy tale. The night, for instance, is "a batter poorly mixed, a batter into which bagged blueberries had been introduced by an amateur baker, a woman who had never worked at a bakery, who shook the berries from the bag and folded them, still frozen, into the batch, so that two distinctive types of muffins resulted from the oven, the one type heavy with fruit, the other dry and light, almost a biscuit." Ruocco's prose, much like her micro-galactic world building, is spectacular. At once lurid and dreamy, at other times completely absurd, her sentences are synchronous black holes and star explosions: They pull you in and burst. Under the whimsical cloak of magical invention, *Dan* is a serious novel that is not afraid of playing or pleasure or glut. "[Melba] concentrated on the paper sliding beneath her, the incessant soft abrasions and electric tingles along her scalp," and so will the reader—squirm and delight under all the imperceptible paper cuts of Ruocco's creation. [LILY HOANG]

Joshua Corey. *Beautiful Soul: An American Elegy.*
Spuyten Duyvil, 2014. 369 pp. Paper: $18.00.

Poets know that plot is at best an accomplished divertissement, at worst a distraction, a self-justifying invitation to ignore the exotic, coaxing lure of words—the evocative musical surface of the text, the immediacy of vowels and consonants at serious play—and to ignore the clean world-ness of images themselves—the density of immersion in event, the collisions of angles, forms, and color that become, within the curious dynamic of memory, the past that, in turn, shapes (and distorts) the integrity of the self. Make no mistake—Joshua Corey is a poet, testified to not only by his four volumes of spare and brittle poetry but by his achievement here, his first novel. What starts as an homage to narrative noir—Ruth seeks the help of a private investigator when she starts to receive letters from her dead mother—boldly crosses genre boundaries into cultural biography as the detective follows a trail through Europe that leads to the mother's involvement in the 1968 Paris student uprisings and then reaches back into the horrors of Hitler's rise. The pleasure, as one character intones, comes from tangling in mystery. With the deft confidence of an accomplished novelist, Corey structures a darkening narrative, every revelation rendered ironic by layerings of secrecy. Was Ruth's mother a heroic figure of the student resistance or are the letters part of some narrative that Ruth struggles to assemble; are they her own ghosts or history's ghosts that she is desperate to constellate into sentences, paragraphs. The closing hundred pages are best described as conceptual—Corey abandons the pedestrian logic of plot and the pretentious clichés of neorealism to immerse us in a fine, clean webbing of images that discloses only reluctantly, reveling rather in language that lifts and terrifies. [JOSEPH DEWEY]

Josef Winkler. *When the Time Comes.* Trans. and intro. Adrian West. Contra Mundum, 2013. 228 pp. Paper: $16.00.

Josef Winkler. *Natura Morta: A Roman Novella.* Trans. Adrian West. Contra Mundum, 2014. 124 pp. Paper: $16.00.

The self-proclaimed "eternal altar boy" of Austrian literature, Josef Winkler stands in peculiar relationship to his contemporaries. Where Gert Jonke and Peter Handke sought to bend the pastoral novel with postmodern wit and ingenuity, Winkler's project might better be cast as an act of arson on the quiet form, setting fire to the provincial beauties and traditions with the embers of Catholic orthodoxy and National Socialist ideology. Contra Mundum Press's new editions of *When the Time Comes* and *Natura Morta*, deftly translated by Adrian West, serve as fitting introductions to Winkler's narrative aesthetic. *When the Time Comes* takes on the form of a village's necrology, framed by a brutal refrain that swells with each new accident, murder, or suicide, adding yet another skeleton to the village's bone stock: "In the very bottom of the clay vessel where the putrid-smelling bone stock was rendered from the bones of slaughtered animals . . . lie the arm bones of a man, torn from his body in a trench on the battlefield." Tragedy piles upon tragedy, skeleton upon skeleton, until the vessel brims with the stories of a village's mounting deaths. The relentlessness of the ghastly images and their growing repetitions bring to mind the call and response of a Catholic liturgy, albeit one transfigured by Nazism's mass graves.

Natura Morta hides similar themes beneath a veneer of vibrant life. Winner of the 2001 Alfred Döblin Prize, Winkler's novella is the brief but dense story of a young man's tragic death told through a series of colorful scenes in a present-day Roman street market. The repetitions are now more subdued. Still lifes of herbs, flowers, and fruit—rosemary, white peaches, apricots, red and white broom—appear again and again, beautiful and sensuous and always, in Winkler's hand, serving as reminders of inevitable rot and decay. These images are set against the blood and offal of the butcher's table: "A *macellaio* in Piazza Vittorio, with a white surgeon's glove stretched over his right hand . . . broke open a sheep's head that had already been split with a cleaver." The constant return to death amid a setting so teeming with life renders a curious sense of stasis, where the sensual and the mortal aim to even one another out. It's narrative as incantation, summoning up and then exploding its objects—flesh, flower, and otherwise. Indeed, in their focused repetition and clarity of purpose, both of these books evidence a writer working at the edges of the novel's form, pushing his prose out into startling new territories. If, in Winkler's view, death is life's only answer, then it is still up to literature to frame our living questions. [HAL HLAVINKA]

Sergio De La Pava. *Personae.*

University of Chicago Press, 2013. 216 pp. Paper: $17.00.

Sergio De La Pava's latest novel begins, more or less, like your average, run-of-the-mill metaphysical detective novel: Former musical prodigy, teen doctorate, and homicide detective Helen Tame is called to the scene of a dead John Doe. At age 111, Doe is an unlikely victim of foul play, but Tame senses more to the case than at first meets the eye. She gets a break after recovering a cache of documents—including a notebook and a story written in the margins of a *TV Guide*—ostensibly authored by Doe. Then things get really weird. To call it a collage is to understate the density of voice and allusion permeating the narrative even at the sentence level. Tame's noirish musings are equal parts

Raymond Chandler and Roland Barthes: "The apartment I responded to . . . was a Manhattan special, meaning you cannot believe a human being who is not incarcerated is not entitled to more space." Ranging from poetic aphorism to absurdist drama, the contents of the cache, transcribed in chapters alternating with Tame's investigation, reveal clues to Doe's identity; however, by the time readers get to the concluding novella, *Energeias: Or Why Today the Sun May Not Rise in The East, Set in The West*, the plot has thickened to implicate Colombian history, the human capacity for good and evil, the divine, and the nature of art. The most surprising twist is how much of this holds together, from the detective's shrewd asides to her victim's literary ruminations, culminating in a thinly veiled autobiographical sequence that is as moving as it is unexpected. More than stylistic affectation, De La Pava's play with genre is an earnest inquiry into riddles that will haunt readers long after they turn the last page. [PEDRO PONCE]

Jason Schwartz. *John the Posthumous.*
O/R Books, 2013. 148 pp. Paper: $17.00.

Jason Schwartz's stark and mysterious *John the Posthumous* is described by its publisher as a "novella in objects," which accurately captures the brevity and strangeness of this book. Like the hornbook or personalized primer to which its first section title refers, it feels like a macabre curio, picked up by chance in a dusty corner of a rummage sale. If pressed to name its genre, under threat of the bodily harm described in its pages, I would say prose poetry, but the superbly poised language also recalls older forms—the chronicle, the miscellany, the verse. *John* is worth reading solely for the perfection of its prose; it is almost flawlessly written on the sentence level. The eerily disembodied voice seems at times to verge on personal confession without ever quite crossing over. The narrator seems to have been cuckolded or is at least obsessed with forms of betrayal and retributive violence. A stray fact or dubious etymology will lead him into agonized description of domestic interiors: bedposts, doorframes, knobs and fittings. The voice hovers around these themes, returning to them again and again with an unhurried, melancholy obsession. Brutal customs are cheerfully explained, grim facts reported with unsettling neutrality: "The common wasp measures roughly two hundred hertz. This is well below the frequency of, say, a human scream." It's as if a house is telling its own version of a horror novel, or the ghost of a betrayed husband brooding over the deaths of his wife and children. Schwartz's method of oblique assertion makes it impossible to offer any definitive reading, leaving narrative ligature to the reader's imagination. The stubborn refusal to over-explain gives the book a unique texture, like a museum in which all the explanatory placards have been removed. What we are left with are the objects themselves: the implements, the rubbed weapons, the ruined bodies. *John the Posthumous* powerfully creates a mood of dark evanescence, leaving the suspicion that further horrors might be uncovered on rereading. Whether that is possible, or even advisable, is another question. Admiring the shifting shadows in his child's bedroom, the narrator confronts a distorted version of himself, noting: "My form on the wall: it now assumes a more gruesome shape." [ERIC LUNDGREN]

John A. Scott. *N.*

Brandl & Schlesinger, 2014. 599 pp. Paper: $34.95AU.

When this extraordinary novel appeared in Australia last April, one reviewer grouped it with "postmodernist maximalist opuses such as *Infinite Jest*, *The Recognitions*, *2666*, *A Naked Singularity* and *Gravity's Rainbow*." The Pynchon reference is probably the most relevant: The novel takes place during the same World War II period, veers from documentary realism to outlandish fantasy, and indicts industrialists as the real warmongers, putting profits over patriotism. And like Pynchon's *V.*, Scott's *N* is a quest for the meaning of a mysterious initial by an individual driven to expose the secret history of his country. *N* is an alternative history along the lines of Sinclair Lewis's *It Can't Happen Here* or Philip Roth's *The Plot against America*: Scott imagines a rightwing takeover of Australia in 1942 and an invasion by the Japanese, both of which entails persecution of the dissenting artists who dominate the first half of the novel. A civil servant named Telford dominates the second half as he begins to realize the nature of the fascist regime for which he works. Linking the two halves are two redhead women who resemble each other, and uniting the lengthy novel is a web of intertextual references to classic works of fiction like *Gulliver's Travels*, *Great Expectations*, "The Purloined Letter," *Through the Looking-Glass*, and *Journey to the Center of the Earth*, not to mention a few references to Joyce's *Ulysses* and a cameo by Gertrude Stein and Alice B. Toklas, sitting out the war in the wilds of Australia (a comic episode conveyed in the style of *Great Expectations*). Formally and politically, *N* resembles Dos Passos' *USA*, alternating between the personal stories of a dozen or so characters and a variety of documents, each in a different font, privileging heterogeneity over the homogeneity demanded by conservative regimes and aesthetics. This bold, important novel is worth seeking out. [STEVEN MOORE]

Marek Waldorf. *The Short Fall.*

Turtle Point Press, 2013. 369 pp. Paper: $16.95

At the center of Marek Waldorf's darkly mesmerizing debut novel is an unconsummated national tragedy. The speechwriter for a charismatic presidential nominee takes the bullet in a botched assassination attempt and is left in a near-vegetative state. Drifting from the past to the present and back, the wounded man's interior monologue navigates through the campaign stops, polling games, and stump speeches that led to his body's intersection with the bullet, eventually bringing him to the conclusion that he himself was the intended target. All this is told in a manic, digressive style reminiscent of Thomas Bernhard's compulsive screeds. In dense passages of block text, the speechwriter details his journey toward finding his—or the candidate's—voice, only to fall out of grace with the campaign's shadowy orchestrators. The novel achieves a kind of poetry when Waldorf weaves his prose through the lattice of a politician's public persona: "What appeared real at any given time was but the reality of a given appearance: the rapture of abbreviated flight, a timely slogan, the vision thing." Indeed, in the tangled realm of political image-crafting, language, charisma, rhetoric, and stagecraft are joined together in the Gordian knot of authenticity, with no hope of a sword to sort them out. When the speechwriter's theory narrows in on the conspiracy's architects, his real vitriol focuses not on the perceived plot behind his undoing, but on the terrifying realities of a political machine that seeks always to "replace America with Americana," on a government whose candidate is simply a cipher for disparate special interests—"the least human of all of us." Waldorf has crafted a novel about the fantasies we pour into one body every four years, lyrically told and meticulously structured, with a cynicism straight out of American politics. [HAL HLAVINKA]

Peter Grandbois. *Domestic Disturbances.*
Subito Press, 2013. 112 pp. Paper: $16.00.

Domestic Disturbances, the first short story collection from Peter Grandbois, takes the inspiration for its surreal landscapes from the paintings of the Clayton Brothers, echoing their revelation of the persistent strangeness lurking beneath every surface. The collection opens with a cosmology: "School Bus" takes place on a school bus, or a universe that *is* a school bus. The bus driver rules this world like a slapstick Norse god, and the children on board, representative tropes from playgrounds real and fictional, are transformed, often literally, into objects and animals, through some not-quite-symbolic alchemical process. Tone is everything here, and Grandbois combines the charm and whimsy of some classic school stories (Louis Sachar's *Wayside School* stories, *The Magic School Bus*) with a haunted terror. The stories that follow, short pieces collected under the heading "Disturbances," are marked by a narrative distance. Mostly titled after household chores, and set in a bland and barely described suburban landscape (Grandbois knows we've heard it all before, and is interested only in troubling the familiar), these stories indeed disturb the domestic. Told with humor and distance, they nonetheless make the skin crawl. Strange things emerge: electricity, insects. Though not technically interconnected, the stories seem to take place in the same universe, and while the POV is variable, a watchful tone permeates the collection, inviting the reader to consider it as a unified work. Grandbois troubles the now-familiar "suburban we" by constantly shifting its location—what contemporary literature has conditioned readers to understand as the voice of a town can here be anything and anywhere, including witness, voyeur, bird, caterpillar. This collection unsettles and delights, and Grandbois's is a welcome and refreshing voice. [CAROLINE ROTHNIE]

Yuriy Tarnawsky. *View of Delft: Five Mininovels.*
(*The Placebo Effect Trilogy, Volume Three / Journal of Experimental Fiction* 53.3.)
JEF Books, 2013. 236 pp. Paper: $17.00.

Tarnawsky grapples with alienation, attenuation, and fear of death in this carefully interwoven collection. In "The Idiot," Eugen Winter, living arrangements in disarray, dutifully attending Fear and Trembling scream therapy, meets a disabled boy who brings him home. Welcomed into the household, Eugen soon moves in. At length the family perform a hilarious version of *Hamlet*. Afterward Eugen lingers, still in costume, whittling, staring vacantly off into space. In "Years of Travel," Franz cannot make sense of the world of appearances. He thinks to consult a priest, but his faith falters. Eventually Franz dreams he has become a drawing, trying to jump from one line to another. In "The Albino Syndrome" Detlev, overawed by his austere father, is drawn to an albino boy who plays the cello but drowns, possibly due to Detlev's neglect. In successive encounters with his withdrawn mother, his anorexic sister Nora, a dead hare, and a ghostly postman, Detlev moves in a bewildered fog. After his father's funeral he meets an army officer who asks to shoot Detlev. Consenting, he finds that "being dead isn't bad at all." In "Karla and Georg or The Ambiguous Nature of Clouds" the couple live in adjoining rooms, much in love. Watching clouds approach one day, Karla says they will permeate each other, as Georg scoffs. Eventually the lovers drift imperceptibly toward a similar fate, resulting in Karla's unexpected death. Distraught, Georg trudges into a swampy landscape of lakes that resemble eyes staring skyward.

In "The School" RR enters an institution where he is fitted for a mysterious role which includes taking part in exercises ultimately intended to prepare, it would seem, for death. In group sessions punctuated by screams, he joins in urging his fellow participants to undertake impossible feats. Tarnawsky's unsettling world mimics the fitful dream called life, overlaid with deceptions, furnished with all the trappings imagination can afford. [MICHAEL PINKER]

Zhong Lihe. *From the Old Country: Stories and Sketches of China and Taiwan.* Trans. and ed. T. M. McClellan. Foreword Zhong Tiejun. Columbia University Press, 2014. 293 pp. Cloth: $35.00.

Even within the often insular world of modern Taiwanese fiction, Zhong Lihe stands out as a writer bound to a very particular piece of turf. Most of his fiction and essays consist of semi-autobiographical accounts of life as a Hakka, a Chinese minority with a history of migration and discrimination analogous to that of the Jews, in rural Meinong county in southern Taiwan—a subculture in a backwater of a province that, until sixty years ago, was on the margins of the Chinese cultural world. Yet in Zhong Lihe's case, insularity is another word for specificity: the specificity that is the soul of narrative. Like James Baldwin—although, as reflected in T. M. McClellan's translation, not the prose stylist Baldwin was—Zhong's marginality made him a keen observer of the painful irony that accompanies the distance between who we think we are and where life places us. Park Shin-jun in "In the Willow Shade" is a typical Zhong character: a Korean patriot and romantic, fluent in Japanese and an admirer of Tolstoy, Park ends up a student at a driving school in Manchuria. And in his works set closer to home, Zhong always retains an awareness of how the macrophenomena of politics and history can manifest themselves within the personal lives of even the most isolated villagers. In his novella "Rain," Taiwan's post-war land reform policy serves as the catalyst for a tragic cascade of private resentments in a Meinong farming hamlet. The global scope of his local stories—particularly his own story, which saw him driven by war, politics, and his own romantic convictions from Meinong to Manchuria to Beijing and back—sometimes reminds the reader of the tale of another native of a tiny island. Zhong was a twentieth century Odysseus, pushed onto an epic journey by the great winds of his age. [DYLAN SUHER]

Louis Armand. *Cairo.*

Equus Press, 2014. 366 pp. Paper: $10.00.

Cairo is a near-future, speculative-fiction romp, touching on nearly every hot-button theme of our paranoid milieu. Five concurrent narratives involve bioengineering, burning high-rises, the surveillance state, extralegal rendition and torture, black helicopters, identity hacking, serial murder, drugs, and class war. The main plot driver is a downed satellite and a chase after world-altering data, comingled with a murder mystery and multiple abductions. The five main characters operate in emotional registers from the overtly funny to the grimly, hopelessly desperate, but they are all severely diminished by the novel's end: one a drug-addicted shell of her former self; another captured and tortured by shadow operatives; and two more ultimately destroyed by forces beyond their comprehension. Armand negotiates this sprawling, kinetic narrative with élan, showing his kinship with such genre writers as Charles Stross, Ken MacLeod, and Iain M. Banks. Armand is especially effective at evoking the various settings of this globetrotting novel, from the red deserts of the Australian outback to a snow-bound Manhattan, a future version of Cairo, domed and surrounded by terminal shanties to the hypermodern alienation of a five-star hotel in Prague. Armand makes all of this scene-shifting and furniture-moving look easy, and though the plotting of *Cairo* is complex to the point of inscrutability, the reader is always able to follow the action, even though the novel doesn't offer the narrative payoffs of genre fiction. The reader is left to think of *Cairo* in different, more formal ways. Armand gives us a clue toward the end of the novel: "Consider the weary Traveler . . . Like you, he is in search of something, but how will he know if he's found it? Or what *it* is . . . Perhaps *he's* the thing he seeks . . . to connect missing elements in a puzzle he alone constitutes . . . As if his journey has been to make a constellation of the coordinates. Provide the missing link . . . One question leads to another. But are the questions adequate to what he seeks?" [GARY LAIN]

George Melly. *Don't Tell Sybil: An Intimate Memoir of E. L. T. Mesens.* Atlas Press, 2014. 176 pp. Cloth: $25.95.

"English Surrealism" may seem, like the "English Riviera" referred to in *Fawlty Towers*, a contradiction in terms. Still, George Melly's sprightly memoir foregrounds an experimental dimension in twentieth-century English life that is different from the declarative innovation of figures such as Henry Green, B. S. Johnson, and Ann Quin, yet charts its own path through perception and imagination, unimpeded by the conventionality represented in the title by Sybil, wife of Belgian-born artist and impresario E. L. T. (Édouard) Mesens and symbol of all that is safe and respectable. Melly, well known to the educated British public as a jazz musician, media personality, and charming gadfly, is the perfect mixture of insider and outsider needed to tell this tale. While this book is ostensibly a biography of E. L. T. Mesens, who in Melly's eyes set the tone for an incipient English Surrealist movement that never quite materialized, *Don't Tell Sybil*—like its cousins *The Autobiography of Alice B. Toklas* and *The Quest for Corvo*—is, however, as much about Melly as it is about its putative subject, with Mesens proving to be a mask for Melly's comic self-discourse. If the true founders of English Surrealism might be said to be Edward Lear and Lewis Carroll, Melly, through his winning and debonair portrait, conveys its spirit in whimsical if bittersweet honesty, as Mesens declines in a series of "aggressively clean white rooms" with a mournful insouciance at once his own and his chronicler's. Perhaps, we muse, England itself is so surreal it may not even need a declared surrealism. [NICHOLAS BIRNS]

Patrick Greaney. *Quotational Practices: Repeating the Future in Contemporary Art.* Univ. of Minnesota Press, 2014. 240 pp. Paper: $27.50.

What better genre to explore Patrick Greaney's *Quotational Practices* than the book review, which defines itself by interacting with preexisting texts. Greaney's new book considers the aesthetic use of quotation in contemporary art and literature. Drawing from voices such as Michel Foucault, Walter Benjamin, and Theodor Adorno, Greaney examines the "quotational works" of authors and artists Guy Debord, Marcel Broodthaers, Heimrad Bäcker, Sharon Hayes, Vanessa Place, and Glenn Ligon. In his masterful explication and translation of key works that rely on quoting other works, Greaney cracks open an unstable, uncomfortable place in which to evaluate the conflicting texts and contexts that form human history. In the study of the artistic and political role of quotation, the central question might not be whether the quotational author/artist constructs something new and original, but rather how quotation functions in the deconstruction of comfortable identities. Greaney explains that important contemporary artworks exist within and push against the historical contexts in which they surface and continue to resurface. In his analysis of Bäcker's 1986 book *transcript*, for example, Greaney shows how Bäcker, a member of the Hitler Youth and later of the Nazi Party, quotes National Socialist texts as a way of exposing and protesting a problematic past that he helped to create and dismantle. For Greaney, the aesthetic use of quotation, which involves repeating texts out of context in a fissured present, forces the quotational author/artist to disrupt prevailing binaries between original/unoriginal, individual/society, us/them, subject/object, gay and lesbian/queer, white/black, normal/abnormal, good/evil. This is the brave work of quotational art. It reproduces texts and dissolves contexts. It criticizes, eclipses, and rejects a linear view of history that precludes creativity, revealing the possibility of multiple futures that may, actually, have already happened. [KAREN MAUK]

BOOKS RECEIVED

al-Ma'arrī, Abū l-'Alā'. *The Epistle of Forgiveness, Volume II: Hypocrites, Heretics, and Other Sinners*. Trans. and eds. Geert Jan van Gelder and Gregor Schoeler. New York University Press, 2014. Cloth: $35.00. (F/NF)

Amdahl, Gary. *Across My Big Brass Bed*. Artistically Declined Press, 2014. Paper: $16.00. (F)

Amdahl, Gary. *The Intimidator Still Lives in Our Hearts: Stories*. Artistically Declined Press, 2013. Paper: $14.00. (F)

Armand, Louis. *Cairo*. Equus Press, 2014. Paper: €8.00. (F)

Asquith, Mark. *The Lost Frontier: Reading Annie Proulx's* Wyoming Stories. Bloomsbury, 2014. Paper: $29.95. (NF)

Ball, Hugo. *Flametti, or the Dandyism of the Poor*. Trans. Catherine Schelbert. Intro. Marc Dachy. Illus. Tal R. Wakefield Press, 2014. Paper: $17.95. (F)

Baxter, Jeannette and David James. *Andrea Levy*. Foreword Lawrence Scott. Bloomsbury, 2014. Paper: $29.95. (NF)

Bengtsson, Jonas T. *A Fairy Tale*. Trans. Charlotte Barslund. Other Press, 2014. Paper: $16.95. (F)

Bernheimer, Kate. *How a Mother Weaned Her Girl from Fairy Tales*. Coffee House Press, 2014. Paper: $15.95. (F)

Bolger, Robert K. and Scott Korb, eds. *Gesturing Toward Reality: David Foster Wallace and Philosophy*. Bloomsbury, 2014. Paper: $29.95. (NF)

Boscagli, Maurizia. *Stuff Theory*. Bloomsbury, 2014. Paper: $24.95. (NF)

Boyko, C. P. *Novelists*. Biblioasis, 2014. Paper: $16.95. (F)

Brayfield, Celia and Duncan Sprott. *Writing Historical Fiction: A Writers' and Artists' Companion*. Bloomsbury, 2014. Paper: $24.95. (NF)

Carpenter, Lea. *Eleven Days*. Vintage Books, 2014. Paper: $15.95. (F)

Catanzano, Amy. *Starlight in Two Million: A Neo-Scientific Novella*. Noemi Press, 2014. Paper: $15.00. (P/F)

Cleary, Suzanne. *Beauty Mark*. BkMk Press, 2013. Paper: $13.95. (P)

Cobb, Lauren. *Boulevard Women*. BkMk Press, 2013. Paper: $15.95. (F)

Cooke, Carolyn. *Amor and Psycho: Stories*. Vintage, 2014. Paper: $15.00. (F)

Crawford, Stanley. *Travel Notes*. Calamari Press, 2014. $14.00. (F)

Cuenca, J. P. *The Only Happy Ending for a Love Story is an Accident*. Trans. and afterword Elizabeth Lowe. Tagus Press, 2014. Paper: $19.95. (F)

DeShell, Jeffrey. *Expectation: A Francesca Fruscella Mystery*. FC2, 2014. Paper: $14.95. (F)

Dewey, Joseph. *Understanding Michael Chabon*. Univ. of South Carolina Press, 2014. Cloth: $39.95. (NF)

Dickinson, Stephanie. *Heat: An Interview with Jean Seberg*. New Michigan Press, 2014. Paper: $9.00. (F)

Dones, Elvira. *The Sworn Virgin*. Trans. Clarissa Botsford. Foreword Ismail Kadare. Paper: $15.95. (F)

Duchamp, Marcel, Henri-Pierre Roché, and Beatrice Woord. *3 New York Dadas* and *The Blind Man*. Trans. Chris Allen. Intro. and commentary Dawn Ades. Atlas Press, 2013. Cloth: $26.95. (F/NF/P)

Ehrlich, Gretel. *Facing the Wave: A Journey in the Wake of the Tsunami*. Vintage Books, 2014. Paper: $15.00. (NF)

Elliott, Julia. *The Wilds*. Tin House Books, 2014. Paper: $15.95. (F)

Ernaux, Annie. *A Man's Place*. Trans. Tanya Leslie. Intro. Francine Prose. Seven Stories Press, 2014. Paper: $13.95. (NF)

Farner, Geir. *Literary Fiction: The Ways We Read Narrative Literature*. Bloomsbury, 2014. Paper: $34.95. (NF)

Fernández-Pintado, Mylene. *A Corner of the World*. Trans. Dick Cluster. City Lights, 2014. Paper: $14.95. (F)

Frankoni, Anker. *Mexican Eskimo Book 1: Exmikan*. An Anker Frankoni Book, 2014. Paper: $14.95. (F)

Freedman, William. *Joseph Conrad and the Anxiety of Knowledge*. Univ. South Carolina Press, 2014. Cloth: $49.95. (NF)

Grandbois, Peter. *Wait Your Turn* and *The Stability of Large Systems*. Wordcraft of Oregon, 2014. Paper: $12.00. (F)

Greaney, Patrick. *Quotational Practices: Repeating the Future in Contemporary Art*. University of Minnesota Press, 2014. Paper: $27.50. (NF)

Genovesi, Fabio. *Live Bait*. Trans. Michael F. Moore. Other Press, 2014. Paper: $15.95. (F)

Gunn, Eileen. *Questionable Practices*. Small Beer Press, 2014. Paper: $16.00. (F)

Hernandez, Lolita. *Making Callaloo in Detroit*. Wayne State Univ. Press, 2014. Paper: $18.99. (F)

Hist, Hilda. *Letters from a Seducer*. Nightboat Books & A Bolha Editora, 2014. Paper: $15.95. (F)

Hobson, Brandon. *Deep Ellum*. Calamari Press, 2014. Paper: $14.00. (F)

Hubble, Nick and Aris Mousoutzanis. *The Science Fiction Handbook*. Bloomsbury, 2014. Paper: $29.95. (NF)

Hughes-Hallett, Lucy. *Gabriele d'Annunzio: Poet, Seducer, and Preacher of War*. Anchor Books, 2014. Paper: $18.95. (NF)

Ingersoll, Earl G. *Understanding Steven Millhauser*. University of South Carolina Press, 2014. Cloth: $39.95. (NF)

Jasieński, Bruno. *The Legs of Izolda Morgan*. Trans. Soren A. Gauger and Guy Torr. Twisted Spoon Press, 2014. Cloth: $23.95. (F)

Jaffe, Harold. *Othello Blues*. Paper: JEF, 2014. Paper: $16.00. (F)

Joyce, Laura Ellen. *The Luminol Reels*. Calamari Press, 2014. Paper: $13.00. (F)

Joyce, Michael. *Twentieth Century Man*. Seismicity Editions, 2014. Paper: $12.95. (F)

Knapp, Kathy. *American Unexceptionalism: The Everyman and the Suburban Novel after 9/11*. Univ. of Iowa Press, 2014. Paper: $45.00. (NF)

Knausgaard, Karl Ove. *My Struggle: Book Three*. Trans. Don Bartlett. Archipelago Books, 2014. Cloth: $27.00.

Kraft, A. Van. *Sleepy Hollow: The Secret Life and Legend of Ichabod Crane*. Art Kraft Studio, 2013. Paper: $7.99. (F)

Lackey, Michael. *Truthful Fictions: Conversations with American Biographical Novelists*. Bloomsbury, 2014. Paper: $29.95. (NF)

Lamprell, Mark. *The Full Ridiculous*. Soft Skull Press, 2014. Paper: $15.95. (F)

Lenzo, Lisa. *Strange Love*. Wayne State Univ. Press, 2014. Paper: $18.99. (F)

Lieder, Tim, ed. *King David and the Spiders from Mars*. Dybbuk Press, 2013. Paper: $12.75. (F)

Lihe, Zhong. *From the Old Country: Stories and Sketches of China and Taiwan*. Ed. and trans. T. M. McClellan. Foreword Zhong Tiejun. Columbia University Press, 2014. Cloth: $35.00. (F)

Linforth, Christopher. *When You Find Us We Will Be Gone: Stories.* Lamar Univ. Press, 2014. Paper: $17.95. (F)

Lock, Norman. *The Boy in His Winter: An American Novel.* Bellevue Literary Press, 2014. Paper: $14.95. (F)

Long, Maebh. *Assembling Flann O'Brien.* Bloomsbury, 2014. Paper: $32.95 (NF)

Louÿs, Pierre. *Pyrbac.* Trans. Geoffrey Longnecker. Wakefield Press, 2014. Paper: $13.95. (P)

Lyon, Annabel. *The Sweet Girl.* Vintage, 2014. Paper: $15.00. (F)

Mack, Michael. *Philosophy and Literature in Times of Crisis: Challenging our Infatuation with Numbers.* Bloomsbury, 2014. Paper: $29.95. (NF)

Mandel, Oscar. *Otherwise Fables.* Prospect Park Books, 2014. Paper: $16.00. (F)

Mantel, Tara. *Elemental.* Livingston Press, 2014. Paper: $18.95. (F)

Manto, Saafat Hasan. *Bombay Stories.* Trans. Matt Reeck and Aftab Ahmad. Vintage International, 2014. Paper: $16.00. (F)

McEvilley, Thomas. *The Arimaspia: Songs for the Rainy Season.* Preface Charles Bernstein. McPherson & Co., 2014. (F/P)

Melly, George. *Don't Tell Sybil.* Atlas Press, 2013. Cloth: $25.95 (NF)

Miles, Valerie, ed. *A Thousand Forests in One Acorn: An Anthology of Spanish-Language Fiction.* Open Letter, 2014. Paper: $19.95. (F)

Minor, Kyle. *Praying Drunk: Stories, Questions.* Sarabande Books, 2014. Paper: $15.95. (F)

Mishler, Susanna J. *Termination Dust.* Boreal Books, 2014. Paper: $18.95. (P)

Montoya, Maceo. *The Deportation of Wopper Barraza.* University of New Mexico Press, 2014. Paper: $19.95. (F)

Morano, Lodovico Pignatti. *Nicola, Milan.* Semiotext(e), 2014. Paper: $14.95. (F)

Mozina, Andy. *Quality Snacks.* Wayne State Univ. Press, 2014. Paper: $18.99. (F)

Must, Dennis. *The World's Smallest Bible.* Red Hen Press, 2014. Paper: $15.95. (F)

Normand, Lawrence and Alison Winch, eds. *Encountering Buddhism in Twentieth-Century British and American Literature.* Bloomsbury, 2013. Cloth: $110.00. (NF)

Ohle, David. *The Blast.* Calamari Press, 2014. Paper: $12.00. (F)

Olsen, Lance. *Theories of Forgetting.* FC2, 2014. Paper: $22.95. (F)

Ondjaki. *Granma Nineteen and the Soviet's Secret.* Trans. Stephen Henighan. Biblioasis, 2014. Paper: $15.95. (F)

Page, Kathy. *Paradise and Elsewhere.* Biblioasis, 2014. Paper: $15.95 (F)

Parkison, Aimee. *The Petals of Your Eyes.* Starcherone Books, 2014. Paper: $14.00. (F)

Piafsky, Michael. *All the Happiness You Deserve.* Prospect Park Books, 2014. Paper: $15.00. (F)

Pron, Patricio. *My Father's Ghost is Climbing in the Rain.* Vintage Books, 2014. Paper: $15.95. (F)

Pozner, Vladimir. *The Disunited States.* Trans. Alison Strayer. Seven Stories Press, 2014, Paper: $22.95. (NF)

Rabaté, Jean-Michel. *Crimes of the Future: Theory and Its Global Reproduction.* Bloomsbury, 2014. Paper: $29.95. (NF)

Rahman, Zia Haider. *In The Light of What We Know.* FSG, 2014. Cloth: $27.00. (F)

Renek, Nava and Natalie Nuzzo, eds. *Wreckage of Reason II: Back to the Drawing Board: An Anthology of Contemporary XXperimental Women Writers.* Spuyten Duyvil, 2014. Paper: $20.00. (F/P)

Richmond, Michelle. *Hum.* FC2, 2014. Paper: $16.95. (F)

Rippberger, Robert. *Escape to Anywhere Else.* Intro. Mariel Hemingway. Regent Press, 2014. Paper: $12.95. (F)

Roberson, Matthew. *List.* FC2, 2014. Paper: $17.95. (F)

Russell, Richard Rankin, ed. *Bernard MacLaverty: New Critical Readings.* Bloomsbury, 2014. Cloth: $110.00. (NF)

Sacheri, Eduardo. *Papers in the Wind.* Trans. Mara Faye Lethem. Other Press, 2014. Paper: $17.95. (F)

Sandri, Giovanna. *Only Fragments Found: Selected Poems 1969–1998.* Trans. Guy Bennett, Faust Pauluzzi, and the author. Intro. Giulia Niccolai. Seismicity Editions, 2014. Paper: $14.95. (P)

Schutzer, Amy. *Spheres of Disturbance.* Arktoi Books, 2014. Paper: $16.95. (F)

Scott, Paulo. *Nowhere People.* Trans. Daniel Hahn. & Other Stories, 2014. Paper: $15.95. (F)

Sebbar, Leïla. *Sherazade.* Trans. Dorothy S. Blair. Interlink Books, 2014. Paper: $17.95. (F)

Segura, Mauricio. *Eucalyptus*. Trans. Donald Winkler. Biblioasis, 2014. Paper: $15.95. (F)

Seidenberg, Steven. *Itch*. RAW ArT PRESS, 2014. Paper: $15.95. (F)

Shoemaker, Karen Gettert. *The Meaning of Names*. Red Hen Press, 2014. Paper: $15.95.

Skemer, Arnold. *H*. Phrygian Press, 2013. Paper: $10.00. (F)

Steidle, Beth. *The Static Herd*. Calamari Press, 2014. Paper: $12.00. (F)

Suceavă, Bogdan. *Miruna, a Tale*. Trans. Alistair Ian Blythe. Twisted Spoon Press, 2014. Paper: $15.00. (F)

Sweeney, Carole. *Michel Houellebecq and the Literature of Despair*. Bloomsbury, 2014. Cloth: $120.00. (NF)

Tingle, Tim. *House of Purple Cedar*. Cinco Puntos Press, 2014. Paper: $16.95. (F)

Upton, Lee. *The Tao of Humiliation: Stories*. BOA Editions, 2014. Paper: $16.00. (F)

Villa, Emilio. *The Selected Poetry*. Trans. and intro. Dominic Siracusa. Contra Mundum Press, 2014. Paper: $33.50. (P)

Villalobos, Juan Pablo. *Quesadillas*. FSG, 2014. Paper: $14.00. (F)

Vint, Sherryl. *Science Fiction: A Guide for the Perplexed*. Bloomsbury, 2014. Paper: $24.95. (NF)

Vizenor, Gerald. *Blue Ravens*. Wesleyan University Press, 2014. Cloth: $27.95. (F)

Zamorano, Désirée. *The Amado Women*. Cinco Puntos Press, 2014. Paper: $16.95. (F)

Ziegler, Alan, ed. *Short*. Persea Books, 2014. Paper: $16.95. (F)

Order Form

Individuals may use this form to subscribe to the *Review of Contemporary Fiction* or to order back issues of the *Review* and Dalkey Archive titles at a discount (see below for details).

Title	ISBN	Quantity	Price

Subtotal __________

Less Discount __________
(10% for one book, 20% for two or more books, and 25% for Scholarly titles advertised in this issue)

Subtotal __________

Plus Postage __________
(U.S. $3 + $1 per book; foreign $7 + $5 per book)

1 Year Individual Subscription to the Review __________
($17 U.S.; $22.60 Canada; $32.60 all other countries)

Total __________

Mailing Address ____________________

xxxii/1

Credit card payment ☐ Visa ☐ Mastercard

Acct. # ____________________ Exp. date __________

Name on card ____________________ Phone # __________

Billing zip code ____________________

Please make checks (in U.S. dollars only) payable to *Dalkey Archive Press.*

mail this form to: Dalkey Archive Press,
3404 North Ben Wilson Street, Victoria, TX 77901